DISCIPLESHIP
IN A WORLD
FULL OF NAZIS

Discipleship in a World Full of Nazis

Recovering the True Legacy of Dietrich Bonhoeffer

MARK THIESSEN NATION

WITH CONTRIBUTIONS BY
Scot McKnight and *Stanley Hauerwas*

CASCADE *Books* · Eugene, Oregon

DISCIPLESHIP IN A WORLD FULL OF NAZIS
Recovering the True Legacy of Dietrich Bonhoeffer

Copyright © 2022 Mark Thiessen Nation. All rights reserved. Except for brief quotations in critical publications or reviews, no part of this book may be reproduced in any manner without prior written permission from the publisher. Write: Permissions, Wipf and Stock Publishers, 199 W. 8th Ave., Suite 3, Eugene, OR 97401.

Cascade Books
An Imprint of Wipf and Stock Publishers
199 W. 8th Ave., Suite 3
Eugene, OR 97401

www.wipfandstock.com

PAPERBACK ISBN: 978-1-7252-9508-7
HARDCOVER ISBN: 978-1-7252-9509-4
EBOOK ISBN: 978-1-7252-9510-0

Cataloguing-in-Publication data:

Names: Nation, Mark Thiessen, 1953– | McKnight, Scot, foreword.

Title: Discipleship in a world full of Nazis: recovering the true legacy of Dietrich Bonhoeffer / Mark Thiessen Nation; foreword by Scot McKnight.

Description: Eugene, OR: Cascade Books, 2022 | Includes bibliographical references and index.

Identifiers: ISBN 978-1-7252-9508-7 (paperback) | ISBN 978-1-7252-9509-4 (hardcover) | ISBN 978-1-7252-9510-0 (ebook)

Subjects: LC | Bonhoeffer, Dietrich, 1906–1945.

Classification: BX4827.B57 .N40 2022 (paperback) | BX4827 (ebook)

03/23/22

To Stanley Hauerwas—
wise mentor, faithful friend

Contents

Foreword by Scot McKnight | ix
Acknowledgments | xi
Abbreviations | xiv
Introduction: It Is Important to Do Theology and Only Theology | xv

1. Toward Retrieving the True Legacy of Dietrich Bonhoeffer | 1
2. "Only the One Who Cries Out for the Jews May Sing Gregorian Chants" | 24
3. "We Should Not Balk Here at Using the Word 'Pacifism'" | 51
4. *Discipleship* in a World Full of Nazis | 87
5. "A Blanket License to Commit Evil Acts"? | 116
6. Discipleship amidst the Rubble | 134

EPILOGUE "Invisibility Is Ruining Us!" | 150

Appendix 1: Whose Bonhoeffer? Which Hermeneutic? Toward Preserving the "Whole Cloth" | 165

Appendix 2: "Christianity Stands or Falls with Its Revolutionary Protest against Violence": How Could Dietrich Bonhoeffer, a Lutheran, Make Such a Claim? | 177
—MARK THIESSEN NATION AND STANLEY HAUERWAS

Appendix 3: Jesus, Bonhoeffer, and Christoform Hermeneutics | 193
—SCOT MCKNIGHT

Appendix 4: *A Hidden Life*: Directed by Terrence Malick (Fox Searchlight Pictures, 2019) | 214

Bibliography | 223

Foreword

It takes boldness to challenge the Niebuhrian consensus ruling the academy on how best to interpret Dietrich Bonhoeffer's life, legacy, theology, and ethics. In your hands is such boldness. I admire it because I have been reading Bonhoeffer for more than forty years in a way that is more like Nation's reading than like many others'. Anyone who challenges the dominant view that Bonhoeffer participated in the plot to assassinate Hitler and was imprisoned and eventually hung for it has my attention because I sense, as Nation does, too much tension. Bonhoeffer's *Discipleship* as well as his *Life Together*, not to ignore statements by friends, his christoform theology, and the consistency of his theology are on the line here. Yes, as Nation will challenge the consensus, one has to deal with Bonhoeffer's closest friend, Eberhard Bethge, who overtly describes a changed mind in Bonhoeffer to what is called a more realist ("a man for his times"), as opposed to a pacifist or (as I would prefer) a christoform ethic. I am unaware that anyone has offered such a forthright challenge of the Bethge-inspired and Niebuhrian consensus.

While I was writing a commentary on the Sermon on the Mount, my editor said I had too much Bonhoeffer in it. To which I replied that I was not aware that was possible! When I had a rough draft done, I sent it to Mark Thiessen Nation for comments and he challenged me to think again about the trajectory of Bonhoeffer's thought. I have since then done that. In fact, I have read all sixteen volumes of Bonhoeffer's works twice since those days (and wish I had done that before writing the commentary). This book makes me want to read them again! Nation's challenge and my rereading of Bonhoeffer have convinced me that Bonhoeffer did not become a Niebuhrian realist but remained a christoform kind of pacifist. He didn't operate with the *Prinzip* of pacifism but the paradigm of Philippians 2:6–11, now turned into the term "cruciformity" by Michael Gorman. I don't know how the man so consistently christoform in his theological ethics could have participated in the plot to assassinate Hitler (or anyone else). Bonhoeffer, let it be said over and over, was not arrested for participating in any assassination attempts. He was arrested for helping to save the lives of fourteen Jews and was imprisoned for subverting the military's power to conscript him into service.

Theologians tend to divide systematics from ethics or theology from morality. One of Bonhoeffer's major interpreters today, Charles Marsh, brings into the theology classroom what he calls "lived theology," and contends that theology that is lived is every bit the theology that is called systematic. His hero is Bonhoeffer, and no one embodied lived theology better than Bonhoeffer (though I'm quite sure Bonhoeffer would have some questions for Marsh). But dissidents, like Bonhoeffer himself in modern-day classrooms, often don't fit into the room where it all happens. Nation's book is the voice of a dissident when it comes to how to read Bonhoeffer. Nation thinks for himself with constant attention to the details that only Bonhoeffer specialists have mastered, and what makes this book valuable is how Christocentric it is in grasping Bonhoeffer's theological ethics. Nation's approach depends on his reading of Bethge, and I hope you give him the hearing he (and Bonhoeffer) deserve. I have on occasion challenged Nation's reading—after all, Bethge was Bonhoeffer's best friend—and this book answers that challenge. I think Nation has successfully dismantled the consensus with a consistent Bonhoeffer ever focused on Christ.

Scot McKnight
Northern Seminary
March 2021

Acknowledgments

As I finish this manuscript on Bonhoeffer, I think of all of those who have influenced and supported my work in many ways over the last four decades. My mother, of blessed memory, was always a practical support to me. It's not at all clear to me how I could have done my earlier research on Bonhoeffer without her support. My children, Michael and Christina, have been a constant source of joy to me during this journey with Bonhoeffer (as are the four grandchildren they have given us). I am so grateful for who they are and that they also are followers of Jesus. For eighteen years, my wife, Mary, lived a kind of costly discipleship in South Central Los Angeles that I will likely never know. Because of her experiences there, she will never allow me to imagine that loving our neighbors as ourselves—especially caring for the least among us—can ever be merely an empty cliché. It is always related to real people, with real needs. I am frequently reminded that ever since she lived in L.A., her "cloud of witnesses" is largely populated by black faces. I am also grateful to the various, vibrant churches that have given me a spiritual home—from my beginnings in the First General Baptist Church, McLeansboro, Illinois; to New Covenant Fellowship, Champaign-Urbana, Illinois; and to Early Church, a Mennonite Church here in Harrisonburg, Virginia.

I won't repeat the details already given in my essay on hermeneutics and Bonhoeffer. Everyone named there could be mentioned here. I simply want briefly to mention others who have been important in my theological journey as related to this book. I have studied under two professors who wrote their doctoral theses on Bonhoeffer. One was my very first theology professor, Richard B. "R. B." Smith. He may have been responsible for the bookstore at Oakland City College carrying Bonhoeffer's *The Cost of Discipleship*. In any event, I bought it there, probably in 1972, which was where my interest in Bonhoeffer began. In the fall of 1980, I wrote my master's thesis at the Associated Mennonite Biblical Seminaries on nonviolent forms of resistance within Nazi Germany under the direction of LeRoy Friesen, who had also written his doctoral thesis on Bonhoeffer. The same semester I wrote a long paper on the Confessing Church, at the University of Notre Dame, in a course taught by John Howard Yoder, who studied with Barth.

The idea for this book began shortly after *Bonhoeffer the Assassin?* was published, in 2013. The early version of the first chapter was originally presented as a lecture in November 2014 at a Bonhoeffer session at the American Academy of Religion meeting. Between then and 2019 this lecture was presented, with revisions along the way, in several venues: the Young Center for Anabaptist and Pietist Studies, Elizabethtown College, Pennsylvania; at a conference on "Christian Love and National Interest," co-sponsored by Patrick Henry College and *Providence Journal*; at the University of Aberdeen; and at Oakland City University. Three of the six chapters were given as lectures at Bethesda Mennonite Church, Henderson, Nebraska, thanks to the invitation from Seth Miller, their pastor and my former student. Early versions of all six main chapters were presented as lectures at Eastern Mennonite University. I am grateful for all of these opportunities, which prodded me to articulate and clarify my views.

I am also grateful for the support given by Eastern Mennonite University in various ways, but especially for a sabbatical that made it possible to do much of the research that has led to this book. I am very grateful that I was able to teach a course on Bonhoeffer at Eastern Mennonite Seminary. The students who have taken my course over the years have certainly enriched my understanding, not least the two men who coauthored my 2013 book, Dan Umbel and Anthony Siegrist.

Two essays in this book were previously published. An early version of chapter five was published in *Perspectives in Religious Studies*, a special issue devoted to honoring my longtime friend, the late Glen Stassen. And a very similar version of the essay in the Appendix written with Stanley Hauerwas, with a different title, was published in the online Australian journal, *ABC Religion and Ethics*.

I am grateful for the good work done by the various folk who work with Wipf & Stock Publishers. I knew John Wipf and Jon Stock before Wipf & Stock existed. It has been a pleasure to have Rodney Clapp as my editor at W & S. Rodney was the acquisition editor for my book *Bonhoeffer the Assassin?* back when he worked with Baker Publishing House. But my relationship with Rodney goes back at least as far as the mid-90s when I read the manuscript for his fine book *A Peculiar People* on my honeymoon. Rodney is a gifted writer; it is a pleasure to work with him. I appreciate it that Scot McKnight was willing both to contribute an essay of his on Bonhoeffer and write the foreword. I have known for many years that I deeply resonate with

Scot's theology. More recently I have come to know (not surprisingly) that he has a deep interest in Bonhoeffer. David Graybill provided help with the formatting and proofreading of the main six chapters and the bibliography. I also want to thank John Nugent for reading the whole manuscript at a late stage, making many helpful suggestions for improvement.

But finally, I want to say something about the person to whom I am dedicating this book. I first encountered Stanley Hauerwas's thought through the book *A Community of Character*, which I discovered in the University of Illinois bookstore in Urbana, Illinois, where I lived and directed an ecumenical peace and justice organization. I realized as I sought to absorb this book that this was not simply one among a thousand books. This book was inaugurating a journey I would be on for the rest of my life. Over the next couple of years, I purchased *The Peaceable Kingdom*, *Vision and Virtue*, and *Truthfulness and Tragedy*. I was hooked. In the midst of my excitement, I corresponded with Hauerwas. But I would never have imagined, in the mid-1980s, that a few years later I would begin an editing relationship with Stanley that would last ten years (producing three book manuscripts, two of which would be published). Nor would I have imagined that I would have a virtual seminar with Stanley by phone during those same years. Since I got to know his secretaries, I knew that he was an incredibly busy man. But he was quite generous with his time. He has been an absolutely wonderful mentor to me—wise, patient, instructive, always opening up new avenues of intellectual exploration. And I've always known that this is hardly unique to me. I'm sure he won't remember this, but the first time I met Stanley was in a restaurant in Chicago, during the annual Society of Christian Ethics meeting in January 1987. John Yoder had invited me to join him and Stanley as they met with present and former doctoral students (mostly Stanley's). The personal bonds Stanley had with these people were obvious. Many of my relationships in professional organizations have come through connections to Stanley. And, among many other admirable qualities, Stan seems to have worked at relationships in such a way so as to prevent the need for competition among either his former doctoral students or the many others who count him as a friend. I know I am grateful simply to have been one among his friends.

Abbreviations

DBWE 1:   *Dietrich Bonhoeffer Works 1: Sanctorum Communio*
DBWE 2:   *Dietrich Bonhoeffer Works 2: Act and Being*
DBWE 3:   *Dietrich Bonhoeffer Works 3: Creation and Fall*
DBWE 4:   *Dietrich Bonhoeffer Works 4: Discipleship*
DBWE 5:   *Dietrich Bonhoeffer Works 5: Life Together and Prayerbook of the Bible*
DBWE 6:   *Dietrich Bonhoeffer Works 6: Ethics*
DBWE 7:   *Dietrich Bonhoeffer Works 7: Fiction from Tegel Prison*
DBWE 8:   *Dietrich Bonhoeffer Works 8: Letters and Papers from Prison*
DBWE 9:   *Dietrich Bonhoeffer Works 9: The Young Bonhoeffer, 1918–1927*
DBWE 10: *Dietrich Bonhoeffer Works 10: Barcelona, Berlin, New York, 1928–1931*
DBWE 11: *Dietrich Bonhoeffer Works 11: Ecumenical, Academic, and Pastoral Work, 1931–1932*
DBWE 12: *Dietrich Bonhoeffer Works 12: Berlin, 1932–1933*
DBWE 13: *Dietrich Bonhoeffer Works 13: London, 1933–1935*
DBWE 14: *Dietrich Bonhoeffer Works 14: Theological Education at Finkenwalde, 1935–1937*
DBWE 15: *Dietrich Bonhoeffer Works 15: Theological Education Underground, 1937–1940*
DBWE 16: *Dietrich Bonhoeffer Works 16: Conspiracy and Imprisonment, 1940–1945*

Introduction
It Is Important to Do Theology and Only Theology

Toward the end of his life, in one of his many interviews, Karl Barth commented: "Don't forget to say I was always interested in politics."[1] There were understandable reasons why he felt the need to say that to his interlocutor. Certainly, by the mid-1960s Barth was known more than anything else as a systematic theologian. Because of that, many were unaware of the ways in which he had been involved in politics, and in relation to some of the most important events in the twentieth century. He wanted this misperception corrected. Because of the ways in which Barth articulated his theology, some even imagined that he was generally uninterested in ethics. And again, this is not totally surprising. In fact, the heart of one of Barth's first writings that addressed the Nazi situation can be captured by the following line: "It was important to do 'theology and only theology—as though nothing had happened.'"[2] Years later Barth still stood by this statement. However, so that he not be misunderstood, he elaborated on what he meant by putting it that way:

> I did not have anything new to say in that first issue of *Theological Existence Today* apart from what I had always endeavoured to say: that we could have no other gods than God, that holy scripture was enough to guide the church into all truth, that the grace of Jesus Christ was enough to forgive our sins and to order our life. The only thing was that now I suddenly had to say this in a different situation. It was no longer just an academic theory. Without any conscious intention or endeavour on my part, it took on the character of an appeal, a challenge, a battle-cry, a confession. It was not I who had changed: the room in which

---

1. I hope my memory is accurate here. I have not been able to track down the reference.
2. Busch, *Karl Barth*, 226.

I had to speak had changed dramatically, and so had its resonance. As I repeated this doctrine consistently in this new room, at the same time it took on a new depth and became a practical matter, for decision and action.[3]

It is perhaps important to note that within this 1933 essay in that first issue of *Theological Existence Today*, Barth also said that one "has to proclaim the gospel 'even *in the* Third Reich, but not *under* it nor in *its* spirit.' Thus, church membership, he said, is not determined 'by blood, nor by race either.'" He quite bluntly referred to the ideology that was giving rise to the new Nazi-aligned "German Christianity" as heresy. Moreover, he claimed that the attitude that Christians needed to adopt was at least "indirectly . . . a political attitude."[4] In fact, as he had stated, his theology was always intended to elicit "decision and action." When I used to quote these statements in my annual lecture on Barth, in a course on Christian Tradition, I would always add something like the following. In "doing theology and only theology, as though nothing had happened," Barth spoke publicly on behalf of labor unions, spoke against the nationalism of his former theological professors, managed to get himself exiled from Germany during the Nazi era, refused to join Reinhold Niebuhr in being a cold warrior, and spoke out against the nuclear weapons buildup in the late 1950s (to mention a few highlights).[5]

Gustavo Gutiérrez, the father of Liberation Theology, has said: "Barth, the theologian of God's transcendence . . . is sensitive to the situation of exploitation in which these broad segments of humanity live. . . . The one who starts with heaven is sensitive to those who live in the hell of this earth; whereas the one who begins with earth is blind to the situation of exploitation upon which the earth is built."[6] That is one way to put it. But it is really New Testament scholar C. Kavin Rowe who has put his finger precisely on the heart of Barth's theology. "It is Barth above all others in our time who has clearly seen a central theological point without which the historical dynamics involved in Christian origins are virtually unintelligible: God is the measure of all things. To speak properly of God in Barth's sense is not to speak of the grandest object within our horizon but of the reality that constitutes the total horizon of all human life." Rowe continues, "the hermeneutical corollary of Barth's insight is of momentous consequence and can be simply stated: what we think about God will determine what we think about

---

3. Busch, *Karl Barth*, 227.
4. Busch, *Karl Barth*, 226.
5. For an account of Barth's involvement in politics (in the narrow sense) see Jehle, *Ever against the Stream*.
6. Gutiérrez, *Power of the Poor*, 203.

everything else. . . . Theology, that is, is never merely ideation. It is always and inherently a total way of life."[7] Yes, indeed, this is key for understanding what Barth meant by saying we should "do theology and only theology."

Sometimes after I have attended another Bonhoeffer session at the American Academy of Religion meeting, I can almost imagine Bonhoeffer saying something parallel to what Barth said in that late interview, although in his case it would be the reverse. "Don't forget to tell them that I too believed, with Barth, in doing theology and only theology." Partly because Bonhoeffer said pithy, memorable things on very many topics, partly because his writing style is often evocative rather than straightforward, and partly because he felt compelled to address himself to issues of the day in public, authors not infrequently address topics in Bonhoeffer's name while ignoring the core of his theological commitments.

Bonhoeffer was fundamentally with Barth on theological method. But their styles were different. Barth in his own way acknowledged this when he wrote a letter to Eberhard Bethge after reading his biography of Bonhoeffer. He confessed his guilt to Bethge for not having spoken out on behalf of the Jews "with equal emphasis during the church struggle."[8] Barth's initial responses to Hitler, in 1933, were to write strictly theological tracts, speaking of idolatry and the need to "do theology and only theology." Bonhoeffer certainly agreed with these writings. But one of the first pieces he composed after Hitler came to power, though framed theologically, was calling on his fellow Christians to act on behalf of the Jews. And when he helped compose a confession for the emerging Confessing Church, in August 1933, the confession not only affirmed those things which should be confessed, it also denied those false beliefs promoted by the pro-Nazi German Christians—beliefs that, among other things, promoted nationalism and anti-Semitism. The Barmen Confession, composed largely by Barth eight months later, concisely named the positive theological tenets to be confessed, without including denials of false beliefs directly.[9]

So, one way to put this is that Bonhoeffer completely agreed with Barth that what is called for as we Christianly navigate whatever world we live in is to always be defined by theological convictions, centered in Christ—to "do theology and only theology." However, perhaps Bonhoeffer would not have

---

7. Rowe, *World Upside Down*, 17. Also see the profound book by Wannenwetsch, *Political Worship*.

8. Barth, "Letter to Eberhard Bethge," in *Fragments Grave and Gay*, 119-22, here 119.

9. Though Barth was probably right that the delegates at Barmen would not have affirmed a confession that directly challenged anti-Semitism (Barth, "Letter to Eberhard Bethge," 119).

added "as if nothing had happened." This was because, as is obvious, Bonhoeffer was always very attentive to the challenges presented by the culture and felt compelled to address them, both through speaking publicly and through shaping disciples, equipping them to faithfully navigate the world in which they lived. So then, Bonhoeffer's challenge was to make sure, in the midst of addressing specific issues, that he underscored the need to keep the God revealed through Jesus Christ central. Put another way, both Barth and Bonhoeffer did not believe in "hyphenated Christianities"—social Christian, social evangelical, religious socialist, and the like. All produce "dangerous short circuits" that implicitly deny that trust in God always entails "a total way of life." In other words, it was tempting to take the "shortest step with Christ into society," to see Christ representing the ideal for peace or social justice so that, e.g., identifying with a "progressive movement" is *truly* what animates us and shapes our involvement in society.[10] But *no* says Bonhoeffer in *Discipleship*: "[To be a disciple] is nothing other than being bound to Jesus Christ alone. This means completely breaking through anything preprogrammed, idealistic, or legalistic. No further content is possible because Jesus is the only content."[11]

So, the main way to see this book is that it places the emphasis on the practical side of Bonhoeffer, while simultaneously seeking to keep the theology that was so central for him front and center. To put it differently, I resonate in many ways with the theological approach of John Webster, Philip Ziegler, and Brian Brock in relation to Bonhoeffer (and in significant ways, Clifford Green and John Godsey). However, my book places the emphasis on the practical outworking of Bonhoeffer's central theological commitments (without, I hope, ever losing the theological center). This is done through the six chapters that comprise the book, along with the epilogue and appendices.

The first chapter will likely elicit the most controversy. It makes three claims, all related to Eberhard Bethge's account of Bonhoeffer's life and thought. And as I say in the chapter, it took me more than thirty years of living with and accepting Bethge's account before I had the confidence to challenge some of his interpretations. But by 2010 honesty compelled me to do so. First, Bethge denies that Bonhoeffer was ever a pacifist, which flies in the face of Bonhoeffer's own claims (both directly and indirectly). Second, Bethge portrays Bonhoeffer as having shifted rather dramatically in his theology by the beginning of the 1940s—becoming a practical realist in the last phase of his life. I have come to realize that this problem with

---

10. Gary Dorrien on Barth in Dorrien, *Social Democracy in Making*, 243.
11. Bonhoeffer, DBWE 4, 58–59.

Bethge's interpretation is the most serious. For it entails Bonhoeffer's having fundamentally changed from a Barthian to a Niebuhrian-type realist, which would entail a dramatic shift from his Christ-centered theology. But there is simply no evidence for such a shift. In fact, I hope to have shown the continuities in Bonhoeffer's life and thought from 1931 (or even more, 1935) until the end of his life. And third, there are problems with Bethge's interpretation in terms of facts. He implies that Bonhoeffer was executed for being involved in attempts to kill Hitler (and that he was personally involved in such attempts). Most now simply take this as a given. And yet when one examines the details in Bethge's biography, all we have are vague innuendos (except for the sorts of "involvement" I acknowledge as true in my chapter).

In chapter two I have offered my account of Bonhoeffer's opposition to anti-Semitism, beginning in April 1933. This is a subject that has been covered frequently. But I thought it important in this book to provide an account of Bonhoeffer's consistent, bold, and courageous opposition to anti-Semitism from early in the Hitler regime until the time he was arrested ten years later. Among other things, it shows that he never understood discipleship to be merely about "private virtuousness."

In chapter three I offer an account of Bonhoeffer's views on war. Typically, when the subject of nonviolence in relation to Bonhoeffer is treated, it is in relation to his pacifist-sounding views in the mid-1930s (especially in *Discipleship*) as contrasted with his later involvement in attempts to kill Hitler (and then searching for passages in *Ethics* that might explain the shift). But what I show in this chapter is the consistent trajectory of Bonhoeffer's views on war and conscientious objection from 1931 to the end of his life. For it is this larger trajectory that we need to notice if we are to grasp Bonhoeffer's views on violence and nonviolence. Although, again, the primacy here does not belong to nonviolence. It belongs to the centrality of Jesus Christ (as is made clear in both *Discipleship* and *Ethics*)—which, then, has theological and moral entailments.

Chapter four can be seen as the heart of the book. Too often the book *Discipleship* is seen not as a serious book but rather as a "devotional" book suited mostly for young enthusiastic Christian disciples (during their naïve "Bonhoeffer phase"). Without in any way disparaging how this rhetorically powerful work can speak to the souls of young zealous believers, I hope my chapter has demonstrated that the book was definitely intended to shape mature Christian disciples in ways suitable for the harsh challenges of the Third Reich *and* that it is, in its own way, a serious work of theology. As much as any of his writings, *Discipleship* reveals how Bonhoeffer has come to clarity regarding putting first things first (while naming with clarity and passion the moral entailments of these central commitments).

The fifth chapter, on *Ethics*, shows the continuities between the theology Bonhoeffer had arrived at by the mid-1930s and his writings of the 1940s. This is accomplished by looking at what the editors have (I believe accurately) guessed to be the first four chapters. The first three chapters offer a substantial theological framing that then lead into the more focused examination of chapter four in which Bonhoeffer dramatically, christologically reframed dominant ethical concepts, like realism and responsibility.[12]

During a few months in prison in 1944 Bonhoeffer, ever the theologian, offers remarkable reflections on a variety of topics, some of which seem simply the momentary imaginative and speculative cogitations of a brilliant theologian seeking to come to grips with a world that has been turned upside down. Who knows what he might have said on the same topics a few years later, if he had made it out of prison alive? I, like many others, have over the years found these reflections to be fascinating and provocative. I have in the brief scope of chapter six, however, reined in my curiosity in a way that serves the overall theme of the book (without, I hope, distorting what Bonhoeffer said during his time in prison).

Through the epilogue, I hope to have indicated what it means to think about Christian witness with Bonhoeffer in such a way that its ongoing relevance is obvious. This essay has three sections. The first draws signals from early in Bonhoeffer's theological existence that indicate the importance of the church to him (which supplements what was said in the chapter on *Discipleship*). In the second section, I draw from an essay by John Webster. Deeply influenced by Barth, Webster's approach to thinking about the Christian community's social witness largely coincides with Bonhoeffer's. There is something vitally important to take note of here. If I am right, then Bonhoeffer's understanding of the Christian community's service and witness to the larger community should be fundamentally theological. And for this identity to be sustained there must be vigilance in this regard. Webster captures this well in his brief essay. However, for Bonhoeffer, this witness and service should always give rise to concrete expressions, embodied faithfulness. Thus, the third section of this essay briefly describes a Christian community living out—faithfully embodying—what Bonhoeffer taught to his students, pastors in training in the midst of Nazism.

---

12. I considered going through the entirety of *Ethics*. However, since there are so many different avenues Bonhoeffer is exploring, I decided that going through each essay would in itself be complicated and would detract from the overall purpose of the book. Having recently reread the whole of *Ethics* I am convinced it is all, in varying ways, in line with the sorts of claims made within my ch. 5 (and the argument of this book as a whole).

Let me briefly comment on the four appendices that offer supplements to the main argument of the book. The first appendix responds to the claim that my interpretation of Bonhoeffer is forcing him into an "Anabaptist/pacifist" framework. This appendix is important, especially as a supplement to my first chapter on Eberhard Bethge. The second appendix, co-authored with Stanley Hauerwas, is a response to an essay written by Michael DeJonge, who argues that Bonhoeffer was definitely not committed to nonviolence. So, this essay briefly summarizes the evidence to the contrary. The third appendix is an essay by Scot McKnight, who is known as a New Testament scholar and writer of popular-style theological books on various topics. I also learned that he knows a considerable amount about Bonhoeffer. This appendix is a thoughtful essay by him that complements what is said in this book. Among the various qualities of the essay, I especially found his reflections on vicarious representative action to be a wonderful supplement to chapter five. The fourth and final appendix is a movie review. This review, among other things, offers a brief portrait of an Austrian Catholic who uniquely, so far as I know, refused to kill in Hitler's military or give an oath of allegiance to him (on pain of death) for reasons largely consonant with Bonhoeffer, albeit with a Catholic rationale and, apparently, as a non-pacifist.

Finally, as I conclude this introduction, I should say a few words about the relationship between this book and my 2013 book, *Bonhoeffer the Assassin?*. There is some overlap between the two books—especially in relation to my three biographical chapters within that book. However, this book is not dependent on that book. Nor does it simply repackage what is said there. This book began with my realization that I had to deal with Eberhard Bethge's claims regarding Bonhoeffer's pacifism (and related interpretive issues). I also saw the need to go through Bonhoeffer's writings on war in detail, which I hadn't previously done. Our earlier book hadn't separately treated Bonhoeffer's writings and actions in relation to anti-Semitism nor his writings from prison. And the chapters on *Discipleship* and *Ethics* in this book, which were also discussed in the 2013 book, have different foci from the previous book. The essay presented here as appendix 1—"Whose Bonhoeffer? Which Hermeneutics?"—is an essay I could only have written after being pressed by critics to reflect on my own journey with Bonhoeffer.

I

Toward Retrieving the True Legacy of Dietrich Bonhoeffer

Introduction

If one asks the average English-speaking Christian what she or he knows about Dietrich Bonhoeffer, it is quite predictable that what will be named is that he was executed for his involvement in attempts to kill Hitler. If this individual knows a bit more about Bonhoeffer, such a person might offer some version of the alluring words on the cover of the *New York Times* best-selling biography of Dietrich Bonhoeffer by Eric Metaxas:

> As Adolf Hitler and the Nazis seduced a nation, bullied a continent, and attempted to exterminate the Jews of Europe, a small number of dissidents and saboteurs worked to dismantle the Third Reich from the inside. One of these was Dietrich Bonhoeffer—a pastor and author, known as much for such spiritual classics as *The Cost of Discipleship* and *Life Together*, as for his 1945 execution in a concentration camp for his part in the plot to assassinate Hitler.[1]

The biography by Metaxas may not be well respected in the academy, but I think this quote in fact reflects what are generally believed to be the two best known—and thereby, centrally defining—facts about Bonhoeffer. First, he was executed for being involved in attempts to kill Hitler. Second, he was the author of two widely read books. One of them—*Nachfolge*, now translated

---

1. Metaxas, *Bonhoeffer*, inside flyleaf.

simply as *Discipleship*—seems to suggest that in the mid-1930s he sounded like a pacifist. Therefore, it follows that his later involvement in attempts to kill Hitler either reveals that he was never really a pacifist or shows that he underwent a shift in his ethics and had, by the beginning of the 1940s, embraced a realism similar to that of his former teacher Reinhold Niebuhr. For he realized that when you are confronted by the horrendous realities of a violent and cruel Nazi regime—especially the murder of millions of Jews—you are morally compelled to become a realist, willing to employ violence to stop those who perpetrate such gross injustices. In fact, precisely because of this shift in ethics, he is often seen as one of the most powerful exemplars of the Niebuhrian realist approach.[2]

But what if there is no evidence that he was executed for his part in the plot to assassinate Hitler? What if, instead, there is evidence that he was arrested, imprisoned, and executed for other reasons? Would that make a difference in the way we understand Bonhoeffer and his legacy?

If there is no evidence that he was executed for his involvement in attempts to kill Hitler—if in fact there is no evidence that he was in any meaningful way personally involved in attempts to kill Hitler—then why do so many, including educated theologians and ethicists, believe that he was?

That is a question that has haunted me since the publication in 2013 of our book *Bonhoeffer the Assassin?*[3] As I have pondered the question and reexamined texts, I have become clearer about what I believe are the two sources of the myth regarding Bonhoeffer's involvement in attempts to kill Hitler—an involvement that supposedly revealed his substantial shift in theological ethics and led to his execution. The first source is simply repetition, the almost ubiquitous claim in writings about Bonhoeffer that he was in fact executed for his part in the assassination plot.[4] When this unsubstantiated claim is repeated often enough, most people understandably will believe it is true. However, more significantly, I have come to believe that the origin of this myth is Eberhard Bethge, one of Bonhoeffer's closest friends and *the* most important biographer of Bonhoeffer. I have become convinced that Bethge wanted his readers to believe that by 1940 Bonhoeffer

---

2. Larry Rasmussen, in 2008, echoed my experience: "Not a single Bonhoeffer class I have taught, indeed no substantial conversation about Bonhoeffer I have been part of, fails to raise the question of how he moved from pacifism to tyrannicide, from the nonviolence of *Discipleship* to the subtle rationale for conspiracy and regime change in *Ethics*" (Rasmussen, "Response to Clifford Green," 168).

3. Nation et al., *Bonhoeffer the Assassin?* This book was co-authored with Anthony G. Siegrist and Daniel P. Umbel. Sometimes I will refer to it as our book, sometimes as my book. I conceived it and served as overall editor.

4. This is true in academic as well as popular-style books and articles.

had embraced a realist ethic. And once we are convinced that Bonhoeffer was executed for his involvement in attempts to kill Hitler, then we read his whole life story (and theology) in light of this knowledge.[5]

So, my task in this chapter is threefold: first, to show how Bethge leaves this impression in his biography and several essays; second, to summarize the evidence that we should rather see Bonhoeffer's life and thought in light of the actual reasons why he was arrested, imprisoned, and executed. And thus, third—and most importantly—I want to help us begin to appropriate the life and theological legacy of Bonhoeffer in light of a very different starting point.

Before I begin my summary of Bethge, let me be clear. Anyone working seriously to understand Dietrich Bonhoeffer is deeply indebted to his close friend and biographer, Eberhard Bethge. His lengthy biography is an indispensable source for understanding Bonhoeffer's life. Moreover, Bethge's fierce loyalty to his friend and his legacy is highly commendable. His commitments and the commitments of other Bonhoeffer scholars have culminated in, among other things, what is now the comprehensive collection of sixteen volumes of Bonhoeffer's writings (all now available in English).

It should not be surprising, however, that it is precisely these volumes that provide the resources for scholars to question some of Bethge's interpretations. My questions in particular have emerged after more than four decades of living with his biography and doing research. This has included reading most of the sixteen volumes of Bonhoeffer's writings and grappling with much of the most relevant secondary literature on the subject (which includes reading numerous detailed accounts of the attempts to remove Hitler from power). Within the last decade, this research has caused me to change my mind. The following is my attempt to provide a brief summary of Bethge's account of Bonhoeffer's role in the conspiracy and the implications for his theology.

---

5. One could offer many examples, in addition to the biography of Metaxas already mentioned. Let me cite two others. Ferdinand Schlingensiepen, in his 2010 biography, refers to Bonhoeffer's decision to become involved in attempts to kill Hitler as "the central decision of his life, to which everything else had been leading" (*Dietrich Bonhoeffer*, 285). In fact, he claims that after Bonhoeffer decides to get involved in attempts to kill Hitler, he returns to his views expressed in 1929, that "even murder can be sanctified" (286). But perhaps Charles Marsh is the biographer who most straightforwardly links him to Niebuhrian realism, expressed most fully through Bonhoeffer's involvement in the conspiracy. See Marsh, *Strange Glory*, 108, 274–80; 315.

Bethge's Template for Our Reading of Bonhoeffer & the Conspiracy[6]

Bethge discusses Bonhoeffer's role in the conspiracy in part 3 of his one-thousand-page biography.[7] However, to make sure the readers see what Bethge wants them to see, at the end of part 2 there is a short section entitled "Christian and Man for His Times," which provides the readers with a template, a guide if you will, for reading part 3.[8]

By telling us that Bonhoeffer "became a man for his times" beginning in 1939, Bethge apparently wants the readers to agree with his assessment of Bonhoeffer's experiment in "life together" with his students at Finkenwalde, the Confessing Church seminary he founded and directed from 1935 to 1937.[9] Now of course Bethge had a deep appreciation of the pastoral training Bonhoeffer offered at Finkenwalde. After all, this is where the two of them met, and it is where their friendship began. And he acknowledges that at the time there was something exciting about Bonhoeffer's lectures on following Jesus that became the book *Discipleship*. Nonetheless, with hindsight, Bethge came to believe that the approach to discipleship that Bonhoeffer taught his seminarians was expressive of a temporary phase in his teacher's short life. It did not truly engage the real world, did not reflect a man who was truly relevant to his times (especially to the public realm).

Thus Bethge wants us to see, with him, that it was also necessary for Bonhoeffer to enter a new phase, to become "a man for his times" after his second brief stay in New York City in the summer of 1939. The world he entered when he returned to Germany after this second stay in the United States called for a significantly different form of existence for Bonhoeffer, with a parallel adjustment to his theological ethic. As Bethge puts it, "in 1939 [Bonhoeffer] entered the difficult world of assessing what was expedient—of

---

6. The following essays/lectures by Bethge supplement the interpretive grid he placed on Bonhoeffer's involvement in the conspiracy and his shifts in theology as described in the biography: "Turning Points," "Christian Political Involvement," "Resistance and Terrorism," "Bonhoeffer's Pacifism," and "Dietrich Bonhoeffers Weg."

7. Bethge, *Dietrich Bonhoeffer*. Page numbers in parentheses refer to this text; the most directly pertinent section is 681–797. In what follows I am attempting to give a fair summary of what Bethge says, while deliberately framing it in a way that highlights the impressions I believe are often left with the reader. In other words, there are details in Bethge's biography that would counter certain impressions. But I've come to believe that, in the grip of Bethge's dominant interpretive grid, many of these particulars are simply lost or forgotten within the alluring tale of intrigue with its innumerable details.

8. Bethge, *Dietrich Bonhoeffer*, 676–78. The following essay provides more detail for this "template" for understanding Bonhoeffer: Bethge, "Turning Points."

9. Also see Bethge, "Turning Points," 7.

success and failure, tactics and camouflage" (678).¹⁰ In other words, Bethge encourages us to see that beginning in 1939 Bonhoeffer left behind some of the theological commitments he had named so compellingly in his books *Discipleship* and *Life Together*. The time to imagine being "only a Christian, a timeless disciple" was over for Bonhoeffer. Focusing on discipleship now "suddenly appeared to keep one in a realm of respectable but irrelevant privacy, and its structure appeared to be virtually an abstraction."¹¹ Put differently, in this new context discipleship was a "costly privilege" Bonhoeffer could no longer afford (678). This became ever more obvious to Bonhoeffer as he saw what was being done to the Jews by the Nazi regime.¹² The times required that he allow even "his innermost commitments, such as his stand for Christian pacifism" to be transformed.¹³ "The resister who had now agreed to the *coup d'état*," says Bethge, "no longer discussed questions like 'violence or non-violence.'"¹⁴ Concerns about expediency, "tactics and camouflage" would now define his approach to ethical issues.

In October 1940 Bonhoeffer became an agent with the German military intelligence agency, the Abwehr. From Bethge's account it appears that the Abwehr was mostly a front for conspirators. For we are told that though the agency "was not staffed solely by resistance people," it nevertheless was a "nest of resistance" (725). And we are informed that what was "most important" about Bonhoeffer's involvement in this military intelligence agency is that "it freed [him] for the work of the conspiracy in [Hans] Oster's and [Hans von] Dohnanyi's circle," a network of conspirators clearly involved in plots to kill Hitler (698). Early on in Bethge's account he lets us know that "for a long time [Bonhoeffer] merely knew and approved of what was going on [in terms of plans for a coup], until his knowledge and approval led to cooperation" (621). Furthermore, we are told that Bonhoeffer was eventually sent to prison because of being "a member of Military Intelligence" (685).

As Bethge narrates the story of Bonhoeffer's connections to the conspiracy he peppers his account with signals of Bonhoeffer's specific involvement in attempts on Hitler's life. Thus we are ushered into the secretive world of intrigue, of espionage, of the life of a military intelligence agent who is attempting to undermine his own government. We are told, for instance, that Bonhoeffer ripped pages out of his diaries in 1938 and 1939 because

---

10. Bethge uses this same language in "Turning Points," 13.

11. Bethge, "Turning Points," 18.

12. See especially Bethge, "Dietrich Bonhoeffers Weg," 125–30.

13. Bethge, "Turning Points," 18. This is an odd statement, given that elsewhere he says that Bonhoeffer never became a pacifist.

14. Bethge, "Resistance and Terrorism," 12.

they would be incriminating (626).[15] Moreover, the reader is informed that Bonhoeffer was involved but had "only a small role" in planning coups in 1939 and 1940 (671).[16] Then we are brought "to the third stage of the German resistance movement, that is, the period between the Western offensive in 1940, and the attempted assassination by [Fabian von] Schlabrendorff in March 1943 and Bonhoeffer's arrest on April 5, 1943. It includes," says Bethge, "Bonhoeffer's actual complicity in the plot against Hitler" (723). Thus we see Bonhoeffer intimately involved with the attempts on Hitler's life in March 1943 *and* we know that only a few weeks later Bonhoeffer is arrested. Here is one of Bethge's brief summaries of these tense events as they unfolded:

> [Bonhoeffer's] double life turned finally into a race between the conspiracy and the Gestapo as to who should reach its goal first: the conspiracy returning to destroy the Gestapo and the system which made it possible; the Gestapo to win control over Canaris' Military Intelligence Service—not knowing that by this they actually would desperately affect the conspiracy. Under suspicion of violating certain rules of the Intelligence service, Bonhoeffer, his brother-in-law, Hans von Dohnanyi, and some friends were arrested; but all suspicions were still unprovable. In prison the main point at issue was by all possible diversions to shield the friends who were continuing to act outside. This was successful until the complex plotting came to light after the failure of the attempt on Hitler's life on July 20, 1944.[17]

Though few details are given, Bethge's apparent claim here is consistent with what he implies in an interview clip in the 1982 documentary film *Dietrich Bonhoeffer: Memories and Perspectives*. Bonhoeffer was indeed personally involved in one or both of the efforts to kill Hitler in March 1943; thus his arrest followed on April 5.[18] Deepening our sense of Bonhoeffer's involvement, Bethge also reports various informal discussions in which Bonhoeffer supposedly affirmed the killing of Hitler. One such report is drawn from

---

15. Let me make myself clear. I have no question but that Bonhoeffer knew a fair amount about what was going on in the resistance circles his brother-in-law Hans von Dohnanyi was involved in or knew about. And he may have mentioned names in his diaries. However, the vagueness of Bethge's statement could imply some involvement on the part of Bonhoeffer, which is almost definitely not the case in 1938 and 1939.

16. What specifics is Bethge alluding to by referring to Bonhoeffer having "only a small role" in 1939 and 1940?

17. Bethge, "Turning Points," 17.

18. Bethge, interview, in Boehlke, *Dietrich Bonhoeffer*, beginning at approximately 1:17:00.

a conversation in the home of Hans von Dohnanyi, where Bonhoeffer is reported to have said "that if it fell to him to carry out the deed [of killing Hitler], he was prepared to do so." Bethge goes on to say, "It was a theoretical statement, of course, since Bonhoeffer knew nothing about guns or explosives" (751–52).

In the midst of discussing Bonhoeffer's involvement in the conspiracy, Bethge also notes the parallel shifts in Bonhoeffer's theological ethic by drawing contrasts between the books *Discipleship* and *Ethics* (see esp. 715–22). This helps us to understand how the one who wrote *Discipleship* in 1937—apparently calling on followers of Jesus to renounce the use of violence—can by the early 1940s affirm the killing of enemies. But Bethge had prepared readers for this earlier in his biography by informing us that Bonhoeffer never actually became a convinced pacifist (153; cf. 127, 254, 388).

By the time we are brought to the point where Bonhoeffer is executed by the Nazi regime on April 9, 1945, we are not surprised that he is hanged on the same morning as other well-known conspirators. For he was one of them. They were all executed for their involvement in efforts to assassinate Hitler.

This is no mundane story of the relatively uninteresting life of a theologian. Quite the contrary. Through Bethge's narration of Bonhoeffer's life as a conspirator, readers have been brought into the exciting world of intrigue, the world of spies and counterspies—observing a life involved in world-transforming events at one of the most important moments in modern history.

So, this is my summary of what I believe to be the impressions that are left with most readers of Bethge's biography. That is why many teachers or writers repeat the story that Bonhoeffer was executed for being involved in attempts to kill Hitler. For more than thirty years I too was under the spell of Bethge's narrative. It wasn't clear to me how it all held together, for there seemed to be unresolved contradictions. Nonetheless, I thought to myself: who am I to challenge the authority of Eberhard Bethge?

Beginning around 2010 several factors emboldened me to challenge the narrative I've just recounted. First, I read a number of book-length accounts of the attempts on Hitler's life. Second, as I reread and carefully outlined Bethge's biography, I noticed that throughout his narrative he consistently understated and even contradicted Bonhoeffer's own claims regarding war and what Bonhoeffer referred to on occasion as pacifism. Third, I realized that Bethge seems to be working with a rather common stereotype of pacifism, including Bonhoeffer's. Thus Bonhoeffer is portrayed as being responsibly involved in crucial public issues only after 1939—when according to Bethge he becomes a "man for his times," willing to use violence. Prior to that time, while sounding like a pacifist, he is only concerned with private virtuousness (and thus is publicly irresponsible). Finally, in relation to Bonhoeffer's involvement in attempts on Hitler's life, I concluded that Bethge wasn't so much wrong as he was vague about facts and, because of that, misleading. (Sabine Dramm, in her book *Dietrich Bonhoeffer and the Resistance*, is much more helpful.) So, how would I reframe these key components of Bonhoeffer's life and legacy?

Reading Bonhoeffer with and against Eberhard Bethge

To be fair, it is because of Bethge's honesty about Bonhoeffer's own claims that I have lived with questions for over forty years. What do I mean?

Long before we had the sixteen volumes of collected works by Bonhoeffer in English, Bethge quoted a letter that Bonhoeffer wrote to his longtime friend Elizabeth Zinn on January 27, 1936.[19] In it Bonhoeffer mentions a transformation that happened in his life and thought; he refers to it as "a great liberation" (*grosse Befreiung*). He confesses that he had too often in the past pursued his vocation as a theologian in an overly ambitious way, expressive of his own vanity. Because of that he often found himself alone. He acknowledges that though he is a theologian and a former pastor, neither the church nor prayer had previously been very important to him. In fact, he confesses: "I was not yet a Christian but rather in an utterly wild and uncontrolled fashion my own master." But then his life was dramatically changed; he experienced a "great liberation." What brought about this transformation? Bonhoeffer reports that "the Bible, especially the Sermon on the Mount freed me from all this." Being so liberated, it became clear to him "that the life of a servant of Jesus Christ must belong to the church." A daily reading of the Psalms—and regular prayer—soon became very important to him. He began to have greater clarity about his own vocation. He also explicitly states that through this liberation he came to see "pacifism" as "utterly self-evident," which he acknowledged was a significant shift for him, for he had previously passionately argued against pacifism.[20]

---

19. Bonhoeffer, "To Elizabeth Zinn," DBWE 14, 134–35. The summaries and quotes in this paragraph are from this letter.

20. I don't believe I have ever used the term *deceptive* to refer to someone else's writing. But I don't know any other way to describe the treatment by Eric Metaxas of this letter from Bonhoeffer to Elizabeth Zinn, as it pertains to pacifism. On pages 123–24 in his 2010 biography, Metaxas quotes almost the whole of this 1936 letter. *Almost* the whole. He conveniently leaves out the paragraph where Bonhoeffer says he came to see "pacifism as utterly self-evident." Having left out this important statement, Metaxas is

We can date this transformation as occurring between 1929 and 1931.[21] Bonhoeffer likely began this process through the discovery of the writings of his theological contemporary Karl Barth in the winter of 1924–1925. It was continued in the writing of his two graduate theses, in 1927 and 1930. But his transformation was truly accomplished and solidified through his experiences in New York City in 1930–1931 while a student at Union Theological Seminary. This happened partly through his deep involvement in Abyssinian Baptist Church, a large, dynamic African American congregation. It was also facilitated through his close friendship with the French Reformed student Jean Lasserre, the first pacifist Bonhoeffer had ever met of his own generation. Lasserre apparently convinced him, through a serious reading of the Sermon on the Mount, to become what Bonhoeffer himself referred to as a pacifist. Though he was quite critical of much of the theology at Union Seminary, Bonhoeffer's classes and friendships there, along with his observations of the harsh realities of racism, helped him acquire a new (or deepened) understanding of the social implications of the Christian faith that would remain with him until the day he died.

What distinguishes my view from Bethge's regarding this transformation is that I believe the evidence shows that the "great liberation" that Bonhoeffer experienced was a *substantial* and also, crucially, a *permanent* transformation—spiritually and theologically. That is, it was a liberation that affected the whole of Bonhoeffer's life and thought from 1931 to the time of his death. His basic reorientation to the Christian faith was lasting. The central way to name this permanency is to say that for the rest of his life his faith and theology are centered in—and redefined by—the person and work of Jesus Christ as articulated most fully in the book *Discipleship*. The implications of this are many, as indicated in his letter to Elizabeth Zinn. But all of them remain to the end of his life, including his coming to see "pacifism" as "utterly self-evident."

Bethge would have us believe that sometime between the summer of 1939 and the fall of 1940 Bonhoeffer became "a man for his time," learning

---

then free to make several unsubstantiated claims. First, he claims that during Bonhoeffer's time in New York City he "did not agree with [Jean Lasserre's] strongly pacifist views" (111). Later in his book Metaxas claims that Bonhoeffer did not "make an issue" of conscientious objection to his students at the seminary from 1935 to 1937 (265). The first claim contradicts what Jean Lasserre himself has said. And the second claim directly contradicts the testimony of Bonhoeffer's former students Eberhard Bethge and Joachim Kanitz.

21. We can do such dating because he presented a lecture on "Basic Questions of a Christian Ethic" in Barcelona, Feb. 8, 1929, in which he defended war (DBWE 10, 359–78). According to Jean Lasserre, Bonhoeffer gave a lecture in Mexico in the summer of 1931 defending pacifism; we have texts critical of war beginning in 1932.

to live a publicly responsible life. His interim stage of teaching discipleship was at an end. The time to imagine being "only a Christian, a timeless disciple" was over. He needed to emerge from this "realm of respectable but irrelevant privacy." The times now required him to allow even "his innermost commitments, such as his stand for Christian pacifism" to be transformed. For "in 1939 [Bonhoeffer] entered the difficult world of assessing what was expedient—of success and failure, tactics and camouflage."

But Bonhoeffer is clear in his book *Ethics* that Christians should never shape their ethics around concerns about success. This is not to say that Christians don't live in the realm of reality. But they discern their engagement in the real world as mediated by Jesus Christ—as Bonhoeffer says in *Ethics* and earlier in his book *Discipleship*.

And when did Dietrich Bonhoeffer ever imagine discipleship to be about "private virtuousness," separated from public life? Or to put it differently, when was Bonhoeffer ever not a "man for his times," addressing himself to issues of urgent public concern? His life—so I would argue—was a life of faithful witness and resistance, including in the public realm, from 1931 forward.

What we know is that, following the horrors of World War I, Bonhoeffer spoke powerfully on behalf of peace. His advocacy began in the summer of 1931 and continued through at least the spring of 1940. There is no public or social issue to which he spoke more frequently than the issue of war. And because he spoke before 1935 and to many multinational, ecumenical groups, his opposition wasn't just to the militarism of the Third Reich, it was against war, full stop (as the Brits say). In December 1932, for instance, in a brief lecture on "Christ and Peace," he said: "For Christians, any military service, except in the ambulance corps, and any preparation for war, is forbidden."[22] When he was on planning committees for ecumenical gatherings, he often made sure that conscientious objection was a subject of discussion for the meetings.

Bethge claims, despite his friend's own assertion, that Bonhoeffer never became a pacifist. Or later, acknowledging that Bonhoeffer sounded like a pacifist, Bethge claims that he shifted from his "pacifism" to a realistic assessment of the need for violence. But there are other testimonies regarding Bonhoeffer's teachings and life. Jean Lasserre, who lectured with Bonhoeffer on peace in Mexico in 1931; Lawrence Whitburn, one of his parishioners in London, 1933–1935; Theodore Heckel, a German church authority who heard Bonhoeffer speak on a number of occasions and interacted with him personally during much of the 1930s; Joachim Kanitz and Wolf-Dieter

---

22. Bonhoeffer, DBWE 12, 260.

Zimmermann, both students of Bonhoeffer in Berlin and at Finkenwalde; Herbert Jehle, who was converted to pacifism through Bonhoeffer; Paul Lehmann in the summer of 1939; and Karl Barth, who met with Bonhoeffer at least six times between 1940 and 1942—all claim that Bonhoeffer was an advocate for pacifism.

In 1934 Bonhoeffer secured a personal invitation from Mohandas Gandhi to study with him in India, in order, as Bethge reports, to learn to fight against Hitler in a Christian manner (that is, nonviolently). As it happened, Bonhoeffer was confronted with a difficult choice at the time: study with Gandhi or direct a seminary for the Confessing Church. He made the agonizing decision to direct the seminary. But in doing so he was not choosing against nonviolence. In fact, in letters to both his friend Erwin Sutz and his brother Karl-Friedrich, he emphasized that a part of what he saw as vital to the training of pastors was helping them to take the Sermon on the Mount seriously.[23] Consistent with that commitment, one of the revolutionary components of the seminary's training was Bonhoeffer's powerful lectures on discipleship that were then developed into the book *Discipleship*. The book is fundamentally about the theological and spiritual centrality of Jesus Christ for the Christian life. However, within it Bonhoeffer offers a substantial argument for the call by Jesus to love enemies and renounce the use of violence.[24]

Of course war was not the only public issue that occupied Bonhoeffer long before 1939. During 1933 Bonhoeffer worked diligently to prevent the Protestant Church in Germany from being redefined by Nazism. This meant many things. But it certainly included attitudes toward, relationships with, and public policies toward Jews. Bonhoeffer was one of the first German Protestants to speak out publicly on behalf of the Jews. In April 1933, just as the first anti-Semitic legislation was passed, Bonhoeffer wrote an article on behalf of Jews. He continued both to speak publicly and act personally on their behalf—whether baptized or not—from that point forward. In fact, his students have noted that part of what set Bonhoeffer apart from many others within the Confessing Church was his belief that the Christian community, as the body of Christ in the world, should always act on behalf of others (and not just for itself).

There are two issues here that should not be missed. First, it is a myth to imagine that Bonhoeffer was not speaking and acting publicly on issues of vital importance long before 1939. Militarism, nationalism, and war were such issues, as was anti-Semitism. Second, once we arrive at the year 1939

---

23. Bonhoeffer, "To Erwin Sutz," DBWE 13, 217.
24. See especially 100–110, 120–25, and 131–45 in *Discipleship* (and ch. 4, below).

there is a consistent trajectory within Bonhoeffer's life and public witness. And the evidence clearly confirms that he continued to live consistently in regards to his belief about war (and violence more broadly).

With this trajectory in mind, let us return to 1939. There is little doubt that Bonhoeffer's central motivation for traveling to the United States in June of that year was to avoid being conscripted into military service.[25] However, despite the desires of his American friends, he only remained in New York City for a few weeks. From a letter he wrote to Reinhold Niebuhr we know that his return had to do with his belief that staying in the US would have lacked integrity. For how could he have imagined returning to Germany later, when it was safe to do so, if he was unwilling to suffer with his fellow Germans during this difficult and even dangerous time?[26] As he said to his friend Paul Lehmann, on June 26: "I must go back to the 'trenches' (I mean of the Church struggle)."[27] Lehmann also had a conversation with Bonhoeffer shortly before he boarded the ship for Germany. They had both recently read *The Revolution of Nihilism*, a book on the situation in Germany. Lehmann commented that the book had caused him to abandon his pacifism. Bonhoeffer said it only solidified his commitment to pacifism.[28] However, Bonhoeffer had also realized that however much he wanted to avoid military service, fleeing to America was not the path of costly discipleship he had taught his students. As he had said to others, "Peace is not the way of safety. It must be dared!" Therefore, he returned to Germany within only a few weeks.

Contrary to the way Bethge frames this decision, we see Bonhoeffer continuing the same trajectory he had been on since 1935 (though certainly with a shift in circumstances). Since December 1937, three months after the Finkenwalde seminary had been closed by the Gestapo, Bonhoeffer had begun training pastors in various locations through a makeshift seminary-in-exile. When he returned to Germany in July 1939, he resumed this work until March 1940, when the Gestapo once again closed the seminary (this time permanently). However, the new and ever-present challenge for Bonhoeffer personally was that military officials were seeking to conscript him into the armed forces. This was a reality he had to confront. To avoid killing in war, Bonhoeffer applied to be a chaplain in the military; his application was denied. What was he to do?

25. Bonhoeffer, "To George Bell," DBWE 15, 156.
26. Bonhoeffer, "To Reinhold Niebuhr," DBWE 15, 210.
27. Bonhoeffer, "To Paul Lehmann," DBWE 15, 206.
28. Reported by Rasmussen, *Dietrich Bonhoeffer*, 58.

Apparently German theologian Sabine Dramm and I have come to similar conclusions. In the spring of 1940 Bonhoeffer met with his brother-in-law Hans von Dohnanyi and Dohnanyi's boss, Hans Oster; both had top positions in the Abwehr, the counterintelligence service. Because of Bonhoeffer's extensive contacts throughout Europe, they believed they could make a plausible argument to the relevant authorities that he could be helpful in gathering military intelligence through these contacts. Then he could become an official intelligence agent. Oster would insist that his work was essential for the welfare of Germany, and therefore he would be granted *uk* status by the military and thus be exempt from conscription.[29]

I have seen no evidence to confirm what Bethge implies, namely that Bonhoeffer went to work for the Abwehr in order to join the conspiracy. Rather, if we are paying attention to the trajectory of Bonhoeffer's life and teachings, we should draw the same conclusion that Dramm has:

> At the beginning of Bonhoeffer's participation in the political resistance was the question about his call-up for military service. Bonhoeffer was unwilling to perform military service for reasons of faith and conscience, but he of course knew that the penalty for refusal was death. Helped by Hans Oster, Bonhoeffer's brother-in-law Hans Dohnanyi developed a particular construction that made the necessary 'uk' status possible. . . . In the foreground, therefore, [of Bonhoeffer's decision to work for the Abwehr] was not a unique (let alone datable) fundamental decision by Bonhoeffer to join the resistance. It was because of his personal, difficult, and risky decision to refuse to perform military service that he entered into the political work of the resistance with what was for him (theo)logical consistency.[30]

So, what did he do for the Abwehr? Really, nothing for it as such. He took a number of trips abroad, which could be made to look as if he was gathering military intelligence, though he was not. His role in the Abwehr was an incredible gift. It not only freed him from having to kill in Hitler's military, it also freed him to continue to do work for the church. He in fact was

---

29. *Uk* is an abbreviation for *unabkömmlich*, meaning indispensable, used as shorthand to mean that one's work is indispensable for the welfare of Germany. Someone with this status was serving the war effort indirectly, thus rendering the person ineligible for conscription. (See DBWE 6, 407n67.)

30. Dramm, *Dietrich Bonhoeffer and the Resistance*, 235. Victoria Barnett concurs: "As the correspondence and documentation from 1938 through April 1943 demonstrate, Dohnanyi brought Bonhoeffer into Military Intelligence in order to keep him out of military service" (Barnett, "Bonhoeffer and the Conspiracy," 72.)

commissioned to continue such work.[31] This official role even put him in a position to assist the church, for as Victoria Barnett suggests, "most of the resistance meetings in which Bonhoeffer took part concerned the pressures on the Confessing Church."[32] He also served as an occasional church consultant on specific issues. His time was freed to write letters to former students and their families. He wrote the manuscripts for his book on *Ethics*. Moreover, because his role as an Abwehr agent allowed him to travel throughout Europe, he could continue to visit with his ecumenical friends, especially Karl Barth in Switzerland. In fact, these visits were often very encouraging for Bonhoeffer in those challenging times. As he wrote to a Swedish theologian friend in a letter on April 11, 1942: "The more hopeless the ruptures in the world become, the more strongly Christians must maintain the bond of peace that unites them in Jesus Christ. Only in this way can the peoples someday find their way back to one another."[33]

But even if his primary reason for working with the Abwehr was to avoid military service, did not such work bring him into regular contact with members of the resistance movement? Bethge gives the impression that the Abwehr was comprised mostly of conspirators. The truth is, there were approximately 13,000 employees in the agency, only about fifty of whom were involved in the conspiracy—though this included several of the top officials.[34] The main headquarters were in Berlin; Bonhoeffer was assigned to the Munich office. Nevertheless, there is no doubt that he interacted with some of the conspirators from time to time. At least one of these conspirators—Gertrude Luckner, who gave assistance to and rescued Jews in the Freiburg area—was a fellow pacifist.[35] But the one he interacted with the most was his brother-in-law and close friend, Hans von Dohnanyi. And I have no reason to doubt that Marijke Smid is right that Bonhoeffer played a significant role as counselor and advisor to Dohnanyi (and a more minor role as moral counselor to others, as well).[36] However, just because he was willing to help his brother-in-law in clarifying his own moral understanding

---

31. Bonhoeffer, "To Eberhard Bethge," DBWE 16, 83.
32. Barnett, "Bonhoeffer and the Conspiracy," 69.
33. Bonhoeffer, "To Erling Eidem," DBWE 16, 270.
34. Dramm, *Dietrich Bonhoeffer and the Resistance*, 33.
35. Barnett, "Bonhoeffer and the Conspiracy," 70, mentions this activity on the part of Luckner, a Catholic social worker "active in the Catholic Peace Movement." Luckner, in a speech in 1978, identified herself as "a very old pacifist. That began at the end of the first World War" (Luckner, "Untitled Remarks," 8.)
36. Reported by Barnett, "Bonhoeffer and the Conspiracy," 72–73, 75.

of the conspiracy does not mean that Bonhoeffer necessarily agreed with him.[37]

But what was Bonhoeffer's role in attempts to remove Hitler from power (including assassination attempts)? Peter Hoffman, perhaps the world's foremost expert on resistance movements in Nazi Germany, refers to Bonhoeffer's work among the conspirators as putting out "peace feelers." More specifically, says Hoffman, "[Bonhoeffer] urged his [ecumenical] friends . . . to use their influence to ensure that the Allies would call a halt to military operations during the anticipated coup in Germany."[38] As Bethge puts it: "Parallel to the conspiracy there were efforts at peace contacts. These peace feelers were not a condition for the coup, as has often been asserted, but they could play an important part" (735). Bonhoeffer's first direct effort was in September 1941. However, the most important meeting in this regard, according to Bethge and Sabine Dramm, was on May 31, 1942, in Stigtuna, Sweden, when Bonhoeffer and his fellow German Johannes Schönfeld met with the English bishop George Bell. Here is the way Bethge describes what Bonhoeffer was commissioned to do in this meeting: "The commission was basically the same as in September 1941, but the aims were stated more precisely. In the event of a coup led by certain persons whose names would be disclosed, Bonhoeffer was to give assurances that its underlying position was peaceful, 'however these men may first have had to disguise themselves to the people, before everything can be truly resolved,' and—this was addressed particularly to the British government—'to ask the military commanders not to use that moment to attack, but to give the new government time to restore healthy conditions'" (757).

To my knowledge there is no evidence that Bonhoeffer's involvement in the conspiracy went beyond this quite limited role. Some might believe that this reflects Bonhoeffer's abandonment of pacifism. Or perhaps he continued his opposition to war but not to killing a leader who had become a tyrant. But there is no particular reason to reach either conclusion. As Bethge says, the attempt to remove Hitler from power was not contingent on the success of this effort. This specific task, if successful, would save lives and make it easier to erect a new government. Hans Bernd von Haeften was another German involved in this effort. He had briefed both Bonhoeffer and Schönfeld before their meeting with Bell in Stigtuna. As it happens, according to Dramm, Haeften was "a convinced supporter of nonviolence"; more

---

37. I am reminded that John Howard Yoder, a well-known pacifist, co-taught a course to ROTC students at the University of Notre Dame for fifteen years. He did this because he thought there was value in clarifying the laws of war, the just war tradition, etc. for these military officers in training (even though he himself was a pacifist).

38. Hoffman, *History of the German Resistance*, 218.

specifically, he could not reconcile killing Hitler with his faith.[39] And yet Haeften had no qualms about participating in this effort with Bonhoeffer to ask the Allied forces not to take advantage of Germany in one of its weakest moments (if the coup was successful). Friedrich Siegmund-Schultze, a German pacifist living in exile in Switzerland, was involved in similar efforts (737, 769–70).[40] Yet, so far as I know, Siegmund-Schultze continued to be a pacifist.[41]

To be clear, there is no evidence that Bonhoeffer had any role in the conspiracy to assassinate Hitler itself. Rather, he was involved only in what Bethge refers to as an effort "parallel to the conspiracy," namely, seeking to broker at least a temporary peace agreement with the Allies in the event that one of the attempts on Hitler's life was successful.

Very many believe that Bonhoeffer was arrested on April 5, 1943, because of his involvement in the two attempts on Hitler's life in March 1943. There were indeed two attempts on Hitler's life in March, only a few weeks before Bonhoeffer was arrested. Of course neither attempt was successful. But many are unaware that neither of these two attempts was discovered by the authorities. Thus no one was arrested because of them. Moreover, apart from Bethge's vague narrative, there is nothing to suggest any involvement on the part of Bonhoeffer. These attempts were instigated by Colonel Henning von Tresckow, the chief of staff of the Army Group Center. The men directly involved were connected to Tresckow. Dohnanyi secured the bombs that were used, because he had access to explosives. But nothing suggests any involvement on the part of Bonhoeffer. In order not to be misled by Bethge's vague narrative, it is important that students of Bonhoeffer note the clear statement made by Clifford Green, the executive director of the collected works of Bonhoeffer in English. Green states: "No scholars or serious readers of Bonhoeffer believe that he . . . was personally involved in attempts to kill Hitler."[42]

So, then, why was Bonhoeffer arrested on April 5, 1943? German authorities had had the Abwehr under surveillance for some time, suspecting that some agents were working against the welfare of Germany as they saw it. By the autumn of 1942 they had discovered financial irregularities in the books in the Munich office, just as Bethge says. The irregularities were connected to a successful attempt by several Abwehr agents, including Dohnanyi and Bonhoeffer, to save the lives of fourteen Jews by helping them

---

39. Dramm, *Dietrich Bonhoeffer and the Resistance*, 168.
40. Dramm, *Dietrich Bonhoeffer and the Resistance*, 79–80.
41. On Siegmund-Schultze, see Conway, "Between Pacifism and Patriotism."
42. Green, "Peace Ethic or 'Pacifism,'" 202.

pose as Abwehr agents, escape from Germany, and resettle in Switzerland. In order to relocate them as well as compensate them for property stolen from them as Jews, these fourteen people were given significant sums of money. The anti-Semitic German authorities were furious that Abwehr agents were helping Jews escape. They also assumed that significant portions of these large sums of money were pocketed by the agents. And thus arrests were made on April 5, 1943, including those of Dohnanyi and Bonhoeffer.[43]

Because of the collected works of Bonhoeffer, we now know what the charges were that led to his imprisonment. We have a summary of the court proceedings. There is no mention of any attempts on Hitler's life. Instead, the central issue for the judge in Bonhoeffer's case is that he was effectively living out the life of a conscientious objector to Germany's war through his work with the Abwehr.[44] That is to say, in September 1943 Bonhoeffer was indicted on charges of avoiding the call-up to military service and thus officially "subverting military power."[45] The court records show that the judge realized that Bonhoeffer's involvement in the Abwehr was certainly not essential for the welfare of Germany, as his *uk* status suggested. Rather, it was a cover, a way for Bonhoeffer to exist in Nazi Germany without killing in Germany's war and without giving a personal oath of allegiance to Hitler—and yet still be free to do ongoing work for the church.

Bonhoeffer was executed on April 9, 1945. We don't know exactly why he was hanged on that day. There was no real trial. It is possible his name was found on a list of "conspirators." And without question, as far as the inner circle of the Nazi regime was concerned, what Bonhoeffer did in putting out "peace feelers" in 1941 and 1942, as well as his knowledge of attempts to overthrow the Hitler regime without reporting them, were acts of treason. As historian Anton Gill has said, 7,000 people were arrested and 4,500 executed following the attempt on Hitler's life in July of 1944. He goes on to say that "in their orgy of summary justice and killing, the Nazis brought in many thousands who were innocent of any plot to kill the dictator. . . . The authorities also found themselves with an excuse to execute many more dissidents who had been in prison . . . since before the 20 July attempt."[46] If we look at the trajectory of Bonhoeffer's life, then examine why he was arrested and the charges that led to his imprisonment, then as we think about why he was executed, we might remember the accusation brought against

---

43. Just so I'm clear: Bethge includes a number of these details in his account in the biography. However, I think some key specifics are often lost because of the way the narrative is shaped. And in some of his briefer accounts, he leaves out salient details.

44. See DBWE 16, 435–46.

45. DBWE 16, 444.

46. Gill, *An Honorable Defeat*, xiii.

Bonhoeffer in 1936 by church official Theodore Heckel. In making an argument that Bonhoeffer should not be allowed to train pastors, Heckel said that it was because he was a "pacifist and enemy of the state."[47]

There are two more claims that need to be examined briefly. Bethge asserts that after Bonhoeffer came back to Germany in 1939 there is no more talk of violence and nonviolence. Rather, "[Bonhoeffer] entered the difficult world of assessing what was expedient—of success and failure, tactics and camouflage" (678). But this is simply not true. The primary textual evidence is Bonhoeffer's posthumously published book *Ethics*.

When we attend carefully to the theological framing of Bonhoeffer's working drafts of this book, we see what we have seen before—the centrality of Jesus Christ, with all the implications this claim entails (as Bonhoeffer sees it). It is only if we ignore this theological framework that we miss the redefining that Bonhoeffer is attempting in this extraordinarily creative work (written between 1940 and 1943).[48]

Take the terms *realism* and *responsibility*. These were moral terms that for many academics at the time carried considerable weight.[49] Therefore, Bonhoeffer engaged in radical redefining by insisting that such terms be seen thoroughly in light of the Christ's centrality. For Bonhoeffer, it was no longer *realism* and *responsibility* that were the freight-bearing terms, but rather the God known in Jesus Christ, thus subverting the typical moral framework.

"The source of a Christian ethic," Bonhoeffer says, "is not the reality of one's own self, not the reality of the world, nor is it the reality of norms and values. It is the reality of God that is revealed in Jesus Christ."[50] Put pointedly, "All concepts of reality that ignore Jesus Christ are abstractions."[51] Toward the end of a substantial discussion of pseudo-realism, Bonhoeffer says, "Furthermore, the foundations of this so-called realism are false insofar as they fail to understand the meaning of the Christian concept of love and thus of the concepts of self-denial, forgiveness, suffering, renunciation, love of enemies, and innocence [*Unschuld*]."[52]

Likewise, with the term *responsibility*: "Because of Jesus Christ," Bonhoeffer famously says, "the essence of responsible action intrinsically

---

47. "From Theodor Heckel to the Regional Church Committee," DBWE 14, 148.

48. The following is an abbreviated version of the discussion I offer below, in ch. 5.

49. Among others, this would include writings by Reinhold Niebuhr and Max Weber.

50. Bonhoeffer, *Ethics*, DBWE 6, 49.

51. Bonhoeffer, *Ethics*, DBWE 6, 54.

52. Bonhoeffer, *Ethics*, DBWE 6, 240–41.

involves the sinless becoming guilty."[53] Immediately following this provocative statement, he says, "It is a sacrilege and an outrageous perversion to extrapolate from this statement a blanket license to commit evil acts. Only where a person becomes guilty out of love and responsibility does their action have a part in the justification pertaining to Jesus Christ's sinless guilt-bearing."[54] Furthermore, he says, "The responsibility of Jesus Christ for all human beings has love as its content and freedom as its form. . . . The commandments of God's righteousness are fulfilled in vicarious representation, which means in concrete, responsible action of love for all human beings."[55] "By grounding responsible action in Jesus Christ we reaffirm precisely the limits of such action."[56] "The Sermon on the Mount as the proclamation of the incarnate love of God calls people to love one another, and thus to reject everything that hinders fulfilling this task—in short, it calls them to self-denial. In renouncing one's own happiness, one's own rights, one's own righteousness, one's own dignity, in renouncing violence and success, in renouncing one's own life, a person is prepared to love the neighbor."[57]

Bonhoeffer concludes this chapter by offering ten pages of argument for why the Sermon on the Mount is crucial for understanding our Christian actions within real human history. Toward the end of these reflections—written in 1942 Germany—he says, "The Sermon on the Mount is either valid as the word of God's world-reconciling love everywhere and at all times, or it is not really relevant for us at all."[58]

So we can see that Bonhoeffer's *Ethics* manuscripts refute Bethge's claim that after 1939 concerns about success assumed such importance for him that he no longer spoke of violence and nonviolence. Or that Bonhoeffer abandoned "his stand for Christian pacifism."

The only real "evidence" that Bonhoeffer shifted from the convictions he articulated in various lectures and in his book *Discipleship* is that of memories of informal conversations, in which Bonhoeffer supposedly affirmed the killing of Hitler. But before we assign much weight to these

53. Bonhoeffer, *Ethics*, DBWE 6, 234.
54. Bonhoeffer, *Ethics*, DBWE 6, 234–35.
55. Bonhoeffer, *Ethics*, DBWE 6, 232, translation amended. *Stellvertretung* is an important theological term in Bonhoeffer's writings across his whole writing career. The collected works typically translate it as "vicarious representative action." I think the better translation is "vicarious representation." The term does not in itself refer to action, though it is sometimes connected to action, as is the case here.
56. Bonhoeffer, *Ethics*, DBWE 6, 224.
57. Bonhoeffer, *Ethics*, DBWE 6, 242.
58. Bonhoeffer, *Ethics*, DBWE 6, 243.

memories we should take seriously the lessons learned by Sabine Dramm in her research on Bonhoeffer and resistance. Dramm discovered contradictory accounts, for instance, regarding Bonhoeffer's role in putting out peace feelers at the meeting in Stigtuna, near Stockholm, on May 31, 1942. As she reports, "The reconstruction of the events in Stigtuna repeatedly raises questions about the reliability of specific recollections." She comments on how "matter-of-course assumptions" can distort memories and thus raise questions about "the objective character of human perceptions."[59] Bethge confirms this suspicion when he questions the accuracy of Bishop Bell's memory—even though it's drawn from a diary Bell kept—that Bonhoeffer would have referred to Hitler as "the Anti-Christ."[60]

Let me suggest a contemporary parallel. A colleague of mine at Eastern Mennonite University, a lifelong pacifist, used to live and work in Zimbabwe and other African countries. He tells me that he would not be at all surprised if some friends of his imagined that he would have affirmed the killing of President Robert Mugabe. For on certain occasions, in conversations with trusted friends and allies in the battle against oppression and injustice, he would vent, expressing his empathy with those who wanted to stop Mugabe by any means necessary. Who would not resonate with those who strongly opposed what were obvious forms of power abuse and oppression? That didn't mean it was true that he affirmed the killing of other human beings, even Mugabe. But listeners, with other frameworks for approaching issues such as killing, might easily have heard him in ways that weren't true to his own convictions. The same could have been true for Bonhoeffer. He was aware that none of the men he met with had ever publicly spoken against war and encouraged conscientious objection to war, as he had. No one resonated with his interpretation of the Sermon on the Mount. But he was among friends—friends he could trust. He had no idea his honest expressions of relative support of his friends or his empathy and frustration would be paraphrased and put into print.

Besides, there are contradictory memories. As mentioned earlier, Paul Lehmann reported that Bonhoeffer had reaffirmed his commitment to pacifism in the summer of 1939, just before he set sail to return to Germany.

---

59. Dramm, *Dietrich Bonhoeffer and the Resistance*, 171. It is, e.g., intriguing that Herbert Jehle, who was converted to pacifism by Bonhoeffer, says that Bonhoeffer was a pacifist "without qualification." However, when his widow was interviewed about Bonhoeffer, she speaks for her husband by saying of Bonhoeffer's (apparently active, affirming) role in the conspiracy: "'Oh, he had to do it!'" I would add: this is because she *knows* that a "reasonable" person would of course affirm violence in this situation (Green, "Bonhoeffer's Christian Peace Ethic," 360.)

60. Bethge, *Dietrich Bonhoeffer*, 722.

Emmi Bonhoeffer, one of Dietrich's sisters-in-law, recounts a conversation she had with him sometime after he had returned to Germany in 1939: "How is that with you Christians?" she asks. "You will not kill but that another one does it, you agree and are glad about it. Why is that?" Dietrich responds: "One should not be glad. But I understand what you mean."[61] Bonhoeffer met with Karl Barth on at least six occasions between 1940 and 1942. Barth was a trusted theological ally; Bethge says that Bonhoeffer told him "the whole truth."[62] A decade later Barth summarized his twin perceptions drawn from their conversations. On the one hand, "The Lutheran theologian Dietrich Bonhoeffer belonged to these circles [of those willing to kill Hitler]." On the other, "He was really a pacifist on the basis of his understanding of the Gospel."[63] When Franz Hildebrandt, whom Bethge referred to as Bonhoeffer's "best and most like-minded friend," was told in 1945 that Dietrich had been involved in efforts to kill Hitler, Hildebrandt said that he was sure that Bonhoeffer was not involved.[64]

Conclusion: "A Rather Different Bonhoeffer"

John DeGruchy, in his biography of Eberhard Bethge, says, "Had another of Bonhoeffer's close friends (say, Franz Hildebrandt) become Bonhoeffer's literary executor and written his biography, in all likelihood we would have a rather different Bonhoeffer today."[65] Indeed, what *if* Franz Hildebrandt, a Jewish Christian, had written Bonhoeffer's biography? In 1940 he wrote:

> As a Christian and as a minister of the church I consider my means to fight Hitler different from those employed by the world. I cannot reconcile modern warfare with Christianity though I respect my fellow Christians who are conscientiously able to do so. I would not object to an ordinary police force doing away with the Nazi party. But I fail to see how the killing of thousands of lives on both sides will harm the guilty. . . . I need not say how I feel about any colleagues of mine now fighting in Hitler's army. . . .
>
> Pacifism, therefore, is to me a practical, not a doctrinal question; it is the question of what means the Christian citizen should have in the service of his country. . . .

---

61. Emmi Bonhoeffer, interview, in Boehlke, *Dietrich Bonhoeffer*, beginning at approximately 1:03:00.
62. Bethge, *Bonhoeffer*, 727.
63. Barth, *Doctrine of Creation* (*CD* III/4), 449.
64. Green, "Pacifism and Tyrannicide," 46.
65. DeGruchy, *Daring, Trusting Spirit*, xiii.

My object is to preach the Gospel and to assure my fellow Christians of the prayers and solidarity of our suffering church with them; it is for the cause of Christ I want to work.[66]

Renate Bethge, Eberhard's wife and Dietrich's niece, has said that "when Bonhoeffer and his close friend Franz Hildebrandt met they invariably talked theology, but when Bonhoeffer and [Eberhard] Bethge met they invariably made music."[67] Is it possible that the reason Bonhoeffer and Hildebrandt "invariably talked theology" was because, as Eberhard Bethge himself said, Hildebrandt was indeed Bonhoeffer's "closest and most like-minded friend"—perhaps especially in relation to matters of theological ethics? And that Bethge was a different sort of friend, a friend with whom he enjoyed life, a profoundly trustworthy friend who, among other things, could be entrusted to be a faithful caretaker of Bonhoeffer's writings as he left them in his care? And is it possible that Hildebrandt's "rather different Bonhoeffer," if such had been constructed, might at key points resemble the account offered in *Bonhoeffer the Assassin?* and in this book rather than the account offered to us by Eberhard Bethge?

One critic of my 2013 book, Michael DeJonge, has implied that I have tried to make Bonhoeffer into an Anabaptist.[68] I am fairly sure he meant that I imagine Bonhoeffer to have been like one of the most influential Anabaptist theologians today—say, John Howard Yoder or Stanley Hauerwas. In response to this claim I would mostly say no. Like this critic, I actually see Bonhoeffer very much as a product of his own background and times. More specifically, he was very much influenced theologically by Luther and by Bonhoeffer's contemporary Karl Barth (to mention only two of the most significant influences). Then we have to say that he clearly departed in significant ways from most Lutherans at the time and went beyond the early Barth. In terms of Bonhoeffer's pacifism, I continue to resonate with this wonderful summary offered by Clifford Green (while substituting the phrase "pacifism" for his "Christian peace ethic"):

> Bonhoeffer's [pacifism] is intrinsic to his whole theology. It cannot be separated from his Christology, his understanding of discipleship and the Sermon on the Mount, his way of reading the Bible, and his understanding of the gospel and of the church. It belongs to the heart of his faith. Accordingly, it cannot be reduced to a principle. It is not a discrete option on a menu of ethical "positions." It is not a separate interchangeable part that

---

66. Hildebrandt, quoted in Cresswell and Tow, *Dr. Franz Hildebrandt*, 92–93.
67. Quoted in DeGruchy, *Daring, Trusting Spirit*, 17.
68. For more on this, see appendices 1 and 2 in this book.

can be removed from his theology and replaced by something else called, perhaps, "realism," or even "responsibility." His [pacifism] is woven throughout his theology and discipleship as a whole. It can't be removed without shredding the whole cloth.[69]

This way of putting it matters to me for three reasons. First, I believe it truly does fit with Bonhoeffer and his theology—including beliefs and actions that he, on occasion, named as pacifism. Second, it is a reminder that for Christians, beliefs about matters like peace and social justice should always be integrated into our theology as a whole. In fact, within our present challenges, I believe Bonhoeffer's way of doing this can be quite illuminating. And third, Green's summary poses a challenge to those many interpreters of Bonhoeffer who would make him into a Niebuhrian realist. Bonhoeffer quite clearly was not that. One way to put this is to paraphrase Bonhoeffer's friend Franz Hildebrandt in his introductory comments for a 1959 pamphlet on "Peace without Eschatology":

> What is commonly said [about Bonhoeffer the conspirator] . . . would "be just as possible, if Christ had never become incarnate, died, ascended to heaven, and sent His Spirit." . . . In a theological and ecclesiastical climate . . . where any literal application of the Gospel is suspect of "Schwärmertum" and where only the ex-pacifist is respectable, it will take some time and not a little humility to admit, especially for those trained in the school of the great Reformers, that at this point in question the Mennonite minority has been, and still is right: "not because nonresistance works, but because it anticipates the triumph of the Lamb that was slain."[70]

What difference would it make to our reception of the legacy of Dietrich Bonhoeffer if we quit framing his life and thought in terms of his being executed for his role in the plots to kill Hitler and instead began with the realization that he was executed in Nazi Germany for courageously proclaiming, and seeking to live faithfully in light of, the gospel of Jesus Christ? As a result, he was executed for rescuing Jews, being a conscientious objector to military service, and being perceived as an enemy of the state.[71]

---

69. Green, "Pacifism and Tyrannicide," 45.

70. Hildebrandt, quoted in Nation et al., *Bonhoeffer the Assassin?*, 232. Hildebrandt's original statement was referring to "what is commonly said from pulpits about peace."

71. I had earlier added to this essay some comments on the evolution of my views regarding Bonhoeffer and pacifism, which relates to what I've written in this chapter. However, I've decided to add an appendix that names this more fully; thus, see "Whose Bonhoeffer? Which Hermeneutic?"

2

"Only the One Who Cries Out for the Jews May Sing Gregorian Chants"[1]

Introduction: Entering into Bonhoeffer's World, 1933

You and I know the outcome of twelve years of Hitler's Third Reich. Specifically, we know what this meant for Jews not only in Germany but throughout Europe. And because of this we know viscerally that the words *Hitler* and *Nazism* represent unmitigated evil. But if we are to enter empathetically into the world of average Germans as Hitler assumes power at the end of January 1933, we must attempt to bracket our knowledge. The majority of Germans did not truly know who Hitler was. They had not read *Mein Kampf*.[2] They did not in the beginning know of his vision for the Thousand-Year Reich, which included the elimination of the Jews. To quote Kierkegaard, "Life must be understood backwards.... But it must be lived forwards."[3] And living life "forwards" means living without an awareness of where events are headed.

---

1. Bethge, "Dietrich Bonhoeffer and the Jews," 71. There is no text in which Bonhoeffer says this. The quote, apparently from late 1935, has been passed down in oral tradition (and Bethge believes it to be a reliable memory of what he said to a group of students). I have changed "he" to "the one" in the translation.

2. But I don't want to overstate this. Hitler waived his salary as chancellor, believing he could get by on the royalties from the sales of *Mein Kampf*. So, it must have been selling well. And after he became chancellor, the book was, by governmental mandate, given to all couples who registered their marriages (Bleuel, *Sex and Society*, 1.)

3. Kierkegaard, *Journals of Kierkegaard*, 89.

In other words, if we are to begin to understand average Germans as Hitler took power on January 30, 1933, then we must appreciate the context of Germany at the time. We must be aware, for instance, of the suffering associated with the four and a half long years of World War I. This war not only personally and painfully touched nearly every family in Germany but also was visibly made manifest by 1918 through the many walking wounded who came home from the war. This was followed by the stringent punishment meted out to Germany through the Versailles Treaty, which nearly every German resented. The Treaty not only highlighted the shame of their loss of the war, but the reparations they were forced to pay also crippled the country financially. In the midst of this, Germany experienced extraordinary inflation. For instance, in October 1923, Bonhoeffer reported in a letter to his parents that a loaf of bread cost six billion marks.[4] By the end of the 1920s all of this was capped off by an international economic depression, which led to widespread unemployment, poverty, and tremendous social unrest—including street fights between communists and fascists.[5]

This provides the immediate backdrop for the rise of Adolf Hitler and the National Socialist party. On January 30, 1933, Hitler was legally appointed as Reich chancellor by the aging President Hindenberg.[6] The young, energetic chancellor was a symbol of hope to many. Hitler promised order when chaos seemed to reign, pride when shame dominated the culture, and jobs and financial security when hardship and poverty were the order of the day.

On February 1, two days after he was appointed Reich chancellor, Hitler addressed the nation.[7] Listeners believed almost immediately that this World War I veteran from a working-class background understood their plight. He began by acknowledging that "the misery of our people is dreadful." He elaborated: "Added to the millions of unemployed, starving industrial workers was the subsequent impoverishment of craftsmen and the entire middle class. If this ruinous condition culminates by engulfing farmers, then we will be in the midst of a catastrophe of incalculable consequences."

Before Hitler named his plan to restore Germany to its previous glory, he placed blame for the present situation on the Weimar Republic,

---

4. Bonhoeffer, DBWE 9, 64.

5. This is captured somewhat in the first season of *Babylon Berlin*, the 2018 German television series available through Netflix.

6. There was serious political maneuvering in the background to make his appointment happen, but this was hardly unique within the world of politics.

7. The following quotes are drawn from Hitler's speech in Sax and Kuntz, *Inside Hitler's Germany*, 130–33; cf. Steigmann-Gall, *Holy Reich*, 115–16.

Bolshevism, and mistreatment by foreign countries. Then he held out a stirring vision for the renewal of Germany:

> The national government sees as its first and foremost task the restoration of the unity of spirit and will of our people. It will preserve and protect the fundamentals on which the strength of our nation rests. It will preserve and protect Christianity, which is the basis of our system of morality, and the family, which is the germination cell of the body of the people and the state. It will disregard social rankings and classes in order to restore to our people its consciousness of national and political unity and the responsibilities that entails. It will use reverence for our great and glorious past and pride in our ancient traditions as a basis for the education of German youth. In this way it will declare a merciless war upon spiritual, political, and cultural nihilism. Germany shall not and will not sink into anarchistic communism.[8]

Hitler then moves toward his conclusion: "We are determined, as leaders of the nation, to fulfill as a national government the task which has been given to us, swearing fidelity only to God, our conscience, and our people."[9] These passionate—and to many—reassuring words of Hitler are followed by promises to turn the various sectors of the economy around. Then Hitler asks his listeners to hold him accountable. He says that if he and his administration have not fulfilled their promises in four years, then "put us on trial and judge us."[10] Hitler ends with what I imagine was perceived to be admirable piety: "May God Almighty take our work into his grace, give true form to our will, bless our insight, and endow us with the trust of our people."

Three things should be kept in mind. First, Hitler would repeat this sort of speech many times during the next twelve years. Second, he appeared to believe what he was saying—and was seeking to fulfill it.[11] (It's what he

---

8. Sax and Kuntz, *Inside Hitler's Germany*, 132.

9. Unlike the text I am quoting, I have translated the German word *Volk* simply as people. *Volk* was simply the normal, reassuring word for people, us—"our people." Of course, it has nationalistic overtones, but that hardly is unique to this moment or this country. Troubling connotations come from the context, not from the meaning inherent in the word.

10. Sax and Kuntz, *Inside Hitler's Germany*, 133.

11. I don't believe he truly meant his pious affirmations about Christianity. These utterances are simply a cynical use of religion. See Weikart, *Hitler's Religion*, and Bucher, *Hitler's Theology*. However, I have been convinced by Steigmann-Gall in his book, *The Holy Reich*, that some of those in top positions within the Hitler regime truly believed they were promoting Christianity. Of course, it was precisely this sort of "Christianity"

didn't say that would prove most troubling.) And third, though democratic elections were suspended early in his rule, Hitler remained quite popular during most of his reign.

Hitler was aware that he needed power in order to accomplish his goals. Within a month he was effectively handed a gift. On February 27 the Reichstag—the building housing the German legislative body—was burned to the ground.[12] This event served as a visible reminder that all was not well. There were still enemies of the Reich from whom the German people needed to be protected. Thus, to many Germans, Hitler seemed justified in making a strong move to assure the German people of security in the midst of such threats. The next day Hitler proclaimed the Reich President's Edict for the Protection of People and State. The first paragraph of this edict states: "Therefore restriction of personal freedom, of the right of free speech, including the freedom of the press, of the right of association and public assembly, intervention in the privacy of post, telegraph and telephone, authorization of house searches and the confiscation and restriction of property, beyond the legal limits, will henceforward be admissible."[13] "Historian Karl Bracher, looking back, has described the edict as 'the fundamental emergency law upon which the National Socialist dictatorship . . . was based.'"[14]

Within less than a month, on March 21, the Malicious Practices Act was put into force, "and [with it] the net of judiciary measures was tightened."[15] Two days later, on March 23, the Enabling Act was passed. Officially named the Law for the Removal of the Distress of People and Reich, approved by a vote of 444 to 94 by the Reichstag, this was seen by many to be "the final blow," since it basically freed Hitler from the need to conform to constitutional regulations.[16] In other words, it gave the chancellor unlimited power, destroying parliamentary democracy.[17]

Another week later, on April 1, there was a state-sponsored boycott of Jewish shops throughout Germany. Many Germans ignored the boycott, including Bonhoeffer's ninety-one-year-old grandmother.[18] Nevertheless, this

---

that Bonhoeffer thought should be defeated. (In addition to Steigmann-Gall on this, see Bergen, *Twisted Cross*.)

12. Sax and Kuntz, *Inside Hitler's Germany*, 134–36. As counterintuitive as it may seem, most historians apparently are convinced that the Nazis did not themselves set the fire.

13. Quoted in Bethge, *Dietrich Bonhoeffer*, 263.

14. Bethge, *Dietrich Bonhoeffer*, 265.

15. Bethge, *Dietrich Bonhoeffer*, 266.

16. Bethge, *Dietrich Bonhoeffer*, 268.

17. Sax and Kuntz, *Inside Hitler's Germany*, 136–37.

18. Bethge, *Dietrich Bonhoeffer*, 267. Also see Berenbaum, *Witness to the Holocaust*,

was the first public act aimed specifically to harm Jews. As Avraham Barkai has shown, it was simply the first of many ways in which the Hitler regime attempted to marginalize Jews through economic measures.[19]

On April 7 the first in a series of restrictive laws was passed, bearing innocuous titles such as the Law for the Restoration of the Professional Civil Service. These laws were intended to align all sectors of society—cultural and political—with Nazi ideology, especially by the exclusion of the political left and non-Aryans (most fundamentally meaning Jews). Some exceptions were made in the beginning. But over the next few years these laws would be expanded.[20] And the April 7 law—through what was called the Aryan Paragraph—would come to mean, among other things, that Christians of Jewish ancestry could not be pastors.

So, within six months Hitler managed to pass legislation that gave him almost unlimited, or dictatorial, power. These laws made life challenging, and eventually dangerous, for Jews, but also for those like Bonhoeffer who were unwilling to declare their loyalty to Germany as defined by Hitler and his Nazi collaborators. It also made foreign contact with ecumenical leaders potentially dangerous.

As we begin to focus on Dietrich Bonhoeffer specifically, it should be said that from the beginning of the Hitler regime he knew more than the average German regarding what was going on at the highest levels of government. He was from an upper middle-class family with an aristocratic heritage and thus had many relatives in high positions throughout Germany. His father, Karl, was perhaps the most respected psychiatrist in all of Germany. Both his father and his brother-in-law Hans von Dohnanyi, a lawyer, were involved in the trial of the man accused of burning the Reichstag. By May 1933 Dohnanyi would be working in a high position in the office of the Reich Ministry of Justice.

Thus, with his insider's view of this new government, Bonhoeffer already on February 1, 1933—two days after Hitler assumed power—could offer a brief but insightful radio address on "The Younger Generation's Altered View of the Concept of *Führer*." Toward the end of his talk Bonhoeffer asks pointed, timely questions. "Does the call for a leader arise from knowledge that the power of things over people has become so great and so destructive and so chaotic that only a great figure would be able to restore order and

1–8.
   19. Barkai, *From Boycott to Annihilation*.
   20. Sax and Kuntz, *Inside Hitler's Germany*, 139–50.

unity?" And, again: "To what extent is leading and being led healthy and genuine, and when does it become pathological and excessive?"[21]

Bonhoeffer's Essay: "The Church and the Jewish Question"

Bonhoeffer was also more aware than the average person of what Hitler intended for the Jews. Thus, he began drafting an essay on "the Jewish question" already at the end of March 1933, before either the boycott or the first law regarding non-Aryans had been passed. By early April he had produced a draft for study within a group of pastors meeting under the direction of Gerhard Jacobi (pastor, Kaiser Wilhelm Memorial Church, Berlin).

A number of events, including the passing of restrictive laws, undoubtedly influenced Bonhoeffer before and during the process of writing this essay. But a second and immediate clarifying event occurred as he continued work on the document—the Reich Conference of German Christians, meeting on April 3–4. According to Eberhard Bethge, this conference "triggered radical changes at all levels of the church." "The slogans of the conference were: *Gleichschaltung* (alignment of all sectors with Nazi goals), the *Führer* principle, the Reich church, and racial conformity."[22] Many church leaders and theologians were concerned about their ongoing influence within society and wondered if a Protestant Church unified around commitments to Nazi principles might better sustain its relevance. Bonhoeffer was of the opposite view. He believed that aligning the Protestant Church with Nazi ideology would be devastating to its identity. Thus, he would follow up this conference with several months of active engagement in order to seek to influence the development of the German Protestant Church's identity under Hitler, working diligently to keep the church from aligning itself with Nazism.[23]

Dietrich's mother, Paula, wrote a letter to a daughter and son-in-law on April 4, just as the church conference is meeting. After mentioning "Christ's most urgent command," to love your neighbor as yourself, she says, "'I do worry a lot about Dietrich. It's time for the church to show that it is still a

---

21. Bonhoeffer, "The Younger Generation's Altered View of the Concept of Führer," in DBWE 12, 266–68, here 267. Compare the longer text: Bonhoeffer, "The Führer and the Individual in the Younger Generation," in DBWE 12, 268–82. It is sometimes claimed that Bonhoeffer's address was cut off early for malicious reasons. Bonhoeffer suggests in a letter that it was cut off simply because it ran slightly over the allotted time (Bonhoeffer, DBWE 12, 91).

22. Bethge, *Dietrich Bonhoeffer*, 269, 270.

23. See Bethge, *Dietrich Bonhoeffer*, 257–323, in light of Steigmann-Gall, *Holy Reich*, and Bergen, *Twisted Cross*.

force in our lives, and fills a need in our lives! It's really making it hard for him."[24] Ten days later Dietrich himself wrote to Erwin Sutz, his Swiss pastor friend from Union Seminary days. At this early stage Dietrich expresses hope that the (Nazi-supporting) "German Christians" will feel compelled to withdraw from the "confessional churches." However, he is much less optimistic regarding the specific issue of anti-Semitism. "The Jewish question," he says, "is also giving the church a great deal of trouble, and here the most intelligent people have totally lost both their heads and their Bible."[25]

A very personal event transpired in the middle of Bonhoeffer's writing of his essay on the treatment of the Jews. On April 11 the father of Gerhard Leibholz, died. Gerhard, who was ethnically Jewish, had married Dietrich's twin sister, Sabine, in 1926. The family asked Dietrich to conduct the funeral. Dietrich consulted his superintendent, who strongly advised him against conducting the funeral of a Jew at this time. Dietrich complied. A number of months later, in November, Dietrich wrote to his brother-in-law:

> I am tormented by the thought . . . that I didn't do as you asked me as a matter of course. To be frank, I can't think what made me behave as I did. How could I have been so much afraid at the time? It must have seemed equally incomprehensible to all of you, and yet you said nothing. But it preys on my mind . . . because it's the kind of thing one can never make up for. So all I can do is to ask you to forgive my weakness then. I know now for certain that I ought to have behaved differently.[26]

This letter is clarifying in two ways. First, it lets us know that long before Hitler came to power the Jewish issue was a personal one for Bonhoeffer. Dietrich had knowingly grown up among ethnically Jewish children.[27] But much more important than that, he was part of a close-knit family. When Sabine had married, her new husband had been warmly welcomed into the close circle of this large family like all the other in-laws. Second, the letter suggests that the episode with Gerhard's father's funeral more than likely stiffened Bonhoeffer's own resolve regarding the Jewish question and

24. Bonhoeffer, DBWE 12, 101n8.
25. Bonhoeffer, DBWE 12, 101.
26. Quoted in Bethge, *Dietrich Bonhoeffer*, 275–76. Cf. Bonhoeffer, DBWE 13, 42.
27. According to Kenneth C. Barnes, "Grunewald [Bonhoeffer's neighborhood, beginning age ten] had the highest percentage [13.54 percent] of Jewish residents of any neighborhood in Berlin, a city in which the proportion of Jews [4.3 percent] was nearly five times greater than in Germany as a whole [0.9 percent]. Four out of the ten members of Dietrich's graduating class (his *Abiturklasse*) at the gymnasium came from Jewish households" (Barnes, "Dietrich Bonhoeffer and Hitler's Persecution," 111, 210n4.) Most of these Jews would have been "assimilated"—baptized as Protestants.

clarified that Dietrich would often be in a minority on this issue (as well as other important theological matters).[28]

Now to Bonhoeffer's essay itself, "The Church and the Jewish Question."[29] As stated above, Bonhoeffer originally wrote the essay in order to have a paper to discuss within a small group of church leaders meeting in early April 1933. The essay as we now have it was completed by April 15 and was published in two journals, one in June, the other in July. This essay is the most substantial writing we have from Bonhoeffer on the situation of the Jews in Nazi Germany. It is also one of the earliest and most complete statements issued by a Protestant theologian during the Third Reich.[30] It addresses personal, ecclesial, and political issues.

In his opening paragraph Bonhoeffer names the key questions straightforwardly. In response especially to the April 7 legislation, he asks what it means that "the Jew is subjected to special laws by the state, solely on the basis of race and regardless of the religion to which he adheres." Bonhoeffer says this poses several questions. Very broadly, "how does the church judge this action by the state, and what is the church called upon to do about it?" And more specifically, "what are the consequences for the church's position toward the baptized Jews in its congregation? These questions," says Bonhoeffer, "can only be answered on the basis of a right concept of the church" (362).

The whole essay appears to be framed by Bonhoeffer in such a way as to show his indebtedness to Martin Luther.[31] Thus, as he begins his substantive argument, he says: "There is no doubt that the church of the Reformation is not encouraged to get involved directly in specific political actions of the state." In fact, he continues, "in the midst of the world's chaotic godlessness" the church affirms "the state as God's order of preservation." For these reasons, and with the recognition of the distinction between gospel and law, the church, says Bonhoeffer, refrains from "any moralizing" regarding the state's specific behaviors. For after all, "history is not made by the church but rather by the state" (362–63).

However, Bonhoeffer continues, "it is certainly only the church, which bears witness to God's entering into history [through Christ], that knows what history is and therefore what the state is." Bonhoeffer acknowledges that "one of the historical problems that must be dealt with by our state is the

28. See Gutteridge, *Open Thy Mouth*, and Gerlach, *And the Witnesses Were Silent*.

29. Bonhoeffer, "The Church and the Jewish Question," DBWE 12, 361–70. In the following few paragraphs, references to this essay will be given in parentheses. The emphases are in the original.

30. But see Pangritz, "Dietrich Bonhoeffer and the Jews."

31. See especially Luther, "On Secular Authority."

Jewish question, and without doubt the state is entitled to strike new paths in doing so." However, as the state does so, "humanitarian associations" and "individual Christians who see themselves called to do so," may "accuse the state of offenses against morality." States that are strong acknowledge their need for such individuals and associations and will welcome their advice (363).

Bonhoeffer continues to draw a clear distinction between church and state. "But the true church of Christ, which lives by the gospel alone and knows the nature of state actions, will never interfere in the functioning of the state . . . by criticizing its history-making actions from the standpoint of any sort of, say, humanitarian ideal." Bonhoeffer goes on to acknowledge the state's necessary use of force to correct certain injustices. And in regards to this—even as it relates to the Jewish question—the church, he says, cannot take "*direct* political action." "But that does not mean," says Bonhoeffer, "that the church stands aside, indifferent to what political action is taken. Instead, it can and must . . . keep asking the government whether its actions can be justified as *legitimate state* actions, that is, actions that create law and order, not lack of rights and disorder. [The church] will be called upon to put this question as strongly as possible wherever the state seems endangered precisely in its *character as state* [*Staatlichkeit*], that is, in its function of creating law and order by force." The church will also not discourage "individual Christians . . . from accusing the state of 'inhumanity,'" when they are called to do so (363–64).

Based upon this set of theological reflections, Bonhoeffer then famously names three courses of action for the church (365–67). He has already named the first action. It is "questioning the state as to the legitimate state character of its actions, that is, making the state responsible for what it does." "*Second* is service to the victims of the state's actions. The church has an unconditional obligation toward the victims of any social order, even if they do not belong to the Christian community."[32] "The *third* possibility is not just to bind up the wounds of the victims beneath the wheel but to fall into the spokes of the wheel itself."[33] Such an action, says Bonhoeffer, would

---

32. This directly contradicts the claim of Charles Marsh that "Bonhoeffer's denunciations of the regime's anti-Jewish policies . . . applied strictly to Jews who had converted to Christianity" (Marsh, *Strange Glory*, 169.)

33. "To fall into the spokes of the wheel itself" is my translation of "*dem Rad selbst in die Speichen zu fallen.*" The translation given in the collected works edition is "to seize the wheel itself," which I believe is not justified. See the careful discussion of the translation of this phrase in Pangritz, "To Fall within the Spokes," 102–7. The translation I have given, not incidentally, seems in line with Bonhoeffer's overall approach to discipleship.

"Only the One Who Cries Out for the Jews May Sing Gregorian Chants"   33

be indirect political action on the part of the church.[34] He elaborates on the rationale for this action:

> This is only possible and called for if the church sees the state to be failing in its function of creating law and order, that is, if the church perceives that the state, without any scruples, has created either too much or too little law and order. It must see in either eventuality a threat to the existence of the state and thus to its own existence as well. There would be too little if any one group of citizens is deprived of its rights. There would be too much in the case of an attack, coming from the state, on the nature of the church and its proclamation, such as the obligatory exclusion of baptized Jews from our Christian congregations or a ban on missions to the Jews. In such a case the church would find itself in *statu confessionis* [a state of confessional protest], and the state would find itself in the act of self-negation.... The necessity for immediate political action by the church must, however, be decided by an "evangelical council" as and when the occasion arises and hence cannot be casuistically construed beforehand. (366–67)

As a segue from these clear calls for action to the final section, Bonhoeffer makes comments that many later readers find disturbing. Here are his opening sentences:

> The measures of the state against Judaism, however, have for the church a very particular context. The church of Christ has never lost sight of the thought that the "chosen people," which hung the Redeemer of the world on the cross, must endure the curse of its action in long-drawn-out suffering. [Quoting Luther, he says:] "The Jews are the most miserable people on earth. They are plagued everywhere, and scattered about all countries, having no certain resting place." But the history of suffering of this people that God loved and punished will end in the final homecoming of the people Israel to its God. And this homecoming will take place in Israel's conversion to Christ.... [Bonhoeffer continues:] We know that no state in the world

---

34. The collected works translation has the word *direct* in this sentence, with a footnote saying that the original manuscript has the German word meaning direct, but that the published version has the German word meaning indirect. Given that Bonhoeffer has earlier in the essay said that the church has no right to "direct" political action, it seems that he is in fact drawing a distinction here: the form of action he envisions is indeed substantial, public action, but by Bonhoeffer's lights, *indirect* political action. (It might be significant in this regard that Bonhoeffer was on the editorial board for the publication in which his essay appeared. See Pangritz, "To Fall within the Spokes," 96.)

can deal with this enigmatic people, because God has not yet finished with it. (367)

As noted above, this long paragraph is a transition to the final section where Bonhoeffer deals with what is for him, theologically, the most crucial issue: allowing the state to define who can be a Christian. More specifically, the Aryan paragraph implies that Jews cannot be pastors within the church. Bonhoeffer extrapolates from this that the paragraph is implying—as more than a few are coming to say—that Jews cannot become baptized Christians. Bonhoeffer says that if the state insists on this then the church will find itself in *statu confessionis*—a state of confessional protest where "'the truth of the gospel and Christian freedom are at stake.'"[35] This is an issue that would preoccupy Bonhoeffer over the next number of years. In fact, he wrote a separate memorandum on this specific issue not long after finishing this essay.[36]

Towards Doctrinal Decisions and Confession (and Identifying Heresy)

As stated before, Bonhoeffer had political connections in high places. So, it is hard to know all of those to whom he was speaking or what he was saying or doing throughout 1933 after the rise of Hitler. After the edict for the Protection of People and State, enacted on February 28, we find Bonhoeffer saying in a letter in mid-April: "That I can't write any more today about the situation here is because, as you know, the privacy of the post is no longer in force."[37] In addition to the fact that Bonhoeffer was very busy, Eberhard Bethge suggests that this is why "few original sources remain from his time in Berlin in 1933."[38] We do know that he was helping some individual Jews. We know, for instance, that he worked in conjunction with Friedrich Siegmund-Schultze. As the head of a social work agency, Siegmund-Schultze in 1933 began helping Jews to escape from Germany. He was forced out of his job and exiled to Switzerland by the Gestapo precisely for this work. We have several letters exchanged between Bonhoeffer and Siegmund-Schultze, in which Bonhoeffer is trying to help a Jewish sociologist whose job is threatened because of being a Jew.[39]

---

35. Bonhoeffer, DBWE 12, 366n14.
36. Bonhoeffer, DBWE 12, 371–73.
37. Bonhoeffer, "To Erwin Sutz," DBWE 12, 102.
38. Bethge, *Dietrich Bonhoeffer*, 259.
39. Bonhoeffer, DBWE 12, 134–35.

What we know is that over the course of the next number of months Bonhoeffer was hard at work with key church leaders to prevent the alignment of the Protestant Church with a Nazi ideology and way of life. His efforts included, but were not be limited to, fighting against the move toward a unified church governed by a Nazi-appointed bishop, opposing Nazi-defined racial conformity, and challenging the church's general willingness to submit itself to the Nazi regime. We should note that working with the Protestant Church meant working with an institution that was connected to two-thirds of all Germans. Working on all of these fronts within the church took up much of Bonhoeffer's time—attending meetings, communicating regularly with key leaders, and maintaining general vigilance. Although all of these efforts were geared toward the theological integrity of the church, one should always be reminded that Bonhoeffer continually criticized those who thought of the church only in and for itself. Many of his own writings—and testimony from his students—make it clear that he always thought that the church was to live for others. It apparently is around the time of his move to London in October 1933 that Proverbs 31:8 began to be used as an admonition by Bonhoeffer: "Speak out for those who cannot speak." It became a phrase that he used often.[40]

Bonhoeffer was also actively involved in the ecumenical movement in Europe from 1931 to 1937. Beginning in 1933 he often made sure his colleagues in the leadership of these groups were apprised of what was happening to the Jews in Germany. Sometimes he convinced them to issue statements to challenge the "German Christians" in that regard. A central reason why he left the ecumenical movement is that he couldn't convince them that the only legitimate Protestant church in Germany was the Confessing Church.

On various occasions throughout 1932 and 1933 "Bonhoeffer proposed to his own church and the ecumenical movement that they should rediscover 'council,' 'heresy,' 'confession,' and 'doctrinal decision'—and this at a time when," according to Eberhard Bethge, "skepticism was paralyzing those with more experience."[41] By the summer of 1933 some leaders within the Young Reformation movement, including Martin Niemöller, agreed with him regarding the need for a contemporary confession. Thus, Bonhoeffer and a few others were given the task of formulating a contemporary confession of faith. They set to work on August 15 at Bethel, the church-sponsored community for the disabled in Bielefeld, Westphalia. After five days of work, Dietrich sent a letter to his grandmother:

40. Bethge, "Dietrich Bonhoeffer and the Jews," 69–70.
41. Bethge, *Dietrich Bonhoeffer*, 289.

> Our work here gives us much pleasure but also much trouble. We want to try to make the German Christians declare their intentions. Whether we shall succeed I rather doubt. For even now if they officially make concessions in their formulations, the pressure they are placed under is so powerful that sooner or later all promises are bound to be broken. It is becoming increasingly clear to me that what we're going to get is a big, popular, national church whose nature cannot any longer be reconciled with Christianity and that we must be prepared to enter upon entirely new paths which we will have to tread. The question really is: Germanism or Christianity? The sooner the conflict comes out into the open, the better. Nothing is more dangerous than concealing this.[42]

The Bethel Confession, as it came to be called, was therefore written with two concerns in mind. First, Bonhoeffer believed that they needed a "Confessing Church," a church that was accountable to a contemporary statement of core confessions, rooted firmly in the Scriptures. And second, he wanted to force heretical beliefs out into the open. A contemporary confession should bring to the surface distinctions between "Germanism" and Christianity. Here I will simply highlight elements from this confession that are directly relevant to the Jewish question.[43]

In the first article of the confession, on Holy Scriptures, much is made of the ongoing definitive importance of both Old and New Testaments.[44] Religiously motivated anti-Semitism not infrequently marginalized the role of the Old Testament or dismissed it altogether. Additionally, the first article, along with several others, challenges the attempt to transpose scriptural teaching and figures into symbols of German mythology, Nazi ideology, or present-day German superiority. For instance, the authors "reject the false doctrine that Jesus appeared as a 'flare of Nordic light' in the midst of a world tormented by signs of decay." Or that Jesus is "our Lord because of his heroic devotion." Or again: "We reject the false doctrine that the cross of Jesus Christ may be regarded as a symbol for a generalized religious or human truth, as expressed in the sentence, 'The public interest comes before private interest.' The cross of Jesus Christ," says the confession, "is not at all a symbol for anything: it is rather the unique revelatory act of God, in which

---

42. Quoted in Bethge, *Dietrich Bonhoeffer*, 302; cf. Bonhoeffer, DBWE 12, 159.

43. I offer a fuller discussion of the Bethel Confession in Nation et al., *Bonhoeffer the Assassin?*, 42–49.

44. Bonhoeffer, "The Bethel Confession," in DBWE 12, 374–424, here 378. In the next few paragraphs, references will be given in parentheses.

the fulfillment of the law, the judgment of death on all flesh, and the reconciliation of the world with God are carried out for all people" (397-98).

Race specifically is named in the discussion of "the Orders" within the overall article on creation and sin. Here the authors say that "the Bible and confessions understand the human race as one united race in its origin and its final destination.... A human being is a human being, and this unity of the human race calls for our obedience. In the course of history this unity has unfolded as numerous tribes and peoples. But the modern concept of race is not found in either the Bible or the confessional writings" (388). A few sentences later, they write: "To speak of the Creator God, who made the entire human race, is to speak of the humanity that exists over and above the distinct peoples. That means, 'the stranger that dwells among you shall be unto you as one born among you, and you shall love him as yourself... I am the Lord your God.' (Lev. 19:34)"[45] (389).

A few paragraphs later, in the same article, the authors reflect on the need to obey ruling authorities. They affirm that normally such authorities should be obeyed. However, Christians may be relieved from this obligation if the authorities do not have the "right concept of their worldly office." More specifically, "if a command of the political authority cannot be followed without sin, then we must obey God rather than any human being"—referring both to Acts 5:29 and the Augsburg Confession, article 16 (391).

In their article on Christ, the authors importantly state: "We reject the false doctrine that would make the crucifixion of Christ the fault of the Jewish people alone, as though other peoples and races had not crucified him. All races and peoples, even the mightiest, share in the guilt for his death and become guilty of it every day anew, when they commit outrage against the Spirit of grace" (398).

In the penultimate article of the confession, there is a section specifically on "The Church and the Jews." Here it is clearly stated that "it can never in any case be the mission of any nation to take revenge on the Jews for the murder committed at Golgotha. 'Vengeance is mine,' says the Lord'" (419). Most of the article is intended to protect those ethnic Jews who are part of the church. "A mission to the Jews that refuses altogether to carry out baptisms of Jews because of cultural or political considerations is refusing to obey its Lord" (418). The article continues, "The fellowship of those belonging to the church is determined not by blood, nor, therefore, by race, but by the Holy Spirit and baptism" (419). In other words, "We object to the attempt to make the German Protestant Church into a Reich church for

---

45. The translation of the biblical text in the original is from the KJV; I have changed it to the NRSV.

Christians of the Aryan race" (420). This section concludes with a strong admonition: "The Christians who are of Gentile descent must be prepared to expose themselves to persecution before they are ready to betray in even a single case, voluntarily or under compulsion, the church's fellowship with Jewish Christians that is instituted in Word and sacrament" (421).

Almost immediately after he had coauthored this confession, Bonhoeffer also wrote a set of "Theses on 'The Aryan Paragraph in the Church,'" to be distributed among interested parties before the upcoming Prussian church synod.[46] For Bonhoeffer, as he had stated before, this issue was a matter that he knew would cause a rupture in fellowship. So, he wanted to name that quite clearly in a brief statement for circulation.

Some of the leaders involved in the move toward the Bethel Confession believed that it needed to be vetted by other church leaders. Therefore, it was circulated among about twenty pastors and theologians. By the time it came back to the original authors for review, Bonhoeffer was so unhappy with the changes that he would no longer sign the document. And it seemed simply to die. It was certainly not formally adopted as a confession for the newly emerging Confessing Church. That would have to wait until next May—at the Barmen Synod.

In the meantime, Bonhoeffer was likely both exhausted and disheartened. He had decided he could not explore a pastorate in a church that would not allow Jewish Christians, like his close friend Franz Hildebrandt, to be pastors. Hildebrandt commented later on how such a position was virtually unheard of at the time.[47] Bonhoeffer and Hildebrandt seriously considered—not for the first or last time—totally exiting the established Protestant Church, making this Confessing Church a truly independent "free church."[48] However, for the moment Bonhoeffer needed space to think and to reflect on his future. At the end of July, he had already been presented as a candidate for a pastoral position in London, serving two small German-speaking congregations. He now felt free to take this position. Being in England would give him time and space to reflect on his situation, his theology, and his future. So, in October he moved to London. Hildebrandt would live with him for a couple of months early in his time there.

Bonhoeffer would remain in England for the next eighteen months. While there, he was in frequent communication with friends and family back in Germany. He was kept informed about what continued to unfold.

---

46. Bonhoeffer, "Theses on 'The Aryan Paragraph in the Church,'" DBWE 12, 425–32.

47. Hildebrandt, "An Oasis of Freedom," 39.

48. Bethge, *Dietrich Bonhoeffer*, 308, 320, 325.

However, he would not be present for what might be called the birth of the Confessing Church. In May 1934 Karl Barth, along with Hans Asmussen and Thomas Breit, composed what would become the Barmen Confession. On May 29–31 a synod meeting in Barmen affirmed this confession, which became the rallying point for what came to be known as the Confessing Church.[49] On October 19–20 the Confessing Church agreed on a further statement at the Dahlem Synod. In some ways this document was more radical. It challenged the legitimacy of the German Protestant Church (now dominated by the German Christians), instead naming the Confessing Church as the legitimate embodiment of Reformation Christianity.[50] Though Bonhoeffer was unable to be present for either of these important meetings, he strongly affirmed these moves to provide confessional ballast for this newly forming church.

Toward the end of his eighteen months in London, Bonhoeffer decided to form and direct one of the Confessing Church seminaries. It should be said that through his sermons in London and his lectures at the seminary he was frequently reminding the Christians he was addressing that faithfulness—including risk-taking ways of loving neighbors and enemies—is inherent in what it means to be Christian. This is especially clear in his lectures on discipleship—later to be a book by the same title. And lest anyone imagine otherwise, Bonhoeffer makes it clear that love—the sort of love extended to brothers and sisters within the church—is also to be extended beyond the church community.[51] In a 1934 sermon in London, Bonhoeffer specifically connects the challenges of the Sermon on the Mount to relationships with the "godless, racially different, despised, rejected brother."[52]

On September 15, 1935, the next major piece of restrictive legislation was passed by the Reich. The Law for the Protection of German Blood and German Honor forbade intermarriage or other sexual relationships between Jews and non-Jewish Germans. It also prohibited Jews from employing non-Jews, flying the national flag, or displaying the Reich colors (in other words, "pretending" to be Germans, so far as the Nazis were concerned).[53] Follow-

---

49. For an early account in English, with documents, see Cochrane, *Church's Confession under Hitler*. Also see Scholder, *Churches and the Third Reich*, esp. 2:122–71. For a brief discussion see Barnett, *For the Soul of the People*, 53–65.

50. For the text of the Dahlem agreement see Matheson, ed., *Third Reich and Christian Churches*, 49–51. For a brief discussion of Dahlem, see Barnett, *For the Soul of the People*, 65–73.

51. See, e.g., Bonhoeffer, DBWE 4, 121.

52. Bonhoeffer, DBWE 4, 121n85.

53. Sax and Kuntz, *Inside Hitler's Germany*, 406–8. Also see Berenbaum, *Witness to the Holocaust*, 24–30.

ing this in a few months was a clarifying law stating that a Jew could not be a citizen of the Reich and offering precise definitions of who was a Jew.[54]

It is important to remember that less than 1 percent of the German population was Jewish. There were concentrations of Jews in certain larger cities and neighborhoods within those cities and within certain occupations.[55] Therefore, what happened to the Jews was not something that was especially visible to most Germans. This changed for a moment on April 1, 1933, with the boycott of Jewish shops and businesses. And violent anti-Semitism was on full display on November 9 and 10 of 1938—the infamous *Kristallnacht*, the night of broken glass. However, again we need some context. Life had become frightening for many throughout Germany. Already in 1933, some pastors had been arrested for challenging the Reich directly. Later, parents could be arrested for complaining that their children had to join the Hitler Youth. In 1937 more than 700 Protestant pastors were arrested. And by 1938 Hitler and his inner circle were already engaged in the early stages of war. Increasingly, anything considered unpatriotic—listening to foreign radio broadcasts, complaining about having to eat margarine rather than butter—could lead to an arrest. Fear was a significant motivator for encouraging people to keep their heads down. And once Germany was fully and openly engaged in war, beginning in September 1939, most Germans were focused on the effects of the fighting. They were not thinking about what was happening to the Jews—which became especially lethal on a large scale through the formulation of the "final solution" at the beginning of 1942.[56]

We Are Not Christ, But We Engage in Responsible Actions

And what about Bonhoeffer? In addition to the essay he wrote in April 1933 on "The Church and the Jewish Question"—and his considerable involvement throughout that year to prevent the Protestant Church from becoming the religious wing of the Nazi party—what else did he do? It is important to acknowledge that there is much we do not know. As noted earlier, Bonhoeffer was already aware by April 1933 that phone calls and letters were no longer necessarily private communications. And he lived in England for eighteen months. But he did not remain silent or inactive. It would be interesting to know what lay behind his passing comment to Ernst Cromwell,

---

54. Sax and Kuntz, *Inside Hitler's Germany*, 404–6.

55. Schleunes, *Twisted Road to Auschwitz*, 38–41.

56. Sax and Kuntz, *Inside Hitler's Germany*, 432–41. For a detailed account see Browning, *Origins of the Final Solution*.

a former church member in London, when Bonhoeffer said in an October 1935 letter, "Recently I've been making myself pretty unpopular over the issue of the Jews [*Judensache*], but with success as well."[57] This statement was made shortly after the egregious Nuremburg Laws for the Protection of German Blood and Honor were passed. Could it be that Bonhoeffer was alluding to his advocacy to church leaders on behalf of Jews and indicating that this is making him unpopular? What we know is that before the year was out, according to some of his students, he would utter the now well-known words: "Only he who cries out for the Jews may sing Gregorian chant."[58] Bonhoeffer was totally convinced by this point that true Christians—and a genuine church—could not remain silent in the face of what was being done to the Jews in Germany.

We should also not underestimate his efforts to help the Protestant Church see that it was theological heresy to imagine that ethnic Jews could not be Christians. More than one out of every six ethnic Jews in Germany considered himself or herself a Christian.[59] Thus working on behalf of Jewish Christians was hardly insignificant. For instance, the Grüber Bureau, founded by Confessing Church pastor Heinrich Grüber, saved more than 1,000 Jews beginning in the fall of 1938. It was staffed by more than fifty volunteers who worked mostly with Christian Jews.[60] There were other Confessing Church pastors who were empowered by the leadership provided by people like Bonhoeffer. During the eighteen months while he was in London, Bonhoeffer himself continued to press leaders in the Confessing Church to keep that Church's opposition to the Aryan paragraph clear. He also helped numerous German Jewish refugees get resettled in the United Kingdom.[61]

In July 1937 Bonhoeffer's close friend Franz Hildebrandt, a pastor of the Confessing Church in Dahlem, on the outskirts of Berlin, was arrested because of his boldness in opposing Nazism. Bonhoeffer and others realized that Hildebrandt could be in grave danger because of being ethnically Jewish. They worked hard to get him released. They accomplished that within a month and helped him to emigrate to the United Kingdom by way of

---

57. Bonhoeffer, DBWE 14, 109. The editor guesses in a footnote what Bonhoeffer might be referring to, but we don't really know.
58. Bethge, "Dietrich Bonhoeffer and the Jews," 71.
59. Schleunes, *Twisted Road to Auschwitz*, 38; and Ludwig, *Suddenly Jews*, 12.
60. Ludwig, *Suddenly Jews*.
61. Bethge, "Dietrich Bonhoeffer and the Jews," 70–71.

Switzerland.⁶² On September 9 of the following year, Dietrich also helped his sister, Sabine, and her husband, Gerhard Leibholz, emigrate to Britain.⁶³

By this time, the Confessing Church had suffered numerous blows since its founding three years earlier. Among other things, Karl Barth had been exiled from Germany in 1935. But 1937 was especially tough for the Confessing Church. Hundreds of pastors were arrested, including Martin Niemöller and his assistant, Hildebrandt. In September the Finkenwalde seminary was closed by the Gestapo. Yet Bonhoeffer likely felt personally encouraged to see pastors willing to suffer and to see students who continued to inspire him with their commitment. It was different after 1937.

On Kristallnacht, in November 1938, the Nazis unashamedly unleashed violent public acts against the Jews, making clear their intentions. This was the most visible expression before the war and within Germany itself of the anti-Semitic hatred. During this twenty-four-hour period, bonfires were lit in every Jewish neighborhood. Tens of thousands of homes and shops were looted. Stormtroopers set fire to 191 synagogues. Ninety-one Jews were killed, and more than 30,000—one in every ten of those Jews who remained in Germany—were arrested and sent to concentration camps.⁶⁴ All of this was, of course, officially sanctioned by government authorities.

During the twenty-four-hour period of Kristallnacht, Bonhoeffer was in a remote village where he was teaching students at a clandestine seminary.⁶⁵ There were no violent actions in the area where he was. November 9 was a Wednesday. By sometime on Thursday, Bonhoeffer was getting word of what had happened. That evening he had a coded phone conversation with his parents in Berlin, 300 kilometers away. He then traveled to the city to find out more. On November 14 he returned to the students, who had heard about the burning of synagogues. One student reported: "A great discussion now arose among us about this deed, and how to assess it. Meanwhile Dietrich Bonhoeffer had returned. Some of us spoke of the curse which had haunted the Jews since Jesus' death on the cross. Bonhoeffer rejected this with extreme sharpness. . . . He utterly refused to see in the destruction of the synagogues by the Nazis a fulfillment of the curse on the Jews."⁶⁶

In the Bible that Bonhoeffer used daily, the date "9.11.38" is penciled in the margin beside Psalm 74, which says: "They said to themselves, 'We shall utterly subdue them'; they burned all the meeting places of God in the

---

62. Bethge, *Dietrich Bonhoeffer*, 581.
63. Bethge, *Dietrich Bonhoeffer*, 631–33.
64. Berenbaum, *Witness to the Holocaust*, 40–68.
65. The following account is drawn from Bethge, *Friendship and Resistance*, 58–71.
66. Bethge, *Friendship and Resistance*, 62.

land. We do not see our emblems; there is no longer any prophet, and there is no one among us who knows how long. How long, O God, is the foe to scoff? Is the enemy to revile your name forever? Why do you hold back your hand; why do you keep your hand in your bosom?"

By this point Bonhoeffer knew he had to be cautious about what he said in letters. But when he sent out his next "circular letter" to former seminary students on November 29, 1938, he said: "During the last few days I have been thinking a lot about Psalm 74; Zechariah 2:8; Romans 9.3f. and 11:11–15. That really makes one pray."[67] In this same letter he encourages his former students to continue to embody "patient endurance . . . in Jesus." And he urges them to be willing to suffer, if faithfulness requires it.[68]

As 1939 begins Bonhoeffer was also continuing to teach his seminary students in clandestine locations. He knew that Germany was moving toward a full-scale war. Soon he would be aware that avoiding conscription into the military was not going to be easy. By the spring of 1940, two things had happened. His clandestine seminary had been permanently closed by the Gestapo, and his brother-in-law Hans von Dohnanyi had found a way for him to avoid giving an oath of allegiance to Hitler and being a soldier killing on the front lines. He could become a civilian agent for the Abwehr, the intelligence agency where his brother-in-law now worked. His bosses would make the argument that his work was essential for the welfare of Germany and then he would receive *uk* status that said he was ineligible to serve in the military. So, from October 1940 to April 1943, when he was arrested, Bonhoeffer was a civilian intelligence agent (and a clandestine conscientious objector).

While working for the Abwehr, he did at least three things in relation to the Jews. First, after the mass deportations of Jews from Germany to concentration camps begin in mid-October of 1941, Bonhoeffer and his colleague Friedrich Justus Perels prepared a detailed report on what was being done, with the hope of encouraging some officers to attempt to stop the deportations.[69]

Second, Bonhoeffer composed writings in which he offered a critique of his society and church. Since October of 1940 he had been working on a book on ethics. Sometime after April 1941 he composed the first draft of a chapter on "Guilt, Justification, Renewal."[70] He opens the chapter with this

---

67. Bethge, *Friendship and Resistance*, 65; cf. Bonhoeffer, DBWE 15, 84.

68. Bonhoeffer, DBWE 15, 83.

69. Dramm, *Dietrich Bonhoeffer and the Resistance*, 119–23; cf. Bonhoeffer, DBWE 16, 225–29.

70. Bonhoeffer, DBWE 6, 134–45.

sentence: "The issue is the process by which Christ takes form among us."[71] Much of the chapter is devoted to ways in which the church—and the Christians who are part of it—have not allowed Christ to take form among them.

> The church confesses that it has not professed openly and clearly enough its message of the one God, revealed for all times in Jesus Christ and tolerating no other gods besides. The church confesses its timidity, its deviations, its dangerous concessions. It has often disavowed its duties as sentinel and comforter. Through this it has often withheld the compassion that it owes to the despised and rejected. The church was mute when it should have cried out, because the blood of the innocent cried out to heaven.[72]

He continues, "The church confesses that it has witnessed the arbitrary use of brutal force, the suffering in body and soul of countless innocent people, that it has witnessed oppression, hatred, and murder without raising its voice for the victims and without finding ways of rushing to help them."[73] "By falling silent," says Bonhoeffer, "the church became guilty for the loss of responsible action in society, courageous intervention, and the readiness to suffer for what is acknowledged as right."[74] Bonhoeffer believes he knows why much of the church has remained silent. "The church confesses," he says, "that it has coveted security, tranquility, peace, property, and honor to which it had no claim, and therefore has not bridled human covetousness, but promoted it."[75] Even though these are serious failings, he also discusses how the church can turn from these sins and enter a path of renewal.

Third, even while reflecting self-critically on moral failures in relation to working on behalf the oppressed and suffering, he and his brother-in-law Hans von Dohnanyi became involved in a successful effort to save the lives of fourteen Jews. They helped these Jews pose as Abwehr agents and escape to Switzerland. This involvement is what would lead to Bonhoeffer's arrest on April 5, 1943.[76]

But I cannot end this chapter without quoting from Bonhoeffer's remarkable essay "After Ten Years," which he wrote for three friends at the end of 1942.[77] In it he reflects on ten years of living under the rule of the Nazis.

71. Bonhoeffer, DBWE 6, 134.
72. Bonhoeffer, DBWE 6, 138.
73. Bonhoeffer, DBWE 6, 139.
74. Bonhoeffer, DBWE 6, 141.
75. Bonhoeffer, DBWE 6, 140.
76. Marsh, *Strange Glory*, 317–18.
77. Bonhoeffer, "After Ten Years," DBWE 8, 37–52.

Here is one of his key lessons: "It remains an experience of incomparable value that we have for once learned to see the great events of world history from below, from the perspective of the outcasts, the suspects, the maltreated, the powerless, the oppressed and reviled, in short from the perspective of the suffering."[78]

Bonhoeffer is acknowledging that such a view shapes our lives and that as Christians we see our lives in light of Christ. Thus he says:

> Certainly, we are not Christ, nor are we called to redeem the world through our own deed and our own suffering; we are not to burden ourselves with impossible things and torture ourselves with not being able to bear them. We are not lords but instruments in the hands of the Lord of history; we can truly share only in a limited measure in the suffering of others. We are not Christ, but if we want to be Christians it means that we are to take part in Christ's greatness of heart, in the responsible action that in freedom lays hold of the hour and faces the danger, and in the true sympathy that springs forth not from fear but from Christ's freeing and redeeming love for all who suffer. Inactive waiting and dully looking on are not Christian responses. Christians are called to action and sympathy not through their own firsthand experiences but by the immediate experiences of their brothers, for whose sake Christ suffered.[79]

Bonhoeffer cannot conclude his essay without reflecting honestly on the remarkable failure of the Christian witness—at times perhaps his own failure—in the midst of the challenges of Nazi Germany. Thus, in the penultimate paragraph, he utters these memorable words:

> We have been silent witnesses of evil deeds. We have become cunning and learned the arts of obfuscation and equivocal speech. Experience has rendered us suspicious of human beings, and often we have failed to speak to them a true and open word. Unbearable conflicts have worn us down or even made us cynical. Are we still of any use? We will not need geniuses, cynics, people who have contempt for others, or cunning tacticians, but simple, uncomplicated, and honest human beings. Will our inner strength to resist what has been forced on us have remained strong enough, and our honesty with ourselves blunt enough, to find our way back to simplicity and honesty?[80]

---

78. Bonhoeffer, DBWE 8, 52.
79. Bonhoeffer, DBWE 8, 49.
80. Bonhoeffer, DBWE 8, 52.

In August 1944, in prison, Bonhoeffer composed an outline for a book he hoped to write. At the beginning of the final section he said: "The church is church only when it is there for others."[81] This was a persistent theme for Bonhoeffer from 1931 forward. Referencing the Catholic tradition, but echoing the sentiments of the prophets of old—who said that the Lord would not tolerate worship that did not give rise to embodied day-to-day faithfulness—Bonhoeffer had, in 1935, uttered the prophetic words of warning: "Only the one who cries out for the Jews may sing Gregorian Chants."

Clarifying Afterthoughts

A friendly critic of an earlier version of this chapter wondered, especially because of my opening paragraphs, whether I had let typical Germans off the hook too easily for their support of Hitler and, more specifically, their anti-Semitism. I understand why he asked that. But nothing could be further from my intention.[82] My concern is rather about anachronism. I believe it is virtually impossible for us to bracket our vivid awareness of the evil of Nazism and the Holocaust as we begin thinking about "the Jewish issue" as it was actually presented to Germans in the early 1930s. That is, it is very difficult not to be anachronistic as we think about these issues in that context. But we should try. Therefore, briefly, I have attempted to show why it was that many Germans were attracted to Hitler as he ascended to power in 1933. If we are honest with ourselves, perhaps we can see why the early speech of Hitler that I referenced was so appealing, especially in the context of the extreme challenges of the day. Furthermore, in conjunction with this realization, it is important to know that, especially early in the Hitler regime, Bonhoeffer was not a typical German. He had access to knowledge of the inner workings of the Third Reich from its inception in a way that most Germans simply did not. (Of course, that did not automatically lead people with his level of knowledge to become resisters.)

None of this frees Germans (including those who were Christians) from responsibility. It is simply an attempt to provide some sense of context for 1930s Germany, providing nuance in relation to the challenges. I was convinced decades ago by Beate Ruhm von Oppen that after the Nazi

---

81. Bonhoeffer, DBWE 8, 503.

82. For very helpful retrospective accounts of what was actually happening, see, e.g., Burleigh and Wippermann, *Racial State*, and Gordon, *Hitler, Germans, and the "Jewish Question."*

regime was fully underway it took courage to want to know.[83] Not far into the regime, fear became a main instrument of control to encourage people to stay silent regarding acts of violence and injustice that they observed. Keep your head down and your mouth closed or *you* might be next.

Thus, the pertinence of the retrospective reflections attributed to pastor Martin Niemöller: "First they came for the socialists, and I did not speak out—because I was not a socialist. Then they came for the trade unionists, and I did not speak out—because I was not a trade unionist. Then they came for the Jews, and I did not speak out—because I was not a Jew. Then they came for me—and there was no one left to speak for me."[84] One might say that this well-known epigraph provides insightful words of enlightened self-interest, after the fact. However, Bonhoeffer did not think that Christians should act on behalf of those who were being harmed primarily because they personally could be next. Instead, he believed that one should know and live out what it means to be a faithful Christian in daily life. Among other things, discipleship—following after Jesus faithfully—requires us to speak up for those who cannot speak for themselves. We should do that even if we have to suffer, even if it costs us our lives. This requires a trust in God—a reverence before God—that could overcome fear. Therefore, it was prescient of Bonhoeffer to preach a sermon on fear already on January 15, 1933.[85] By the mid-1930s he was well aware that fear was destructive of true, active discipleship. Thus, in his book *Discipleship* he says: "Human beings should not be feared.... The disciples are to overcome fear of death with fear of God.... Anyone who is still afraid of people is not afraid of God. Anyone who fears God is no longer afraid of people. Daily reminders of this statement are valuable for preachers of the gospel."[86] And this was why, in the 1940s, reflecting on why the church had stayed silent when it should have spoken out for those who were persecuted, Bonhoeffer says: "The church confesses that it has coveted security, tranquility, peace, property, and honor to which it had no claim."[87] Such concerns led to silence, both because of disordered loves and out of fear of persecution by the Nazis.

And finally, some further comments about Bonhoeffer's 1933 essay "The Church and the Jewish Question." In 2017, the 500th anniversary of the beginnings of the Reformation, my wife and I were in Germany. Berlin

---

83. Ruhm von Oppen, *Religion and Resistance to Nazism*, 35. Also see Johnson, *Nazi Terror*.

84. But note the questions raised about attributing this to Niemöller in Hockenos, *Then They Came for Me*, 179–80, 200–202.

85. Bonhoeffer, DBWE 12, 454–61.

86. Bonhoeffer, DBWE 4, 196.

87. Bonhoeffer, DBWE 6, 140.

featured two special museum exhibits commemorating Luther. One was on Luther's influence throughout the world. The other was on Luther's destructive influence in Nazi Germany—especially in relation to anti-Semitism. The title for this latter exhibit was a quote from Bonhoeffer: *"Luther's Words Are Everywhere . . . ,"* with the subtitle *Martin Luther in Nazi Germany*.[88] Bonhoeffer was in fact one of the key Protestant Church leaders highlighted in the exhibit who as an atypical Lutheran opposed the Nazis.

I have in this chapter basically agreed with Eberhard Bethge and the museum exhibit curator that in the midst of Nazi Germany, Bonhoeffer stands out with considerable clarity as one who opposed anti-Semitism. Though I have not in this chapter substantively engaged opposing viewpoints, I am well aware that not everyone is so positive about Bonhoeffer's witness regarding the Jews and anti-Semitism.[89] One of the central targets is Bonhoeffer's long paragraph in his 1933 essay, the one that I described earlier as a segue from the first to the second section in his essay.[90] In closing this chapter I want to offer reflections on this paragraph, placing it within Bonhoeffer's life and his broader theological considerations.

There are two fundamental concerns regarding this paragraph. The first is that Bonhoeffer refers to the Jews as a people who have "hung the Redeemer of the world on the cross." And therefore, this people "must endure the curse of its action in long-drawn-out suffering." Israel is, says Bonhoeffer, God's "chosen people." But their suffering is a sign of the judgment of God. This leads into the second concern. "The history of suffering of this people that God loved and punished will end in the final homecoming of the people Israel to its God." Drawing a parallel with the church, Bonhoeffer reminds the reader that the church has also been "unfaithful to its Lord over and over again, and that it shares in the humiliation that it sees in this outcast people." The only hope that the church has for itself or Israel is that they have "faith in the one true God in Christ." This then leads into his discussion in the second section about ethnic Jewish Christians and to his challenging of the Nazi attempt to say Jews cannot be pastors or Christians.

I would suggest that there is no way to completely remove the offense of these views. However, to be properly understood, the theological claims in this paragraph should be contextualized within Bonhoeffer's theology more broadly and related to his life from April 1933 forward.

First, it seems important to notice that Bonhoeffer believed that God acts in history, including through judgment. So, for instance, in a lecture on

---

88. Bucholtz et al., *"Luther's Words Are Everywhere."*
89. See the helpful survey in Haynes, *Bonhoeffer Legacy*.
90. Bonhoeffer, DBWE 12, 367.

"Only the One Who Cries Out for the Jews May Sing Gregorian Chants"   49

war that he delivered several times in the fall of 1930 in New York City, he spoke of God's judgment on Germany in World War I: "Christian people in Germany, who took the course and the end of the war seriously, could not help seeing here a judgment of God upon this fallen world and especially upon our people. Before the war we lived too far from God, we believed too much in our own power, in our almightiness and righteousness."[91] These are strong words coming from someone who in the same speech admitted that still, in 1930, the Treaty of Versailles was the most painful remaining wound of the war, "which still is open and bleeds in Germany."[92]

It may be that in his 1933 essay Bonhoeffer says that the Jews have suffered because they are responsible for the crucifixion of Jesus. However, for him, this is clearly about the judgment of God. In no way does it justify human actors punishing the Jews. Thus, the Bethel Confession that Bonhoeffer coauthored says: "It can never in any case be the mission of any nation to take revenge on the Jews for the murder committed at Golgotha. 'Vengeance is mine,' says the Lord."[93] And, as previously mentioned, in November 1938, soon after Kristallnacht, that horrible night of violence against Jews within Germany, one student reported on a conversation that ensued with their teacher: "A great discussion now arose among us about this deed, and how to assess it. Meanwhile Dietrich Bonhoeffer had returned. Some of us spoke of the curse which had haunted the Jews since Jesus' death on the cross. Bonhoeffer rejected this with extreme sharpness. . . . He utterly refused to see in the destruction of the synagogues by the Nazis a fulfillment of the curse on the Jews."[94]

Again, in terms of theology, we should note an important paragraph in Bonhoeffer's essay "Heritage and Decay" in *Ethics*. I believe Andreas Pangritz is right to say that there is a key sentence in this 1941 essay that either represents a change in Bonhoeffer's theology or a naming of something that was left unnamed in his 1933 essay: "Western history is by God's will inextricably bound up with the people of Israel, not just genetically but in an honest, *unceasing encounter*."[95] This seems to be a tacit affirmation of the importance of the ongoing existence of Jews as Jews (and not just as Christian Jews). Pangritz is also right that there are two sentences early in this essay that likely reflect Bonhoeffer's awareness of the deportation of

91. Bonhoeffer, DBWE 10, 415.
92. Bonhoeffer, DBWE 10, 414–15.
93. Bonhoeffer, DBWE 12, 419.
94. Bethge, *Friendship and Resistance*, 62.
95. Bonhoeffer, DBWE 6, 105; emphasis added. See Pangritz, "Dietrich Bonhoeffer and the Jews," 174–78.

Jews from Germany to concentration camps, even as he wrote and revised this essay: "The Jews keep open the question of Christ; they are the sign of God's free, gracious election and of God's rejecting wrath; 'see the kindness and the severity of God' (Rom. 11:22). Driving out the Jews from the West must result in driving out Christ with them, for Jesus Christ was a Jew."[96]

But most importantly, in the midst of our discomfort with some of the theology included in Bonhoeffer's 1933 essay, we must not forget the clarity of its threefold call to action—questioning the state's actions, serving the victims of the state's actions, and being willing to "fall into the spokes of the wheel" in order to stop the abusive behaviors. Had this call been taken up by leaders of the Protestant Church in Germany in any wholehearted way, the fate of the Jews in Europe would have been dramatically different. Despite the indifference of most church leaders, Bonhoeffer did what he could to resist the anti-Semitic acts within Germany until his arrest in April 1943—an arrest that happened precisely because of his effort to save the lives of fourteen Jews.

---

96. Bonhoeffer, DBWE 6, 105.

3

"We Should Not Balk Here at Using the Word 'Pacifism'"[1]

Introduction: Raised to Be a German Patriot

When we think of Dietrich Bonhoeffer in relation to war, we probably think first of World War II. However, it is important to realize that he was a child of World War I. In fact, looking back in 1929, the young adult Dietrich was undoubtedly right that the First World War was in many ways a crucial, formative experience for Germans during this time. Born in 1906, he was among those he described as the "revolutionary youth," those who matured during and just after the war.[2]

The beginning of the war, when Dietrich was eight years old, was exhilarating to the children in the Bonhoeffer home.[3] We are told that "the first German successes [of the war] filled Dietrich with boyish excitement" (26). However, his parents discouraged their children's understandable enthusiasm from becoming anything like celebration. When one of the children shouted "Hurrah, there's war!" she had her face slapped. Perhaps that was because the adults knew the tragedy and mourning that always accompany real war—suffering that would soon come close to their own family (26).[4]

---

1. This is a quote from a lecture by Bonhoeffer in 1932 (Bonhoeffer, DBWE 11, 367).

2. Bonhoeffer, DBWE 10, 360–61.

3. The account that follows is taken from Bethge, *Dietrich Bonhoeffer*, 25–28, unless otherwise noted. Page numbers are in parentheses.

4. The child who is reported to have had her face slapped was a girl. It is also possible

As Sabine, Dietrich's twin sister, recounts, "very bitter losses were soon being suffered by our wider circle of relations." She remembers that "my mother felt these with all her heart, while for our father, too, the very first months of the war in 1914 brought much sorrow. We were told that three cousins had fallen in the West, that our cousin Lothar Bonhoeffer had his leg crushed and an eye shot out, and that another cousin had had to have his leg amputated."[5]

Given their many connections in high places, it is quite likely that Dietrich's parents could have secured for their sons less dangerous roles within the military. However, as in most families, doing one's patriotic duty was unquestioned in the Bonhoeffer household. Therefore, when Dietrich's older brothers, Karl-Friedrich and Walter, were called up for military service in 1917, they enlisted in the infantry, where the need was greatest. On April 23, 1918, Walter was wounded; five days later he was dead. "His death," says Eberhard Bethge, "seemed to break his mother's spirit" (27). According to Sabine, "it was a long time before my mother recovered" from this loss.[6] Sabine also mentions that one of the effects that the reality of death and dying had on little Dietrich was that he and Sabine, as they were falling asleep, developed a nightly ritual, imagining with all earnestness what death was like and then what eternity was like.[7] According to Bethge, "the death of his brother Walter and his mother's desperate grief left an indelible mark on the child Dietrich" (28). Reflecting on this time from the vantage point of 1930, the young adult Dietrich said, "Although I was then a small boy, I never can forget those gloomy days of the war."[8] "Death stood at the door of almost every house and called for entrance. . . . Germany was made a house of mourning."[9]

The war ended on November 11, 1918. The following summer, when Dietrich was thirteen, he joined the Boy Scouts. He remained a Scout until sometime in 1920 (31). "On Sunday mornings," Dietrich reported, "we always drill, have mock battles and that sort of thing. It is always nice"[10] (32).

By the summer of 1923, Bonhoeffer had become a student at the University of Tübingen. "His first terms there coincided with ominous political

---

that that sort of elation was unacceptable in a girl.

5. Leibholz-Bonhoeffer, *Bonhoeffers*, 4.
6. Leibholz-Bonhoeffer, *Bonhoeffers*, 24.
7. Leibholz-Bonhoeffer, *Bonhoeffers*, 38.
8. Bonhoeffer, DBWE 10, 412.
9. Bonhoeffer, DBWE 10, 581–82.

10. Bethge comments that Dietrich seemed oblivious to the fact that some families attended church services on Sunday mornings.

and economic events: the French occupation of the Ruhr, unrest in Bavaria and Saxony, the declaration of a state of emergency throughout the Reich, and rampant inflation" (47). In the midst of this, Dietrich, like his father before him, joined the Hedgehog Fraternity, a club "devoted to the patriotic ideas of the new German Reich"[11] (48). "For two weeks [in November 1923] he served with the Ulm Rifles Troop as a member of the so-called Black Reichswehr" (49). Commenting on this achievement, he said in a letter to his parents: "Today I am a soldier."[12]

Barcelona Lecture: "Love for My People Will Sanctify War"[13]

Bonhoeffer transferred from the University of Tübingen to the University of Berlin in June 1924; he took courses at Berlin until July 1927. Bonhoeffer's first substantial public statements on war came after receiving his doctoral degree, while serving as an assistant pastor in Barcelona, Spain, beginning in February 1928.[14] In addition to preaching nineteen sermons, Bonhoeffer in November began a series of three lectures on "Crisis and Hope in the Contemporary Religious Situation." In the last lecture, entitled "Basic Questions of a Christian Ethic," presented on February 8, 1929, Bonhoeffer addressed the topic of war.[15]

Bonhoeffer was well aware as he began these lectures that he was speaking in a time of upheaval and confusion. "In Germany," he says, "the experience of war was joined by the experience of revolution, and the one absolutely unmistakable result seems to be that these historical events have prompted a hitherto unprecedented revolution in morals" (360). He elaborates: "It would be difficult to find a period in history that has experienced as radical a change in, say, literature as has the period between 1910 and approximately 1925. All that seemed solid has become soft, all that seemed certain has become uncertain, all that seemed self-evident has become

---

11. Bethge also notes that Dietrich's brothers had deliberately not joined the Hedgehog fraternity, partly because of its right-wing ideology. When in 1933 Hedgehog as an organization affirmed the Aryan paragraph, both Dietrich and his brother-in-law and fellow theologian Walter Dress publicly dissociated themselves from it (49).

12. Bonhoeffer, DBWE 9, 70.

13 Compare what is said here on this lecture with what is said in Nation et al., *Bonhoeffer the Assassin?*, 101–24.

14. Bonhoeffer does make a very brief statement affirming war in *Sanctorum Communio* (DBWE 1, 119).

15 Bonhoeffer, DBWE 10, 325–78; the lecture on ethics specifically, 359–78. (References to the lectures will be given in parentheses for the next several pages. Emphases are in the original.) For Bethge's comments and summary on Bonhoeffer's lecture on ethics, see Bethge, *Dietrich Bonhoeffer*, 118–20.

questionable—politically, literarily, philosophically, ethically" (361). Put differently: "The rug—or let us say the bourgeois parquet floor—has been ruthlessly pulled out from under our feet, and we must now search for a bit of *earth* on which to stand. We have been utterly and completely shipwrecked and are now horrified to see just how utterly at sea many of us are" (326).

These three lectures were Bonhoeffer's effort, in his early twenties, to try to reestablish a bit of solid (theological) earth on which he and his congregants could stand. But, as would be his trademark, he was not going to make such an undertaking easy. This would be especially apparent in his lecture on "Basic Questions of a Christian Ethic." In fact, one of his earliest claims must have seemed to his congregants to be the opposite of reestablishing solid ground. For he makes what must have seemed to his audience the extraordinary claim that "Christianity and ethics have absolutely nothing to do with each other. There is no Christian ethic" (363; cf. 354). On what grounds does he make such a claim? He accepts the claim that "ethics is a matter of blood and a matter of history." That is, "it is a child of the earth, and for that reason its face changes with history as well as with the renewal of blood, with the transition between generations" (360). Thus, he believes it will not do to let the modifier *Christian* be added to ethics, so that it is simply one more approach to the moral life, along with German ethics, French ethics, etc. No, a Christian approach to life must be different: "Because Christianity speaks of the exclusive path from God to human beings from within God's own compassionate love toward the unholy, the sinful, while ethics speaks of the path from human beings to God, about the encounter between the holy God and the holy human being; in other words, because the Christian message speaks of grace while ethics speaks of righteousness" (362–63).

Even as Bonhoeffer makes this claim, he acknowledges that there appears to be a "so-called New Testament ethic" (363). What significance is there in this? He spends several paragraphs seeking to show that the ethical teachings found in the New Testament offer nothing distinctive in terms of their moral teachings. There are parallels within the contemporary Greco-Roman culture. As he concludes this brief discussion, he poses an obvious question.

> But what is now left of a Christian ethic? Does the Sermon on the Mount really have nothing new to say to us? It has nothing "new" in the sense of new demands, but it does have something completely different to offer. The significance of all of Jesus's ethical commandments is rather to say to people: You stand before

the face of God, God's grace rules over you; but you are at the disposal of someone else in the world. You must act and behave such that in each of your actions you are mindful of also acting before God, mindful that God has a certain will and wants to see that will done. Each particular moment will reveal the nature of that will. (365)

These last two sentences tell us why Bonhoeffer challenges "a [so-called] Christian ethic." For he has observed the tendency to move from teachings in, say, the Sermon on the Mount, to formulating ethics in terms of principles. Principles then become independent of the will of God and our relationship to God, assuming their own, autonomous authority (apart from God). Something more unexpected, more radical is going on through the person and teachings of Jesus, says Bonhoeffer.

> This ongoing relationship to God's will is the great moral renewal Jesus brought about, the dismissal of principles, of fundamental rules—in biblical terms, the law. And precisely this dismissal is a consequence of the Christian idea of God. For if there were indeed a universally valid moral law, following it would involve taking the path from human beings to God. . . . In that case, I would control my own relationship with God, as it were, and there could be ethical action without any immediate relationship with God. But the most important aspect is that I would then become a slave to my principles and would be surrendering the most precious human possession, my freedom. When Jesus places people immediately under God, new and fresh at each moment, he restores to humanity the immense gift that it had lost, freedom. (365–66)

Bonhoeffer does not shy away from some of the radical implications of this view.[16] What a Christian knew to be right yesterday, he says, may not be what he or she knows to be right today (365). Nor does a Christian look around to others, discerning together what it might mean to act morally in a given situation (367). No, "precisely because I am face to face with God in this solitude, I alone can know what is right or wrong for me personally" (367). In fact, "there are no acts that are bad in and of themselves; even murder can be sanctified. There is only faithfulness to or deviation from God's

---

16 Elements of Luther and Barth are, of course, at work in Bonhoeffer's approach to ethics. But perhaps here the influence of Kierkegaard is most apparent, especially in Bonhoeffer's statement that God will sanctify murder, which is likely a reference to Kierkegaard's *Fear and Trembling*. In that book, Kierkegaard cites the story of God asking Abraham to sacrifice Isaac as a way to test Abraham's trust in God and reliance on God's will rather than his own.

will. There is no law with a specific content, but only the law of freedom, that is, bearing responsibility alone before God and oneself" (367).

Throughout the rest of the lecture Bonhoeffer briefly discusses three contemporary issues—sex, economics, and war (with most attention given to war). In the midst of discussing these specific issues he underscores what has already been said. For instance, he briefly recounts the claims of some that Christians should not go to war. The "case for this seems entirely clear and convincing," he says, "yet it suffers at the central issue; it is not concrete and as a result does not look into the depths of Christian decision. It invokes the commandment not to kill and believes that commandment to be the solution" (370). But as Bonhoeffer has already said, it is "the most serious misunderstanding to turn the commandments of the Sermon on the Mount once again into a law by applying them literally to the present" (367). To do so is to be enslaved to such laws rather than realizing the freedom to act situationally in the moment in response to the will of God (372).

With all of this as a theological backdrop, then we have Bonhoeffer's clearest and fullest statement about war in this lecture:

> The situation [as to whether to go to war] seems clear to me. In such cases, I no longer have the choice between good and evil; regardless of which decision I make, that decision will soil me with the world and its laws. I will take up arms with the terrible knowledge of doing something horrible, and yet knowing I can do no other. I will defend my brother, my mother, my people, and yet I know that I can do so only by spilling blood; but love for my people will sanctify murder, will sanctify war. As a Christian, I will suffer from the entire dreadfulness of war. My soul will bear the entire burden of responsibility in its full gravity. I will try to love my enemies against whom I am sworn to the death, as only Christians can love their brothers. And yet I will have to do to those enemies what my love and gratitude toward my own people commands me to do, the people into whom God bore me. (372)

Bethge comments that Bonhoeffer's statements on war made in his Barcelona lecture on ethics "had long been articles of faith among German nationalists in the [Protestant] church."[17] While true, such an observation also gives the wrong impression. It is not as if "German nationalists" were merely a fringe group in the German Protestant Church. Most, if not all, of Bonhoeffer's theological teachers—and other contemporaries

---

17. It can easily be confusing to North Americans to refer to the Evangelical church, which is what the translation has. I realize that is the literal rendering. But Protestant, it seems to me, communicates better in this part of the world.

who populated his world—were nationalists, caught up in what Karl Barth referred to as "the ideology of war." The Australian historian John Moses has made this clear in several writings.[18] It is also true, as Bethge says, that Bonhoeffer was here "not speaking his own language." In fact, he was, at this point in his life, speaking as a rather typical German patriot (albeit, with his own theological rationale).

Eberhard Bethge comments that "excessively nationalist statements such as those in his Barcelona lectures never crossed his lips again."[19] He never repeated such statements, Bethge says, because "he now saw them transformed into nationalistic slogans and interwoven with anti-Semitic agitation" (127). Bethge is quite right to say that Bonhoeffer would never speak like this again. But, once again Bethge's sentence is misleading. How? First, as suggested above, the views that Bonhoeffer promoted might have been "nationalistic," but would not have been perceived as "excessively" so. Their main thrust would simply have comported with the perspectives of typical German theologians at the time. Furthermore, it seems evident that Bonhoeffer's views changed not because of some pragmatic calculation that they would be used by others in ways he didn't agree with. Rather, by his own account, he underwent a transformation in his life and thought, specifically in relation to war, within the next few years.

As it happens, the theological seeds were planted already in these three lectures that would produce fruit in the future, theological fruit that would actually call for a reframing of much of what was said in his lecture on ethics in 1929.[20] In some ways this is summarized in two prescient sentences in the lecture on ethics itself. "But the situation is this, that there is a will toward a new ethical formation and fullness of life, and the only thing lacking is the correct point of departure. Our task, no more and no less, should be the attempt to show this point of departure" (362). The "correct point of departure" is indeed crucial. In his first lecture, on the prophets, we have what would become one of his central emphases: "God guides the nations and is the Lord of history. God bestows grace on whomever he will. Religion is not bound by national boundaries; national boundaries disappear before God"

---

18. For example, see Moses, "Dietrich Bonhoeffer's Repudiation," and Moses, *Reluctant Revolutionary*. Also see P. Jenkins, *Great and Holy War*, esp. 74–85, 172–76, 207–13, and 217–28; and Correll, *Shepherds of the Empire*, 221–61. More broadly see J. Jenkins, *Christian Pacifism Confronts German Nationalism*. For a glimpse of how this continued into World War II, see Stargardt, *German War*.

19. Bethge, *Dietrich Bonhoeffer*, 127. The remaining quotes and paraphrases from Bethge in this paragraph are drawn from Bethge, *Dietrich Bonhoeffer*, 119–20, unless noted otherwise.

20. Quotes in this paragraph are from Bonhoeffer, DBWE 10, 325–78.

(336). However, it is in his second lecture, "Jesus Christ and the Essence of Christianity," that he points to the essential key that would for him truly open new theological (and thus moral) avenues. In the opening paragraph of this lecture, Bonhoeffer says: "We all know that, for all practical purposes, Christ has been eliminated from our lives" (342). In responding to this reality, he anticipates the tenor of his later book, *Discipleship*.

> But if there is something in Christ that makes claims upon my entire life, from top to bottom, and does so with the full seriousness of the realization that it is God who is speaking here, and if it is only in Christ that God's word once became a present reality, then Christ possesses for me not only merely relative but also absolute urgent significance. Although I am still free to say yes or no it can no longer be an ultimately indifferent matter to me. To understand Christ means to understand this claim: taking Christ seriously means taking seriously his absolute claim on human decision. (343)

Here indeed are the seeds for reformulating what it means to be free (in Christ) and how commands and obedience can come to be seen as consistent with such freedom (yet still rooted in a relationship with God).

To New York, to Bonn, Then toward "Acting under the Constraint of Grace"

After returning from Spain, Bonhoeffer would write his *Habilitation* thesis, *Act and Being*. This thesis, submitted to the University of Berlin on March 14, 1930, qualified him to teach in a German university. He would also revise his doctoral thesis, *Sanctorum Communio*; it would be published in September 1930. Only a few days after he received the first copies of the published version of *Sanctorum*, he left Germany for another foreign adventure, traveling to New York City to study at Union Theological Seminary. He could not have imagined the transformation he would undergo during the ten months he was based in New York.

Beginning early in his time in the city, Bonhoeffer was asked to speak on war and peace. In fact, he indicates he "was astonished on being asked again and again, what German people think about a future war."[21] We have two examples of the numerous lectures and sermons he gave, one of them presented on Armistice Day Sunday, November 9, 1930.[22]

---

21. Bonhoeffer, DBWE 10, 583.
22. Bonhoeffer, DBWE 10, 411–18 and 580–84.

Bonhoeffer clearly wanted to convey to his American audiences the pain and suffering endured by Germans during the war. He also spoke about the Treaty of Versailles in quite critical terms, indicating that even twelve years later this was the most painful memory of the war for most Germans.[23] In doing this he did not excuse Germany for its guilt in World War I. But his most critical comments about Germany and the war were when he spoke specifically as a Christian. Bonhoeffer said that Christians in Germany should have been able to see that the war was "a judgment of God upon this fallen world and especially upon our people," largely because of Germany's arrogance and pride—rooted in a lack of trust in God.[24] These comments were certainly a departure from what he had said in Barcelona, but not as different as his concluding remarks.

"Returning to the Christian point of view, it seems to me," Bonhoeffer says, "one of the greatest tasks for our church, [is] to strengthen the work of peace in every country and in the whole world." Further, "we know, it is not enough only to talk and to feel the necessity of peace, we must work seriously. There is so much meanness, selfishness, slander, hatred, prejudice among the nations. But we must overcome it. . . . Let us work together for an everlasting peace." "Our churches have already begun this international work," he continues. "But more important than this is, it seems to me, that every Christian man and woman takes seriously the great idea of the unity of Christianity, above all personal and national desires, of the one Christian people in the whole world, of the brotherhood of mankind. . . . How can the man, who hates his brother, expect grace [from] God?"[25]

We have no more textual evidence from Bonhoeffer's time in New York City regarding his views on war. However, we have the testimony from the French Reformed pastor Jean Lasserre, another international student at Union Seminary, who had become a close friend of Bonhoeffer's. The two men traveled to Mexico and spoke together at "a public conference at which three to five hundred students of the Normal School for Teachers were present." They both condemned war and violence. In fact, says Lasserre, "Dietrich spoke as firmly as I, if not more strongly, on the meaning of pacifism." According to Lasserre, "This was in June or July, 1931, at the end of our stay in America."[26] What seems clear is that by the end of his time in New York, Bonhoeffer's views on war and peace were undergoing a dramatic shift from the views expressed in his Barcelona lecture in 1929.

23. Bonhoeffer, DBWE 10, 412–13, 414–15, 582–83.
24. Bonhoeffer, DBWE 10, 582.
25. Bonhoeffer, DBWE 10, 417–18.
26. Lasserre, quoted in Kelly, "Interview with Jean Lasserre," 152.

Eberhard Bethge mentions that meeting Lasserre was Bonhoeffer's "first encounter with a Christian pacifist of his generation." In fact, says Bethge, "after meeting Lasserre the question of the concrete answer to the biblical injunction of peace and that of the concrete steps to be taken against warlike impulses never left him again." Bethge continues,

> It was also Lasserre who provided the initial impulse for Bonhoeffer's great book *Discipleship*. In Jean Lasserre he found a man who shared his longing for the concretion of divine grace and his alertness to the danger of intellectually rejecting the proximity of that grace. His friend confronted him with the question of the relationship between God's word and those who uphold it as individuals and citizens of the contemporary world. This soon led Bonhoeffer to a new understanding of the Sermon on the Mount. . . . But only now [1931 and beyond] . . . was Bonhoeffer's academic knowledge of Lutheran ethics transformed into a committed identification with Christ's teachings of peace. The biblical-ecumenical belief in the one body of Christ became his foundation. In the years to come he continued to build on this structure.[27]

However, once again, in the midst of offering much help in understanding Bonhoeffer, Bethge's account is misleading. In the midst of saying all of this, Bethge interjects that Bonhoeffer never became "a convinced pacifist."[28] This claim flies in the face of Bonhoeffer's own words, as Bethge well knew.[29] For after all, Bethge quotes the January 1936 letter from Bonhoeffer to his long-time friend Elizabeth Zinn. Bonhoeffer acknowledges in that letter that he truly became a Christian only a few years before Hitler came to power (most likely while living in New York). And what facilitated this transformation? More than likely, Bonhoeffer's deep involvement in the Abyssinian Baptist Church, a large and dynamic African American church in Harlem, was crucial to his "conversion." However, what Bonhoeffer himself names in this letter as crucial to his "great liberation" is "the Bible, especially the Sermon on the Mount." Among the many changes in his life and thought that flowed from this transformation was the belief that "Christian pacifism, which a brief time before . . . I had still passionately disputed, suddenly came into focus as something utterly self-evident."[30]

---

27. Bethge, *Dietrich Bonhoeffer*, 153–54.
28. Bethge, *Dietrich Bonhoeffer*, 153.
29. The letter I am quoting from in this paragraph is quoted, in full, in Bethge, *Dietrich Bonhoeffer*, 204–5.
30. Bonhoeffer, DBWE 14, 134.

High on Bonhoeffer's agenda after returning from the US in July 1931 was to spend time with the theologian Karl Barth. Though he had been influenced by Barth's writings since the winter of 1924–1925, Bonhoeffer had never met him. He thus made plans to spend three weeks, beginning on July 10, in Bonn, knowing Barth taught at its university.

Bonhoeffer was quite taken with Barth's lectures. However, it was the personal interaction with Barth himself that truly captivated him. In a letter to a Union Seminary friend, Erwin Sutz, Bonhoeffer wrote: "I am impressed by [Barth's] discussion even more than by his writing and lectures. He is really fully present. I have never seen anything like it nor thought it possible." Bonhoeffer continues, "There is an openness, a willingness to listen to a critical comment directed to the topic at hand, and with this such concentration and with a vehement insistence on the topic at hand, for the sake of which he can speak proudly or humbly, dogmatically or with utter uncertainty, in a way that is certainly not intended primarily to advance his own theology." In short, "I have, I believe, seldom regretted not having done something in my theological past as much as I now regret that I did not go to hear Barth sooner."[31]

As Bethge comments, "for Bonhoeffer the encounter [with Barth] was even more stimulating because he had changed since 1927 and 1929. His stay in the United States had confronted him with ethical questions as never before. Through Jean Lasserre and [Albert] Frank Fisher [an African American student at Union, who connected him to Abyssinian Baptist Church], his interest in the essential present form of grace had been renewed and transformed into the problem of acting under the constraint of grace and simple obedience."[32] In fact, says Bethge, "it is indisputable that there is no contemporary to whom Bonhoeffer opened his heart so completely as he did to Karl Barth."[33] I believe it is also indisputable that there is no contemporary who exerted more theological influence on Bonhoeffer than Barth.[34] Bethge goes on to say that in the summer of 1931, when Bonhoeffer first met with Barth, "the Sermon on the Mount had moved into the foreground of his thought, and he did not yet find anything helpful in Barth."[35] In terms of direct help that may be true. However, in light of the later framing of the book *Discipleship*, it seems important that toward the end of their

---

31. Bonhoeffer, DBWE 11, 37.

32. Bethge, *Dietrich Bonhoeffer*, 181–82.

33. Bethge, *Dietrich Bonhoeffer*, 186.

34. Bethge offers his fullest discussion of the significance of Barth for Bonhoeffer in *Dietrich Bonhoeffer*, 73–77. However, one sees traces of the significance throughout Bethge's biography. Also see Pangritz, *Karl Barth in Theology of Bonhoeffer*.

35. Bethge, *Dietrich Bonhoeffer*, 185.

conversation in Bonn, Barth said to Bonhoeffer that he "was making grace into a principle and was bludgeoning everything else to death with it."[36] It also seems pertinent that, according to Bethge, at this very time Bonhoeffer was concentrating "on the terrifying proximity of an actively intervening God," but in a way that would "preserve the majesty of God from being cheapened in the pulpit, and sought to proclaim him in the concreteness of grace-filled command."[37] These emphases, and others within Barth's writings, would be crucial for Bonhoeffer's ongoing theological development—including his understanding of the Sermon on the Mount.

Furthermore, given that Bonhoeffer's views on violence would become deeply rooted in his Christology and the grace-filled command of the One who uttered the Sermon on the Mount, is it irrelevant that after Bonhoeffer's time in Bonn he knew that "Barth too [was] among those for whom the experience of war was decisive"?[38] *Decisive* is the right word. For anyone who knows much about the life of Karl Barth, born in 1886, knows that his theology underwent a dramatic transformation during World War I. This change began early in the war and by the end of the conflict led to the publication of the first edition of his famous Romans commentary.[39] Here is Barth's own account of what drove him to rethink his theology from the ground up:

> On [the day of the outbreak of World War I] "ninety-three German intellectuals issued a terrible manifesto, identifying themselves before all the world with the war policy of Kaiser Wilhelm II and Chancellor Bethmann-Helweg.... Among the signatories I discovered the names of almost all my German teachers.... It was like the twilight of the gods when I saw the reaction of [these revered theological teachers] to the new situation" and discovered how religion and scholarship could be changed completely "into intellectual 42 cm cannons." "To me they seemed to have been hopelessly compromised by what I regarded as their failure in the face of the ideology of war. Their ethical failure indicated that their exegetical and dogmatic presuppositions could not be in order." Thus "a whole world of exegesis, ethics, dogmatics and preaching, which I had hitherto held to be

---

36. Bonhoeffer, DBWE 11, 38.
37. Bethge, *Dietrich Bonhoeffer*, 185.
38. Bonhoeffer, DBWE 11, 226.
39. He was also dissatisfied enough with this first substantial articulation of his new perspective that he wrote a new version of the same commentary, which he finished by 1921. It is this second edition for which he is best known.

essentially trustworthy, was shaken to the foundations, and with it, all the other writings of the German theologians."[40]

Had Barth recounted something like this to Bonhoeffer in July 1931? And is that why, less than six months later, Bonhoeffer recounted in a lecture on systematic theology that "Barth too [was] among those for whom the experience of war was decisive"?[41] Bonhoeffer continued: "Hopefully this will be true of every theologian. However, Barth's message does not come from [that experience], nor from the cultural problems, but rather from a new reading of the Bible, a new way of seeing humankind from God's perspective, . . . from God's own word spoken in God's revelation."[42] Bonhoeffer was obviously on this same journey, with Barth, of discovering a new way of reading the Bible—which then opens up new ways of seeing the world.

So, it becomes obvious that Bonhoeffer's time with Barth was pertinent to his views regarding war and—equally important—his theological approach in general (which would then shape his particular approach to war theologically and morally).

Ecumenical Engagement and Peace Lectures

Between the time Bonhoeffer met with Barth and when he attended his first ecumenical conference, he composed a catechism with his close friend and fellow theologian Franz Hildebrandt.[43] A section of it dealt with the question of peace. Bethge says that "the introduction of the subjects of war, peace, or the ecumenical question into the elementary teaching of the church was something entirely new" (187). And what do they say in this catechism? Having framed the discussion a little earlier by talking about "self-preservation," they begin this section by asking: "But doesn't one have to destroy life in war?" The answer: "For that very reason the church knows nothing of the sanctity of war. For in war, the struggle for existence [*Dasein*] is fought with a dehumanized means. The church that prays the Lord's Prayer calls to God only for the cause of peace." They continue, "But isn't that unpatriotic?" Bonhoeffer and Hildebrandt answer that God uses the state for the service of God. And in the midst of daily life, Christians must

---

40. Busch, *Karl Barth*, 81. A very good, recent account of this time is given by William Klempa in Barth, *Unique Time of God*, ix–46. Klempa reminded me that Barth had the date wrong. The statement signed by Barth's former teachers was issued in September, shortly after the war had begun, not at the beginning of August.

41. Bonhoeffer, DBWE 11, 226.

42. Bonhoeffer, DBWE 11, 226.

43. Bonhoeffer, DBWE 11, 258–67. Bethge, in his biography, dates this catechism.

not remain aloof from political struggles. For "the commandment of love urges the Christian to stand up for his neighbor." However, Christians must also recognize "the irreconcilable conflict between the peace of Christ and the hate of the world."[44]

Bonhoeffer's formal ecumenical involvement began in September 1931, when he met with the World Alliance for Promoting International Friendship. He was appointed as one of the three European youth secretaries. As Bethge puts it, "the emerging world of the Protestant ecumenical movement became a vital part of his theology, his role in the church struggle, and ultimately his political commitment" (190). "It was the peace question," says Bethge, "and the new wave of defamation in Germany, that assured [Bonhoeffer's] loyalty to the organization and reconciled him to its slight theological reputation" (194). Put another way, Bonhoeffer had significant doubts about the liberal and humanist theologies that dominated this ecumenical organization.[45] However, because of his commitment to peace, Bonhoeffer would continue his involvement, while continually working to clarify his own Barth-influenced theology for peace through his lectures—coming to clarity, I would argue, only in the mid-1930s.

The first public presentation we have from Bonhoeffer on peace after his return from the United States is a sermon he preached on the evening of Memorial Day, February 21, 1932, in a church in Berlin.[46] Bonhoeffer began this sermon with these words: "The church does not leave anyone alone." He then follows this by saying that on this day everyone is understandably looking for consolation. And God welcomes everyone—no matter the distress, the fear, or the questions—everyone, that is, who truly seeks to know God and God's will. Those seeking God are welcomed in this church on this day.[47]

However, he also wants to make it clear that what is offered within the church differs from what is offered when one stands before state-sponsored war memorials. The church cannot "sing the song of praise of battle and the death of heroes into the listening ears of enthralled young people." In fact, he continues, "on this day the church stands here so strangely without ceremony, so little proud, so little heroic." This means the church should be

---

44. Bonhoeffer, DBWE 11, 262–63.

45. In one of his Barcelona lectures, Bonhoeffer refers to humanism as "the most severe enemy of Christianity" (Bonhoeffer, DBWE 10, 355). However, in his diary earlier the same year, he had said that his theology was becoming more "humanistic" (Bonhoeffer, DBWE 10, 64).

46. Bonhoeffer, DBWE 11, 419–27.

47. Bonhoeffer, DBWE 11, 420.

willing to be unpopular, especially on a day like Memorial Day.[48] For when we as Christians come to the church on Memorial Day, says Bonhoeffer, we "have a right to expect to hear in this place what Christian mourning is and what Christian consolation and Christian hope are."[49]

Bonhoeffer roots everything he says in Christ and his cross. These foundational affirmations are then followed by passionate statements about peace. "And how easy it is in times of confusion like today," says Bonhoeffer, "to fight in the name of Christ against the real Christ.... It is a rebellion against Christ. And the one great power of this uprising is called war! The others are called pestilence and famine." "And [these powers] attack the nations and drag them in. And death goes around and reaps its harvest. It mows down millions. And now comes the great disintegration of Christianity.... The past war caused thousands, caused millions to doubt Christ, and among them especially those who took his word seriously and now saw themselves so bitterly disappointed."[50]

"God's way in the world leads onto the cross and through the cross to life," Bonhoeffer says. "For this reason do not be alarmed, do not be afraid—be faithful!... What does faithfulness of the community of Christ mean here other than calling out into this furious raging again and again—unto exhaustion, unto humiliation, unto martyrdom—the words of Christ that there should be peace, that there should be love, that there should be blessing, and that he is our peace."[51] He concludes:

> Memorial Day in the church! What does that mean?... It means that we can really mourn for the dead of the world war only if we, with the same [devotedness] in which they stood out there, now pass on the message of peace, for the sake of which their death had to be, and preach it more loudly. It means looking out beyond the borders of our own nation, across the whole world, and praying that the gospel of the kingdom, which puts an end to all war, now may come over all nations and that then the end may come, that Christ may draw near.
>
> Memorial Day in the church! That means that God in the cross is near to us. [That] means pointing to Christ on the cross, who won the victory through the cross. Memorial Day in the church, that means knowing that Christ alone wins the victory! Amen.[52]

48. Bonhoeffer, DBWE 11, 420–21.
49. Bonhoeffer, DBWE 11, 422.
50. Bonhoeffer, DBWE 11, 424–25.
51. Bonhoeffer, DBWE 11, 426.
52. Bonhoeffer, DBWE 11, 427. I have translated the word *Treue* as "devotedness"

Several months later, on July 26, 1932, Bonhoeffer gave an address titled "On the Theological Foundation for the Work of the World Alliance" at the organization's meeting in Czechoslovakia.[53] His opening few pages simply uttered the call to clarify the theology undergirding the World Alliance. Without a substantial theology, Bonhoeffer asserted, the Alliance was simply at "the mercy of fluctuations in the political atmosphere." He specifically referenced the "political wave of nationalism among the youth."[54] The alternative was to "reflect on the truth of the gospel."[55] That's what was needed.

He began by saying, "The work of our World Alliance—consciously or unconsciously—is grounded in a very distinct conception of the church."[56] This conception included the realization that Christ is Lord of the entire world—and thus has a claim on the whole world. The church speaks on his behalf because "the church is the presence of Christ on earth." Thus, "the word of the church is the word of the present Christ; it is gospel and commandment."[57]

The rest of the lecture is an elaboration on these claims. Bonhoeffer names what he is against as well as what he is for. He acknowledges that it is tempting to employ principles, for they seem to offer clear guidance in the midst of the complexities of situations. Nonetheless, despite the fact that "this is the path that the churches have almost always taken," he believes they should avoid the temptation to withdraw "to the level of principle."[58] He suggests that the alternative is to be attentive to the commandment of God. But how do we receive this commandment? Not in biblical law. "Even the Sermon on the Mount may not become a literal law for us. In its commandments it is the illustration of that which God's commandment can be, but not exactly what it is today and especially for us. . . . The commandment is not there once and for all; rather it must be always given anew. Thus alone

---

rather than "faithfulness." The latter word is used in the DBWE translation, but I think it can suggest a meaning that doesn't fit with Bonhoeffer's intention here.

53. Bonhoeffer, DBWE 11, 356–69. It is worth noting the discussion of some similar themes in Bonhoeffer's "Report on the Theological Conference of the Provisional Bureau for Ecumenical Youth Work," Apr. 29–30, 1932 (Bonhoeffer, DBWE 11, 346–55). Also see the summary of his lecture in a set of eight theses (Bonhoeffer, DBWE 11, 370–72).

54. Bonhoeffer, DBWE 11, 357.
55. Bonhoeffer, DBWE 11, 358.
56. Bonhoeffer, DBWE 11, 358.
57. Bonhoeffer, DBWE 11, 359.
58. Bonhoeffer, DBWE 11, 361.

are we free from the law that stands between us and God, and thus do we listen to God alone."[59]

Second, Bonhoeffer offers a strong critique of the notion of the "order of creation." He mentions that in his time this is the most common way to think of the commandments of God. Yet in it lies "a special danger." This danger, he says, "is basically that everything can be justified on its basis. One need only portray something that exists as willed and created by God and then everything that exists is justified for eternity: the strife among peoples of humanity, national struggle, war, class distinctions, the exploitation of the weak by the strong, economic competition as a matter of life and death." The fundamental mistake that is made here, as far as Bonhoeffer is concerned, is that this view doesn't take seriously the ways in which sin has affected everything that exists.

Bonhoeffer proceeds briefly to offer an alternative to both the Sermon on the Mount as law *and* to the "order of creation."

> From Christ alone we must know what we should do. Not, however, from him as the preaching prophet of the Sermon on the Mount, but rather from him who gives us life and forgiveness, as the one who has fulfilled God's commandments for us, as the one who brings and promises the new world. . . . With this, we are wholly directed toward Christ. Through this, however, we understand the entire world order of the fallen creation as directed only toward Christ through the new creation. . . . [This is accomplished through the orders of preservation, whose] value does not rest in themselves . . . . Rather they are God's orders of preservation, which have continued existence only as long as they remain open for the revelation in Christ. The preservation is the act of God with the fallen world through which he guarantees the possibilities of a new creation.[60]

Following a relatively lengthy discussion of the orders of preservation, Bonhoeffer says: "The churches bound together in the World Alliance believe that they recognize a very specific order as that commanded us by God today. The order of *international peace* is God's commandment for us today."[61] Having made this clear statement, he distinguishes what he is saying from what he describes as "pacifist humanitarianism" or embracing "the ideal of peace." The former suggests that the call to peacemaking needs to be justified on some ground other than being a command from God, and

---

59. Bonhoeffer, DBWE 11, 362.
60. Bonhoeffer, DBWE 11, 363–64. Really, this whole paragraph is very important.
61. Bonhoeffer, DBWE 11, 364; emphasis his.

the second makes peace into "an absolute" that "has value in itself," divorced from the gospel and commandment of Christ, and thus apparently removed from the need to hear the revelation of God through Christ.[62]

Bonhoeffer follows this by saying:

> The broken character of the order of peace is expressed in the fact that the peace demanded by God has two boundaries: first, the truth; second, justice. A community of peace can exist only when it does not rest on *a lie* or on *injustice*. Wherever a community of peace endangers or suffocates truth and justice, the community of peace must be broken and battle must be declared. If the battle from both sides is really about truth and justice, then the community of peace, even when externally broken, will be realized more deeply and strongly in the battle for this very cause.[63]

Because he knows that the pursuit of truth and justice can often be difficult and hurtful he adds that "the only enduring basis of any community of peace [is] the forgiveness of sins."[64] In other words, he says, "Neither a static concept of peace . . . nor a static concept of truth . . . grasps the evangelical idea of peace in its vivid relationship to the concept of truth and justice."[65] That is to say, equilibrium—external peace—is not necessarily in line with the purposes of Christ. Sometimes struggle is instead called for. "Struggle is not an order of creation, but it can be an order of preservation for the future of Christ, toward the new creation. Should the situation arise, the struggle can protect the openness for the revelation in Christ better than external peace, in that it breaks the hardened, self-enclosed order."[66]

Having introduced the importance of struggle, he knows he may be misunderstood. Therefore, he clarifies:

> Today, however, there is a widespread and extremely dangerous error that says that in the *justification of struggle* there is already the justification for war, that this contains the *fundamental Yes to war*. The right to wage war can be derived from the right to struggle no more than the right to inflict torture can be derived from the necessity of legal process in human society. . . . Today's war destroys soul and body. Because there is no way for us to

---

62. Bonhoeffer, DBWE 11, 365.

63. Bonhoeffer, DBWE 11, 365; emphases his.

64. Bonhoeffer, DBWE 11, 365.

65. Bonhoeffer, DBWE 11, 366.

66. Bonhoeffer, DBWE 11, 366. This is also specifically mentioned in Bonhoeffer, "The Bethel Confession," DBWE 12, 385–86.

understand war as God's order of preservation and therefore as God's commandment, and because war needs to be idealized and idolatrized in order to live, today's war, the next war, must be *condemned* by the church. We do not express any judgment against past deeds, even in the last war—that is not our right— "thou shall not judge"—but we must face the next war with all the power of resistance, rejection, condemnation. Not out of the Enthusiast establishment of a commandment—for example, the fifth above the others—but rather out of the obedience to God's commandment that affects us today, that there should be no more war because it robs us of the view toward revelation. We should not balk here at using the word "pacifism." Just as certainly we submit the ultimate *pacem facere* [to make peace] to God, we too must *pacem facere* to overcome war. Certainly this will not lead to an eradication of strife as such from the world. But we are concerned here with a very specific means of struggle forbidden today by God. Understood this way, the protest of the Alliance could be a genuine listening to God's present commandment.[67]

To remind us: this was a lecture on the need for a theology for the World Alliance. Yet Bonhoeffer spends much of his time explaining what he means in saying that God commands Christians to speak against war—to make peace as the body of Christ. However, at the beginning of the address, he articulates his concern that this can only truly be grasped if we see that the command of God is closely tied to the church. And he concludes by lamenting that there is no clarity within the World Alliance on the meaning of Christ or the gospel. Given this reality, he says, "the truth is torn asunder. And that makes our word powerless, even mendacious."[68]

About a month later, on August 29, Bonhoeffer delivered an address at the International Youth Conference in Gland, Switzerland.[69] It has no title. But perhaps the opening words—"The Church is dead"—can serve as the title. In the opening few pages of this brief address, Bonhoeffer suggests that the church is often perceived to be lifeless. In his reflections he encourages his listeners to accept the diagnosis: the church is dead. And then he points to the fact that God raises the dead. He reminds his listeners that the church is alive—is vibrant and life-giving—only because of Christ. For the church

---

67. Bonhoeffer, DBWE 11, 366–67; emphases his.

68. Bonhoeffer, DBWE 11, 369.

69. Bonhoeffer, DBWE 11, 375–81. Also see his reports on the youth conferences, Bonhoeffer, DBWE 11, 381–98.

"is about Christ and nothing else." What we need to do is "let Christ be Christ."[70]

In the following paragraph Bonhoeffer seems to be addressing a specific deficiency he noticed at the conference. He poses a pointed question: "Has it not become terribly clear, again and again, in all that we have discussed with one another here, that we are no longer obedient to the Bible? We prefer our own thoughts to those of the Bible. We no longer read the Bible seriously. We read it no longer against ourselves but only for ourselves. If this entire conference is to have had a great meaning, it would perhaps be to show us that we must read the Bible in an entirely different way by the time we meet again."[71]

Bonhoeffer asks rhetorically, "Why is the community of brothers in the church of Christ, as it appears in the World Alliance, afraid? Because it knows about the commandment to peace, yet with the clear gaze given to the church, it sees a reality governed by hate, by hostility, by violence. It is as though all the powers of the earth had sworn themselves against peace: money, the economy, the drive to power, yes, even love for the fatherland—all have been pulled into the service of hate, the hatred of the peoples, the hate of compatriots toward their own compatriots."[72]

He briefly describes some of the violent, conflicted, oppressive situations throughout the world. He refers to recent events in South America and East Asia. He refers to "starving people," those "humiliated and degraded nations," "political extremes against political extremes, fanaticized against the fanaticized, false gods against false gods—and behind all this, a world bristling with weapons as never before, a world that is feverishly mobilizing for war, in order to guarantee peace through armaments, a world whose false gods have become the word 'security'—a world without sacrifice, full of distrust and suspicion, because it still feels the terrors of the past in its bones." This is all so horrible and systemic, Bonhoeffer says, that it seems "the demons themselves have taken control of the world, that it is the forces of darkness that here gruesomely conspire and can burst forth at any moment."[73] With this diagnosis, Bonhoeffer means to suggest that such situations will not be changed simply with a "bit of education toward international understanding." No, "Christ alone adjures the false gods and the demons. Only before the cross does the world tremble, not before us."[74]

---

70. Bonhoeffer, DBWE 11, 377.
71. Bonhoeffer, DBWE 11, 377–78.
72. Bonhoeffer, DBWE 11, 378.
73. Bonhoeffer, DBWE 11, 379.
74. Bonhoeffer, DBWE 11, 379.

Having made clear once again that Christian peacemaking is centrally about Christ and the power of his cross and resurrection, he reiterates what he had said in Czechoslovakia, that peace is not the absence of strife. Strife is sometimes crucial as Christians seek truth and justice. However, he once again makes clear that the necessity for strife does not justify war. Quite the contrary. "Today there should no longer be war—the cross does not want it." Present-day war "lays waste to God's creation and obscures the view of revelation.... The church forsakes obedience whenever it sanctions war. The church of Christ stands against war in favor of peace among the peoples, between nations, classes and races."[75]

In December 1932 Bonhoeffer presented a brief lecture to the German Christian Student Association on "Christ and Peace."[76] This talk was built around the double love command: to love the Lord our God with all our heart, soul, and mind and to love our neighbors as ourselves.

Throughout this brief talk, there is a minor theme that Christians should not live with the illusion of creating a peaceful world—especially with humanistic methods. This is not what Christ promises. For as long as there is sin in the world and God allows human freedom, there will be war. "Christ was much more concerned," says Bonhoeffer, "that we should love God, that we become disciples of Jesus, as we are called to do through the promise of the Beatitudes, and that we thus become witnesses for peace."[77] Christ has not given us detailed rules for all of the complex realities in the world that we will confront, Bonhoeffer says. However, "To the simple reader of the Sermon on the Mount, what it says is unmistakable."[78] "The commandment, 'You shall not kill,' the word that says, 'Love your enemies,' is given to us simply to be obeyed. For Christians any military service, except in the ambulance corps, and any preparation for war, is forbidden. The belief that sees freedom from the law as meaning you can do anything you like outside the law is a human belief and defies God. Simple obedience knows nothing of good and evil but lives in discipleship to Christ and does its good works as a matter of course."[79]

Bonhoeffer in this lecture speaks in direct opposition to the book *Moral Man and Immoral Society*, by his former teacher Reinhold Niebuhr. Bonhoeffer does so by addressing himself to the differences between individuals

---

75. Bonhoeffer, DBWE 11, 380.

76. Bonhoeffer, DBWE 12, 258–62. Like some of Bonhoeffer's other writings, such as his Christology lectures, this address is reconstructed from student notes.

77. Bonhoeffer, DBWE 12, 259.

78. Bonhoeffer, DBWE 12, 259.

79. Bonhoeffer, DBWE 12, 260.

and society. "So, when we speak of matters of peace, we must always keep in mind that relations between two nations are deeply analogous with relations between two individual persons. The things that stand in the way of peace are in both cases thirst for power, pride, the drive to seek fame and honor, as well as arrogance and feelings of inferiority, fear of other people, and the struggle for living space [*Lebensraum*] and for bread. What is sinful for an individual person, however, can never be a virtue for a *nation* [*Volk*]."[80] "The Christian's struggle," Bonhoeffer continues,

> is therefore a struggle for the cause. In the conflict with the enemy of the gospel, the Christian's *weapons*, however, are faith and love, which are purified in suffering. How much more so than in quarrels that are only about earthly possessions. What does this greatest and highest commandment tell us? It calls upon us to love and makes the love of our neighbor a *parable* for our love of God. We do not *truly* love God unless we love our neighbor as ourselves. Our love for our neighbor is not *pure* if we do not love God in and with him. Love is self-seeking if it does not seek God and God's commandments. In the pure love with which God first loved us is the peace that Christ gives (John 14:27), which is promised in the Beatitudes. Pure love, however, would rather see a defenseless brother be killed than to see his soul, or our own, stained with blood. Pure love, in obedience to the fifth commandment, gives up its life for a brother, whether he is on this side or the other side. Pure love quite simply cannot lift up a sword against a Christian, because that would mean to lift it against Christ.[81]

This talk was presented in December 1932, shortly before Hitler became chancellor. Following Hitler's ascent to power, at the end of January 1933, Bonhoeffer spent most of his time and energy trying to work with other church leaders to help the Protestant Church in Germany not to become aligned with Nazi ideology. For Bonhoeffer the theological issues at stake—which were great—included implications for nationalism, militarism, and antisemitism.[82] He was one of the theologians who by the end of July had been commissioned to compose a confession for the emerging Confessing Church. Some of his specific concerns are expressed in the

---

80. Bonhoeffer, DBWE 12, 260–61; emphasis his. Cf. Bonhoeffer's comments in a sermon on Gideon, drawn from Judg 6–8: "If you have faith, lay down your weapons" (Bonhoeffer, DBWE 12, 466).

81. Bonhoeffer, DBWE 12, 261–62; emphases his.

82. To better understand the need for his diligent work, it is helpful to read Bergen, *Twisted Cross*. For documents that help tell the story, see Solberg, *Church Undone*.

portions of what came to be called the Bethel Confession that were authored or coauthored by him.[83] For instance, the article on "Creation and Sin," under the sub-category of "Faith in the Creator and Natural Knowledge," says: "We reject the false doctrine that struggle [*Kampf*] is the fundamental law of the original creation, and that an aggressive attitude is therefore God's commandment arising from the original creation. Struggle presupposes the condition of being friend or foe. The condition arises only from the existence of good and evil. The goal of this struggle, to annihilate one another, is a consequence of the fall, according to which good and evil are no longer separate in a human being. Therefore, no struggle with evil, that is, with sin, may ever be aimed at the person who carries the evil, for evil is at work on both sides. The fight must be against evil as such."[84] Then, in writing on the subject of "Orders," Bonhoeffer and his coauthor strategically quote the Augsburg Confession: "'Christians therefore are obliged to be subject to political authority and to obey its commands and laws in all that may be done without sin. But if a command of the political authority cannot be followed without sin, we must obey God rather than any human beings.'"[85] As was mentioned in chapter 2, after revisions to this confession were made by outside consultants, Bonhoeffer himself would not sign it. There would not be an official confession for the Confessing Church until the following May in Barmen.

In October 1933 Bonhoeffer moved to London to pastor two small German-speaking congregations. Bethge says that during his time in London Bonhoeffer was preoccupied with the Sermon on the Mount. He preached a series of sermons on the Sermon on the Mount, which unfortunately are lost. It is likely that these sermons would have been similar to what later would appear in his book *Discipleship*, including what he said there on peace. But we do have some strong statements on peace from Bonhoeffer during these eighteen months. One such statement is from a 1934 sermon on 2 Corinthians 12:9. In it Bonhoeffer makes the extraordinary claim that "Christianity stands or falls with its revolutionary protest against violence.... Christianity has adjusted itself much too easily to the worship of power."[86] One of his church members, Lawrence Whitburn, became Bonhoeffer's friend and frequent conversation partner. Their relationship began with discussions of Bonhoeffer's sermons. But, according to Whitburn, "there

---

83. Bonhoeffer, DBWE 12, 374n2.

84. Bonhoeffer, DBWE 12, 385–86; cf. Bonhoeffer, DBWE 11, 362–67.

85. Bonhoeffer, DBWE 12, 391. In addition to providing the reference to the Augsburg Confession, the editors also reference Acts 5:29.

86. Bonhoeffer, DBWE 13, 402.

soon developed an unaffected friendship and it did not take very long before he was coming and going as freely as one of the family." He observes, "If one really wanted to raise a lively discussion [with Bonhoeffer], one had only to touch on the subject of divorce or pacifism. His opinion against the former and in favour of the latter was so marked and clear in his mind that the discussion soon developed into an argument, presumably as we thought the opposite. Nevertheless, we still remained good friends."[87]

We can also see what Bonhoeffer believed about war and peace during his time in London by noting his address on peace, "The Church and the Peoples of the World," presented at the World Alliance Conference in Fanø, Denmark, in the late summer of 1934.[88] In this brief address Bonhoeffer says very clearly that God has commanded the body of Christ to witness to the peace that together they have in Christ. Apart from the fact that Christians are to keep God's "commandment of peace," he notes that unity in the body of Christ is violated by war. "They cannot take up arms against Christ himself—yet this is what they do if they take up arms against one another."[89] However, Bonhoeffer does not want followers of Jesus to confuse the call of their Lord with safety. "There is no way to peace along the way of safety," Bonhoeffer says.

> For peace must be dared. It is the great venture. It can never be made safe. Peace is the opposite of security. To demand guarantees is to mistrust, and this mistrust in turn brings forth war. To look for guarantees is to want to protect oneself. Peace means to give oneself altogether to the law of God, wanting no security, but in faith and obedience laying the destiny of the nations in the hand of Almighty God, not trying to direct it for selfish purposes. Battles are won, not with weapons, but with God. They are won where the way leads to the cross. Which of us can say he knows what it might mean for the world if one nation should meet the aggressor, not with weapons in hand, but praying, defenseless, and for that very reason protected by "a bulwark never failing"?[90]

Bonhoeffer provided a list of theses to accompany his talk.[91] In this short document he reflects on the conflicted nature of the World Alliance's self-identity and the purposes of the Alliance and names the common belief

87. Whitburn, "Bonhoeffer without His Cassock," 79–80.
88. Bonhoeffer, DBWE 13, 307–9; theses for the same address, 304–6.
89. Bonhoeffer, DBWE 13, 308.
90. Bonhoeffer, DBWE 13, 308–9.
91. Bonhoeffer, DBWE 13, 306.

among members, that "the enemy of work for peace is war." He then lists three ways in which people seek to justify war, followed by three responses to war by secular pacifists. Having named these two responses, he then says that "these two arguments are of equal value and are equally unchristian." He concludes this brief paper with three paragraphs on what he apparently believes should be the Christian church's responses to war (consistent with his talk). Here is the first of three paragraphs:

> The Christian Church answers: (a) The human will must be confronted with the commandment: Thou shall not kill. God does not exempt us from obeying His commandments. Man by his transgressions will be guilty before God. The God of the Sermon on the Mount will judge him. To the objection: The State must be maintained: the Church answers: You shall not kill. To the objection: War creates peace: the Church answers: This is not true, war creates destruction. To the objection: The nation must defend itself: the Church answers: Have you dared to entrust God, in full faith, with your protection in obedience to His commandment? To the objection: Love for my neighbor compels me: the Church answers: The one who loves God keeps His commandments. To the question: What shall I do then? The Church answers: Believe in God and be obedient. But to the secular pacifism the Church answers: The motives of our actions are not the welfare of humanity, but obedience to God's commandments. Even if war meant the good of humanity, God's commandment would remain steadfast.[92]

He begins the second paragraph by saying, "The powers of evil will not be broken by means of organisations, but by prayer and fasting (Mark 9:29)." Having made clear (pacifist) statements in the first paragraph, he concludes by making sure that everyone can see that he is fundamentally making theological claims. "It is not pacifism that is the victory which overcomes the world (1 John 5:4) but faith, which expects everything from God and hopes in the coming of Christ and His Kingdom. Only then will the cause of evil—that is to say, the Devil and the demons—be overcome."[93]

Bonhoeffer had been interested in the teaching and practices of Mohandas Gandhi for about ten years. Once we know this, we can see the influence of Gandhi in the Fanø lecture in questions such as this: "Which of us can say he knows what it might mean for the world if one nation should meet the aggressor, not with weapons in hand, but praying, defenseless?"

---

92. Bonhoeffer, DBWE 13, 305–6.
93. Bonhoeffer DBWE 13, 306.

Not long after giving that address, Bonhoeffer secured a personal invitation from Gandhi to come live with him in an ashram. Eberhard Bethge explains that by 1934 "Bonhoeffer was motivated by the desire to witness Gandhi's exemplification of the Sermon on the Mount—in the spiritual exercises aimed toward a certain goal, and the Indian ways of resistance against tyrannical power." Bonhoeffer, says Bethge, "sought a prototype for passive resistance that could induce change without violence." Or, in other words, "he sought a means of fighting Hitler that went beyond the aims and methods of the church struggle while remaining legitimate from a Christian standpoint."[94]

About the same time he was considering moving to India to learn from Gandhi, Bonhoeffer was asked to direct a seminary back in Germany for the Confessing Church. Soon he made up his mind to direct the seminary. And because he didn't have time to do both, he postponed indefinitely any plans to visit India. But both the possibility of learning from Gandhi and his interest in directing a seminary are framed for Bonhoeffer by what Bethge refers to as Bonhoeffer's "constant concern" with the Sermon on the Mount and discipleship.[95]

In fact, even without training from Gandhi, Bonhoeffer seems to have had hope for resistance on the part of the Confessing Church that would be similar to movements led by Gandhi. He provides a window into this thinking in a letter to Erwin Sutz, his friend of Union Seminary days, in April 1934.

> And while I'm working with the church opposition with all my might, it's perfectly clear to me that *this* opposition is only a very temporary transitional phase on the way to an opposition of a very different kind, and that very few of those involved in this preliminary skirmish are going to be there for that second struggle. I believe that all of Christendom should be praying with us for the coming of resistance "to the point of shedding blood" and for the finding of people who can suffer it through. Simply suffering is what it will be about, not parries, blows, or thrusts such as may still be allowed and possible in the preliminary battles; the real struggle that perhaps lies ahead must be one of simply suffering through in faith.[96]

---

94. Bethge, *Dietrich Bonhoeffer*, 409. On Bonhoeffer's awareness of Gandhi's "passive resistance," see DBWE 11, 250–51.

95. Bethge, *Dietrich Bonhoeffer*, 327, 372.

96. Bonhoeffer, DBWE 13, 135; emphasis his.

On September 11, 1934, he confides again to Sutz, specifically about the conflicting choices confronting him.

> Now, I am back again in our congregation, tormenting myself with trying to decide whether to go back to Germany as director of a preachers' seminary that is soon to be opened there, stay here, or go to India. I no longer believe in the university; in fact I never really have believed in it—to your chagrin! The next generation of pastors, these days, ought to be trained entirely in church-monastic schools, where the pure doctrine, the Sermon on the Mount, and worship are taken seriously—which for all three of these things is simply not the case at the university and under the present circumstances is impossible. It is also time for a final break with our theologically grounded reserve about whatever is being done by the state—which really only comes down to fear. "Speak out for those who cannot speak"—who in the church today still remembers that this is the very least the Bible asks of us in such times as these. And then there's the matter of military service, war, etc., etc.[97]

Bonhoeffer shared these reflections quite openly with Erwin Sutz because he knew he would understand (and perhaps, in some ways, resonate with him). However, it appears that Bonhoeffer also shared similar reflections with some members of his close, extended family. Early in 1935, for instance, Dietrich had apparently shared similar sentiments with his brother Karl-Friedrich. However, his candor seems not to have been well received. Thus, on January 14, 1935, Dietrich defends himself in a letter.

> Perhaps I seem to you rather fanatical and mad about a number of things. I myself am sometimes afraid of that. But I know that the day I became more "reasonable," to be honest, I should have to chuck my entire theology. . . . I think I am right in saying that I would only achieve true inner clarity and honesty by really starting to take the Sermon on the Mount seriously. Here alone lies the force that can blow all this hocus-pocus sky-high—like fireworks, leaving only a few burnt-out shells behind. The restoration of the church must surely depend on a new kind of monasticism, which has nothing in common with the old but a life of uncompromising discipleship, following Christ according to the Sermon on the Mount. I believe the time has come to gather people together and do this. . . . I still have a hard time thinking that you really find these ideas of mine completely mad. Things do exist that are worth standing up for without compromise. To

---

97. Bonhoeffer, DBWE 13, 217.

me it seems that peace and social justice are such things, as is Christ himself.⁹⁸

Similar concerns animate his ongoing involvement in the ecumenical movement, as his memorandum to the Ecumenical Youth Commission on January 29 makes clear. He notes that in the wake of the growing influence of a "military spirit" there seems to be "a readiness to take seriously the Christian message of peace." More specifically, he mentions a group of young Christians who are considering forming a community "on the basis of the Sermon on the Mount. It is felt," says Bonhoeffer, "that only by a clear and uncompromising stand can Christianity be a vital force for our people." He continues, "This group would also make a definite stand for peace by conscientious objection." Bonhoeffer goes on to encourage those planning the next conference to have conscientious objection as one of the topics for discussion.⁹⁹

By April 26, 1935, Bonhoeffer would be back in Germany to begin a new adventure—what he would describe later as the happiest time of his life—directing a seminary for the Confessing Church. A few days into this venture, Hitler gave an address that was broadcast on the radio, to commemorate Labor Day. Among other things he announced the introduction of a general military draft. According to Eberhard Bethge, the seminary students responded enthusiastically to Hitler.¹⁰⁰ They had been willing to suffer in their work for the Confessing Church, yes; but they also wanted it understood that they were all patriotic Germans. They were happy that Hitler was helping Germany to regain its world standing by rebuilding its military capabilities. They would be happy to reassert their patriotism by entering into the military when the time came. More specifically, Bethge says that "Hitler's move to 'remove the shame of Versailles' met with general approval. Even those ordinands who had been among the seven hundred arrested in March 1935 after a celebrated Sunday proclamation ('Against Idolatry') viewed the revival of the 'military ethos' as a matter of course, and some of them volunteered for military service soon thereafter." This reflects the reality that, as Bethge says, "Even within the Confessing Church the Lutheran view of military service was uncontested."¹⁰¹ In the midst of this patriotic unity, Bethge notes the stark contrast of the demeanor of one

98. Bonhoeffer, DBWE 13, 284–85.

99. Bonhoeffer, DBWE 13, 289–90. Bonhoeffer often encouraged Christians to consider being conscientious objectors. See, e.g., Bonhoeffer, DBWE 11, 354–55.

100. Bethge, *Dietrich Bonhoeffer*, 431–32; Bethge, "Dietrich Bonhoeffers Weg," 118–21.

101. Bethge, *Dietrich Bonhoeffer*, 431.

important person: "And yet," he says, "there sat in the corner the Director, Dietrich Bonhoeffer. Pretty obviously he did not at all share our feelings."[102]

Of course this was only a few days into their time together. The students had heard only a few of Bonhoeffer's lectures. Among those first students was Joachim Kanitz, who, like Bethge, was in the inner circle of Bonhoeffer's students. Kanitz reflected years later on these early months in the seminary:

> That semester we worked on the exegesis of the Sermon on the Mount; later he worked this into his book *Discipleship*. It became clear to us on the basis of this Bible study that it is not possible for Christians to justify killing or to justify war. So, of course, we also had to talk about the very immediate question of what we would do if it came to war or even if it didn't come to war, what we would do if we were drafted, since the draft had been introduced.... When it came to the point when we were in fact drafted—I was called up on May 15, 1939—we went in with a bad conscience. It was against our convictions. But the alternative was being lined up against a wall and shot. I remember that when it came to the outbreak of war on September 1st 1939, I was still hoping that the Confessing Church would come out with a loud "no," but by then it was no longer in a position to act at all.[103]

I will discuss the book *Discipleship* in some detail in the next chapter. But it is important to note here that Kanitz is right. In fact, I'm not sure there is much debate that Bonhoeffer in this book was calling on disciples of Christ to be peacemakers. More specifically, Bonhoeffer helps readers to see that Jesus calls on his followers to do the extraordinary, renouncing violence and even rights, as expressions of our new life in Christ and as a way of loving even those who have become enemies. Bonhoeffer continued to teach his students the content of this book until the final seminary-in-exile location was forcibly closed by the Gestapo in the spring of 1940.

Bishop Theodor Heckel, director of the Church Foreign Office of the German Protestant Church, wrote a letter to the Regional Church Committee on March 7, 1936, denouncing Bonhoeffer. Heckel encouraged the committee "to take measures to ensure that he will no longer train German theologians." Why? "Because one could charge him with being both a pacifist and an enemy of the state."[104] Heckel said this after having heard

---

102. Bethge, "Dietrich Bonhoeffers Weg," 120. (Translation of this essay by Timothy Geddert and Mark T. Nation.)

103. Nation et al., *Bonhoeffer the Assassin?*, 11.

104. Bonhoeffer, DBWE 14, 148.

Bonhoeffer present a number of his lectures at ecumenical gatherings, as well as having worked with him in his pastoral appointment in London.

I was gratified that in composing a critical, article-length review of *Bonhoeffer the Assassin?*, the senior Bonhoeffer scholar Clifford Green struggled to find any Bonhoeffer texts that challenged my basic argument.[105] Apparently, the two most significant texts he could find are brief and, really, easily dealt with. They are both from the Finkenwalde period, 1935–1937. One is a short paragraph from a lecture on confirmation instructions. In response to the question "How are Christians to act in war?" the instructions begin the answer by saying: "There is *no* revealed commandment of God here." The instructions continue, "The church can never give its blessing to war and weapons. The Christian can never participate in unjust wars. If the Christian takes up arms, he must daily ask God for forgiveness for this sin and pray for peace."[106] Two paragraphs earlier the instructions offer these reflections on the sixth commandment: "God alone is Lord over all life and has given us friend and foe that we may not harm them, hate them, despise them, be angry toward them, but rather love them, preserve their lives, serve, benefit, forgive them, pray for them."[107]

There are several comments to make about this. First, there is some ambiguity in the meaning here. Second, Bethge says that Bonhoeffer's assistant, Wilhelm Rott, was actually responsible for "the catechetical section of the work" at the seminary.[108] So, Rott may have presented what appears in this lecture. Third, even if these catechetical instructions are derived from Bonhoeffer, the text we have is taken from the reconstruction of what Bonhoeffer said, based on student notes. Fourth, and very importantly, Bethge himself contrasts what is said in this catechetical instruction with what Bonhoeffer had said in 1931, when he composed catechetical instructions with Franz Hildebrandt (as discussed earlier in this chapter). In 1931 Bonhoeffer (and Hildebrandt) clearly spoke against war. Bethge acknowledges that in 1936 Bonhoeffer himself rejected military service and attempted to convince his students likewise to be conscientious objectors. However, in 1936 at Finkenwalde, Bonhoeffer "could not yet make a convincing case to the ordination candidates" to do so. Thus "the 1936 catechism is interesting," Bethge says, "because it summarizes what Bonhoeffer viewed at the

---

105. Green, "Peace Ethic or 'Pacifism'?"
106. Bonhoeffer, DBWE 14, 791.
107. Bonhoeffer, DBWE 14, 790.
108. Bethge, *Dietrich Bonhoeffer*, 441.

time as the absolute minimum of what the congregation's message should be," for those who did not agree with his own views.[109]

The second text is similar in context. Again, it is drawn from student notes. And it is a set of brief comments on how to preach on war in sermons. One sentence captures the essence of what is said: "A final answer to the question of whether a Christian should or should not participate [in war] must be rejected."[110] Again, Bethge's comments, in relation to the catechetical instructions, are pertinent. Bonhoeffer here is not speaking in his own voice, with his own convictions. He is giving advice to students who do not agree with him (assuming the reconstruction from student notes is even accurate). But here my case is even easier because we have a sermon from Bonhoeffer himself, preached on Memorial Day, in February 1932, which was discussed at length earlier in this chapter. There, he is not at all ambiguous about war.

Even clearer is what Bonhoeffer says straightforwardly in 1936 and 1937, right at the time he gives these lectures. After all, it is in January 1936 when he says to Elizabeth Zinn that he sees pacifism as simply self-evident. Joachim Kanitz, who was one of the students who stayed more than the normal term of study, is clear that Bonhoeffer taught them pacifism and connected this to conscientious objection. And there are the more than fifteen pages of *Discipleship* that articulate the call to love enemies and renounce violence, even at great cost to ourselves (as will be discussed in the next chapter).

Finally, I want to comment briefly on a piece of evidence that some might see as counting against my portrait of Bonhoeffer as a pacifist and conscientious objector.[111] This is his comments to or silence regarding soldiers who are involved in combat. By September 1942 more than twenty-one of Bonhoeffer's former seminary students had died on the battlefield. He frequently received letters from students serving on the front lines. Sometimes they reported doing horrible things—murdering captured soldiers and civilians, for instance. He wrote letters to them. He wrote letters to family members of his fallen students. He always wrote with compassion and sensitivity. Does anyone truly imagine that this was because he no longer cared about loving enemies or killing on the battlefield, in the name of Hitler?

---

109. Bethge, *Dietrich Bonhoeffer*, 188–89.

110. Bonhoeffer, DBWE 14, 766.

111. I should mention that there are also some passages within *Ethics* that I will want to engage more fully. I will do that in ch. 5, which is specifically on *Ethics*.

I think we can see that that is certainly not true by listening once more to the testimony of Joachim Kanitz. He recalls a conversation he had with Bonhoeffer in August 1942, while he was on leave from the military. He was wearing his officer's uniform and felt shame wearing it in Bonhoeffer's presence. He remarks on Bonhoeffer's great sensitivity as they spoke, noting that Bonhoeffer said nothing to him to make him feel ashamed. But Kanitz also states his resolve related to what his teacher had taught him. "The reason I tell about this," says Kanitz, "is that through the pacifism that Bonhoeffer had taught us, that we had come to by reading the Bible, the will to resist fascism and dictatorship had been planted so firmly in me that these seven years as a soldier were utter hell for me. Sometimes I was close to insanity because of it. At any rate, the only thing I could conclude for the rest of my life was: never again."[112]

Dietrich Bonhoeffer devoted much of his life—including his teaching and lecturing career—to articulating a "revolutionary protest against violence." He taught and lived these convictions consistently from 1931 to the end of his life. However, his convictions were centered not in his own righteousness but in Christ, the gracious commander who calls believers to faithfulness and offers forgiveness to those who repent. Bonhoeffer's role, like ours, was to point to Jesus Christ—the One who summons by evangelical address and enables us to live by the empowering word of God.

"It Is about Christ and Nothing Else": Toward Discipleship[113]

It seems that ever since Bonhoeffer suggested, in July 1932, that "we should not balk here at using the word 'pacifism,'" most have in fact strongly rejected the use of this very word as a descriptor for his views regarding peace. And this despite his 1936 statement that sometime before 1933 he came to see pacifism as self-evident. Moreover, as I hope this chapter has made clear, these are hardly isolated remarks. They fit into a trajectory in Bonhoeffer's life and thought, a trajectory that represents a departure from convictions he previously held. And he held these pacifist convictions for the rest of his life.

The apparent reason why many have difficulty believing that Bonhoeffer was ever a pacifist—or if he was, that he had changed by 1940—is because of the supposed nature of his involvement in attempts to kill Hitler, an involvement that is inconsistent with pacifism. I have addressed this issue in chapter 1. An ancillary reason for doubting that Bonhoeffer was ever a

---

112. Nation et al., *Bonhoeffer the Assassin?*, 11.
113. Bonhoeffer, DBWE 11, 377.

pacifist is because of his form of argumentation in some of his lectures on peace. That is, since pacifism is typically understood to mean adhering to the principle never to kill (especially in war), then Bonhoeffer could not have been a pacifist since he abhorred a principle-centered approach to ethics. So, this is what will be examined for the remainder of this chapter.

The first point that needs to be made is that there is a consistency in Bonhoeffer's opposition to war from 1931 forward, despite the evolution of his form of argument.[114] To show this, let me simply replay highlights from this chapter's earlier discussion of his public lectures on peace.

In a Memorial Day sermon in February 1932, Bonhoeffer said that the great power of the "uprising against Christ is called war!" Later in the same sermon, he said that we should "pass on the message of peace" with the same devotedness with which wars are fought.

A few months later, in a July 1932 lecture "On the Theological Foundation for the Work of the World Alliance," at a youth conference in Czechoslovakia, Bonhoeffer spoke in the form that is most clearly contextual (and in terms of a formal style of argument most similar to his lecture on ethics in Barcelona). This includes being clear about his opposition to imagining that we need to obey biblical law, including the Sermon on the Mount. And he opposes "humanitarian pacifism," which is justified on grounds other than Christ, as well as "the ideal of peace," which is divorced from the gospel and the command of Christ. However, in the face of these disclaimers, there is no lecture in which Bonhoeffer is clearer on the subject of war.

His foundational affirmation is that "the word of the church is the word of the present Christ; it is gospel and commandment." As a way of preparing the ground for some of the primary entailments of his central affirmation, he strongly criticizes the quite common understanding of "the orders of creation," a belief that, among other things, often leads to active support of one's own country's wars. He offers rather a focus on "the orders of preservation," a condition which presents an openness to "the revelation of Christ." Following this reframing, he affirms that "international peace" is God's commandment today. He makes it clear that peace is not the same as superficial order or equilibrium that simply ignores the need in society for truth and justice. In fact, conflict may be necessary to correct injustices and lies. However, he specifically makes clear that such needed conflict in no way justifies war. In fact, he says, "there is no way for us to understand war as God's order of preservation." Further, "today's war, the next war, must be condemned by the church." Moreover, he says that "we must face the next

114. We don't have a text from 1931. However, as reported earlier in this chapter, Jean Lasserre says that Bonhoeffer advocated against war in the summer of 1931 in Mexico.

war with all the power of resistance, rejection, condemnation." And it is in this lecture where Bonhoeffer says: "We should not balk here at using the word 'pacifism.'"

About a month later, in August 1932, Bonhoeffer spoke to the International Youth Conference held at Gland, Switzerland, on Lake Geneva.[115] Similar to his emphasis in July, he begins with a focus on the church. However, here he begins with a challenge: "The Church is dead." He devotes the first few pages to reflections on this sense that apparently more than a few had. He weighs in by saying that Christians who have faith should not be anxious about a church that appears lifeless. For God raises the dead. Indeed, we should realize, that the church "is about Christ and nothing else." Thus, "We come together in order to hear Christ." However, in conjunction with this emphasis, we might notice something that was not present in the July lecture. For in that lecture, the only straightforward references to the Bible were to say that Christians are not bound by the laws of Scripture. However, in this lecture, reflecting on what he had heard at the conference, Bonhoeffer wonders aloud whether "we are no longer obedient to the Bible. We prefer our own thoughts to those of the Bible. We no longer read the Bible seriously. We read it no longer against ourselves but only for ourselves." Having said this, Bonhoeffer again is clear about war. "Today there should no longer be war—the cross does not want it." He continues, "The church forsakes obedience whenever it sanctions war. The church of Christ stands against war in favor of peace among the peoples, between nations, classes, and races."

By December 1932, in his lecture on "Christ and Peace," given to the German Christian Student Association, we see that Bonhoeffer has now shifted dramatically from the formal approach in his July lecture in Czechoslovakia.[116] He is still saying that discernment is needed for knowing exactly what to do in specific situations. However, on peace, "there is only one *authority* who has spoken definitively on this question, and that is *Jesus Christ*. . . . To the simple reader of the Sermon on the Mount, what it says is unmistakable," Bonhoeffer boldly pronounces. "The commandment 'You shall not kill,' the word that says, 'Love your enemies,' is given to us simply to be obeyed." What follows from this? "For Christians, any military service, except in the ambulance corps, and any preparation for war, is forbidden. The belief that sees freedom from the law as meaning you can do anything you like outside the law is a human belief and defies God. Simple obedience knows nothing of good and evil but lives in discipleship to Christ and does

---

115. Bonhoeffer, DBWE 11, 375–81.

116. Bonhoeffer, "Christ and Peace," DBWE 12, 258–62; emphases his.

its good works as a matter of course." In fact, in almost direct contradiction to what he had said in Barcelona, Bonhoeffer argues that the love we are to have in Christ "would rather see a defenseless brother be killed than to see his soul, or our own, stained with blood. Pure love, in obedience to the fifth commandment, gives up its life for a brother, whether he is on this side or on the other side." This is the first time that both in content and form we see Bonhoeffer anticipating his more fully developed thought in *Discipleship*.

The last lecture I will mention is "The Church and the Peoples of the World" from late summer 1934.[117] This was presented in Fanø, Denmark, to the Ecumenical Council of Christian Churches. This talk is quite brief. In it, we see Bonhoeffer's dual emphasis on Christ and the church. "For the members of the ecumenical Church, in so far as they hold to Christ, His word, His commandment of peace is more holy, more inviolable than the most revered words and works of the natural world." Christians, Bonhoeffer says, "cannot take up arms against Christ himself," which is what they do if the European countries go to war against one another. But his unique emphasis in this lecture is his focus on trust: "There is no way to peace along the way of safety. For peace must be dared. It is the great venture. It can never be made safe. Peace is the opposite of security." He continues, "Peace means to give oneself altogether to the law of God, wanting no security, but in faith and obedience laying the destiny of the nations in the hand of Almighty God." Indeed, "Which of us can say he knows what it might mean for the world if one nation should meet the aggressor, not with weapons in hand, but praying, defenseless, and for that very reason protected by 'a bulwark never failing?'"

I hope the reader can see that there is a consistency in all of Bonhoeffer's public reflections on peace from 1932 through 1934.[118] In all of them, there is an unequivocal call to peacemaking, along with a denunciation of participation in war on the part of Christians. This sort of witness is typically referred to as pacifism; and Bonhoeffer so labels his own approach. Those who imagine Bonhoeffer could not have been a pacifist because he opposed a principle-focused approach to ethics are simply revealing their ignorance of the varieties of pacifism. John Howard Yoder, in his book *Nevertheless*, describes twenty-nine different logical approaches to pacifism. If I were to

---

117. Bonhoeffer, "The Church and the Peoples of the World," DBWE 13, 307–10.

118. We don't have more peace lectures from Bonhoeffer after 1934 because his main venue for such lectures is ecumenical gatherings. By spring 1935 he is very busy directing and teaching in a seminary, which occupies him until spring 1940. But he also becomes disenchanted with the ecumenical movement because most of its leaders won't accept his claim that the Confessing Church is really the only genuine representation of the Protestant Church in Nazi Germany.

choose one type within which to fit Bonhoeffer it would probably be "The Pacifism of Proclamation."[119] But regardless of whether I am right about the type within which he fits, simply perusing *Nevertheless* opens up new ways to grasp Bonhoeffer's own claim that he came to see pacifism as self-evident and to take him at his word.

Yet there is no question but that we can see an evolution in Bonhoeffer's theology in his peace lectures. Even though he had written graduate theses on ecclesiology and Christology, it took him a while to work out how to integrate his insights on the church and Christ with his fresh discovery of the word of God spoken through the Scriptures, especially the Sermon on the Mount.[120] Furthermore, he was determined to do this while sustaining not only an awareness of God's absolute claim on our lives but also our awareness of our ongoing need for God, entailing the existential call for each of us to be disciples—which requires both a lifelong journey of faith and a life lived for the sake of the world.[121] I would argue that without question his clearest and fullest statement regarding the claim that "it is about Christ and nothing else" is presented in his book *Discipleship*, to which we turn next.

---

119. Yoder, *Nevertheless*, 62–67. Cf. Bartsch, "Foundations and Meaning of Pacifism." Also see Yoder, *Karl Barth and Problem of War*.

120. In our 2013 book, *Bonhoeffer the Assassin?*, chs. 4 and 5 address theological shifts from Bonhoeffer's Barcelona lecture to his book *Discipleship*.

121. This of course includes the ways in which he integrates what he considers the best insights from Luther and his ongoing learning from Barth. We can also see that Bonhoeffer is continuing to be influenced by Kierkegaard. Helpful in seeing this is Westphal, *Kierkegaard's Concept of Faith*, especially his first six chapters on *Fear and Trembling*.

4

Discipleship in a World Full of Nazis

Introduction

"Repent and believe in me." Do you know who spoke those words in the first century? Josephus, the Jewish historian. It was his attempt to transform the allegiance of someone who was violently plotting against him, likely because Josephus was seen as collaborating with the Roman oppressors.[1] This is a rather obvious reminder that biblical language, often seen as narrowly religious or spiritual, can be replete with sociopolitical connotations. Might this also be true for some of Bonhoeffer's theological language employed in 1930s Germany?

Nachfolge is the title Dietrich Bonhoeffer chose for his book that was published in Germany in 1937, a book that originated as lectures he delivered to his students at a Confessing Church seminary beginning in the spring of 1935.[2] To convey the spirit of the book, the title, *Nachfolge*, was originally rendered into English as *The Cost of Discipleship*. I have been aware for some time that *Nachfolge*, discipleship, was not a common topic among theologians or pastors within Germany in the 1930s.[3] What I was

---

1. Wright, *Jesus and Victory of God*, 250.

2. Discipleship had also been the subject of sermons he preached in London between 1933 and 1935 and the topic of lectures he presented at the University of Berlin in 1936 (as well as a regular subject for his students at the seminary throughout the time he directed it).

3. But it does seem likely that one of the reasons for Bonhoeffer's use of the term *Nachfolge* as the title and focus of the book was because of his familiarity with the well-known medieval work by Thomas à Kempis, *Imitatio Christi*, translated into German as

not aware of until 2010 was the following, which is reported by Ferdinand Schlingensiepen, the son of a Confessing Church pastor, in his biography of Bonhoeffer: "At all Nazi public events there were speeches about '*Führer* and followers.' During the war these were made into a song with the refrain, '*Führer, befiehl, wir folgen dir*' ['Leader, command, we'll follow you']." Schlingensiepen comments: "When Bonhoeffer called his lecture course [and, later, his book] *Nachfolge* (following, or discipleship), he was not only using a New Testament concept, but also contrasting it expressly with a term widely used by the Nazis."[4]

As we begin reading *Discipleship*, we can see that Bonhoeffer's "prose is powerfully direct." We also notice that this tract for the times "is saturated with biblical language and image, often... set against the ideological horizon imposed on his readers by Nazi illusions of heroic achievement."[5] Written after Hitler's rise to power is accomplished and his attempt to Nazify German society is fully underway, *Discipleship* "serves as Dietrich Bonhoeffer's meditation on the conditions for Christian [faithfulness and] resistance. This meditation is easily misread. Books were censured by Nazi authorities, and Bonhoeffer could not speak directly. Nonetheless, in pointed antitheses, often using the dominant terms and rhetoric of Nazis, Bonhoeffer contrasts the heroic vision of Nazi propaganda with the Christian gospel."[6]

As described in the last two chapters, Bonhoeffer had already for several years been issuing theo-political challenges to Christians, prior to and during the rise of the Third Reich. Prophetic lectures on war, writings and actions challenging anti-Semitism, and the coauthoring of a confrontational confession of faith: all of these were bold calls to attentiveness regarding Christian life in 1930s Germany. That is to say, Bonhoeffer had been calling the church to a life of faithfulness and resistance since 1931. But it was not until he began directing a Confessing Church seminary in the spring of 1935 that Bonhoeffer was given the opportunity to clarify for himself and articulate for others the spiritual and theological foundations of such a call to faithfulness and resistance—in a world that he knew was being ruled by Nazis. He did this through the composition of lectures and subsequently a book on discipleship.

Those who want a directly relevant, political Bonhoeffer will be disappointed by the book *Discipleship* and thus this chapter. But for those willing

---

Nachfolge Christi (mentioned by German editors, DBWE 4, 303).

4. Schlingensiepen, *Dietrich Bonhoeffer*, 206.

5. Hook and Reno, *Heroism and Christian Life*, 180. Hook and Reno's chapter on "Twentieth-Century Antiheroism" was instrumental in helping me see more clearly the theo-political dimensions of *Discipleship*.

6. Hook and Reno, *Heroism and Christian Life*, 194.

to take it for what it was (and is), the book *Discipleship* is incendiary. It was intended to light a fire of faith and resistance strong enough to form lives in the kiln of the Christian community for the rigors of faithful life in the Third Reich. If given enough oxygen, such a fire had the potential to burn down the supporting walls of Nazism.

It is difficult to convey the extraordinary way in which Bonhoeffer in *Discipleship* integrates his God-centered theology into his call to serious faithfulness and resistance, giving rise to public witness. We must never forget that, as he writes this book, as he lives his life, Bonhoeffer is formatively shaped by Luther's passion for the singularity of the gospel of Jesus Christ. And he sees himself in alignment with the God-centeredness of Karl Barth's theology. However, just as Barth discovered the Scriptures as the living, challenging word of God in the midst of World War I—especially through the book of Romans—so Bonhoeffer while in New York City underwent his own transformation through a deep engagement with the Bible—especially the Sermon on the Mount. Following this, he also came to know—existentially *know*—that a God-centered faith defined centrally by Jesus gives rise to a particular embodied faithfulness and resistance in the midst of the world.

In fact, given that he experienced his own liberation through the Scriptures, it should not be surprising that after 1931 most of Bonhoeffer's written work would be in the form of biblical theology. Theologian John Webster is right to suggest that this reality is too frequently lost in the world of Bonhoeffer scholarship. For "students of Bonhoeffer have often gravitated towards other issues: sociality and the ethical, most of all. One result of this is an over-theorized picture of Bonhoeffer; the practical directness of Bonhoeffer's biblical writings, and his sense that biblical exposition is a task of the theologian in which theory may be a hindrance, have been lost from view."[7]

By the mid-1930s Bonhoeffer self-consciously reflected on the approach to theology—and the formation of pastors—he has come to adopt. In September 1934, when he had not yet decided whether he would accept the invitation to direct a Confessing Church seminary—when he was, in fact, still considering studying the tactics of nonviolent resistance with Mahatma Gandhi—Bonhoeffer wrote a letter to his Swiss friend from Union Seminary days, Erwin Sutz, a former student of Karl Barth: "The next generation of pastors, these days, ought to be trained entirely in church-monastic schools, where pure doctrine, the Sermon on the Mount, and worship are taken seriously." Bonhoeffer was aware that the approach to training he had

---

7. Webster, *Word and Church*, 90.

just named did not fit with that of a university, and thus did not fit with the career track Sutz had assumed he was pursuing. So, he explains, "I no longer believe in the university; in fact I never really have believed in it—to your chagrin!" This is certainly not, for Bonhoeffer, an anti-intellectual move. Rather, it is a way to stay faithful to his vocation as a teacher on behalf of the church. And staying faithful requires boldness and courage (which should not be hampered by state-imposed strictures). "It is also time for a final break with our theologically grounded reserve about whatever is being done by the state—which really only comes down to fear. 'Speak out for those who cannot speak.'—who in the church today still remembers that this is the very least the Bible asks of us in such times as these? And then there's the matter of military service, war, etc., etc."[8] One can see in this letter to his trusted friend what he has in mind for the seminary he will direct. Certainly not your standard training center for pastors!

A few months later, in January 1935, after he had decided to move back to Germany and direct the seminary, he wrote to his agnostic brother, Karl-Friedrich. Apparently, Dietrich had already been in conversation with him, probably along the lines of what he wrote to Erwin Sutz. For he is responding to his brother's concern that he is a fanatic. "Perhaps I seem to you rather fanatical and mad about a number of things," writes Dietrich.

> I myself am sometimes afraid of that. But I know that the day I became more "reasonable," to be honest, I should have to chuck my entire theology. . . . I think I am right in saying that I would achieve true inner clarity and honesty by really starting to take the Sermon on the Mount seriously. Here alone lies the force that can blow all this hocus-pocus sky-high—like fireworks, leaving only a few burnt-out shells behind. The restoration of the church must surely depend on a new kind of monasticism, which has nothing in common with the old but a life of uncompromising discipleship, following Christ according to the Sermon on the Mount. I believe the time has come to gather people together and do this. . . .
>
> Things do exist that are worth standing up for without compromise. To me it seems that peace and social justice are such things, as is Christ himself.[9]

Later that same year, Bonhoeffer addressed the need to distinguish his uncompromising stand for peace and social justice from liberal approaches, such as those dominating the ecumenical organizations in which he had

---

8. Bonhoeffer, DBWE 13, 217.
9. Bonhoeffer, DBWE 13, 284–85.

participated. Several times publicly he had in a critical way distinguished his own approach to peace from those in the ecumenical world. And he had on occasion criticized the theological approach of his former teachers at Union Seminary, including specifically the social gospel and the "ethical realism" of Reinhold Niebuhr.[10] However, as the director of a Confessing Church seminary, he wanted to offer not simply a critique but a positive alternative.

Thus, in August 1935 he offered a lecture in which he articulated the approach he was taking in his focus on discipleship. He entitled it "Contemporizing New Testament Texts."[11] The question Bonhoeffer is grappling with here is whether the Bible is only given a contemporary voice—if it is only made relevant—by being justified before the bar of modern knowledge (especially reason, culture, and folklore) *or* whether the contemporizing of the word of God happens through the justification of the present before Scripture.[12] As he speaks, he is aware that the former approach is more common. With Barth, however, he has come to believe that the latter approach is demanded by the gospel. For in making modernity normative as we seek to appropriate Scripture, the word of God is made captive,

> so that the biblical message must pass through the sieve of one's own knowledge ... [that, in fact,] whatever does not pass through is disdained and thrown away, so that one trims and prunes the [Christian] message until it fits the fixed framework, until the eagle can no longer rise and escape into its true element and instead is put on display with clipped wings as a special exhibit among the other domesticated pets. Just as a farmer who needs a field horse passes by the fiery stallion and buys the feeble, tamed horse instead, so also does one purchase a usable Christianity, tamed . . .—and it is only a question of honesty before one quickly loses all interest in this construction, and turns away from it. *This contemporizing* of the Christian message leads directly to paganism, which means that the only

---

10. Bonhoeffer, DBWE 6, 51; DBWE 10, 305–20, esp. 307–8, 318–19; DBWE 12, 236–43, 260–61; DBWE 15, 229–30, 438–62. Of course, this is about much more than a few texts that speak directly about the social gospel and Niebuhr. It is rather that Bonhoeffer's whole approach to social (theological) ethics is quite different from those approaches.

11. Bonhoeffer, DBWE 14, 413–33.

12. I have altered the translation slightly. Where I have used "folklore," the word given in the text is the untranslated *Volkstum*. *Volkstum* means folklore, alluding to cultural or national traditions. In Nazi Germany the term came to be defined partly in relation to Aryanism.

difference between G[erman] C[hristians] and so-called neo-pagans is *honesty*.[13]

As one can see from his strong rhetoric, Bonhoeffer has no use for the taming of the gospel, for domesticating the living voice of God through a contemporizing that transforms the good news into a merely "usable gospel." Put negatively, this is a concern, for instance, that promoting a gospel *because* it is usable for peace and social justice ends up making the purpose for which the gospel is usable centrally defining (which then corrupts the gospel, the foundation of our faith).[14] Put positively, one can see as this lecture unfolds that the key issue for Bonhoeffer is his desire that God's voice—God's functionally authoritative, living voice—be allowed to speak *to*, *for*, and (when needed) *against* us. And he has decided that one way to accomplish this goal is to write rhetorically persuasive biblical theology addressed to followers of Jesus. As John Webster puts it:

> [Bonhoeffer] becomes, in effect, a practical, biblical theologian, writing with what is often drastic simplicity and force. The determined plainness and resistance to intellectual sophistication is to be taken at face value: to read the biblical writings from the 1930s is not to be invited to reflect, but to be summoned by evangelical address. This is why (*contra*, for example, Charles Marsh) it seems to be entirely proper to read writings like *Life Together* or *Discipleship* as "pietistic" or naïve, provided that we use such terms to advertise the fact that Bonhoeffer is concerned to unleash the critical power of the Scriptural word without the mediation of conceptual sophistication.[15]

Webster's insightful comments seem exactly right. However, I worry that words like *pietistic* or *naïve* can be misunderstood (even with Webster's nuance). It seems important to remind readers that the author of *Discipleship* was not only a highly educated theologian but was also very worldly wise. Dietrich was close friends, for example, with his brother-in-law Hans von Dohnanyi, who at the time Dietrich was writing *Discipleship* was a top official in the Ministry of Justice. They not infrequently discussed current events. Moreover, the Bonhoeffer family was generally well connected. This is to say that Dietrich himself was well informed about what was happening within the highest circles in the Nazi regime. Therefore, it is important to remember that undergirding the deceptively simple style in his book

---

13. Bonhoeffer, DBWE 14, 414–15; emphases his.

14. One can see these concerns at work in some of Bonhoeffer's peace lectures, as discussed in ch. 3.

15. Webster, *Word and Church*, 99.

Discipleship is the sociologically, philosophically, and theologically sophisticated work of his two graduate theses, *Sanctorum Communio* and *Act and Being*, along with his considerable knowledge of current affairs. Thus his "naïveté" is, borrowing from Paul Riceour, very much a studied, second-order naïveté.[16] Saying it this way is important because the powerful, naïve-sounding rhetoric of *Discipleship* may cause us to miss the rich, carefully worded theology and awareness of social realities woven into the very fabric of this book, expressive of Bonhoeffer's intention to shape disciples for life—life lived in public spaces, within Nazi Germany. Nonetheless, Webster has clarified *why* Bonhoeffer wrote this important work in such a rhetorically provocative way. He was determined not to allow sophisticated academic scaffolding to get in the way of his desire to "unleash the critical power" of the living word of God spoken through Scriptures—especially given the deep challenges confronting himself and his students in Germany in the mid-1930s.[17]

The rest of this chapter will be devoted to discussing the content of Bonhoeffer's most substantial effort to articulate forceful biblical theology. Through his book *Discipleship*, Bonhoeffer hoped to unleash the living word of God addressed to original and future readers. The result was a work that John Webster named as "perhaps the most potent piece of Christian writing to come out of the German conflict."[18]

Discipleship, the Book

"Cheap grace is the mortal enemy of our church. Our struggle today is for costly grace."[19] These opening words in chapter 1 are a battle cry. They are the opening salvo within a book that, as John Webster says, is "an emergency work, directed to a church in peril."[20] They frame the theme of the whole chapter. Later in the chapter Bonhoeffer's rhetoric intensifies. "Like ravens we have gathered around the carcass of cheap grace. From it we have imbibed the poison which has killed the following of Jesus among us. The doctrine of pure grace experienced an unprecedented deification. The pure doctrine of grace became its own God, grace itself" (53). As he writes these

---

16. On this see Wallace, *Second Naiveté*.

17. In its own way, *Discipleship* is Bonhoeffer's parallel to Barth's *Romans*. And his lecture "Contemporizing New Testament Texts" contains echoes of Barth's "The New World in the Bible."

18. Webster, "Discipleship and Calling," 134.

19. Bonhoeffer, DBWE 4, 43. In this chapter, references to DBWE 4 (*Discipleship*), will be in parentheses in the text.

20. Webster, "Discipleship and Calling," 134.

sentences Bonhoeffer is well aware that he is addressing his fellow Protestants in the land of Luther. He knows that many readers are by this point nervous, worried that "works-righteousness" is lurking around the corner. Thus, he launches a preemptive strike: "The word of cheap grace," he says, "has ruined more Christians than any commandment about works" (55).

If one reads the whole of the chapter, one can see that Bonhoeffer has not abandoned his identity as a Lutheran theologian. That is to say, grace—or more specifically the unconditioned gift of salvation through Jesus Christ—is still at the heart of the faith he is promoting. But the accent is clear: cheap grace kills the identity of the church (and the spiritual lives of the individual Christians who comprise it). Moreover, Bonhoeffer is convinced that cheap grace is a gross distortion of the teaching of Luther.[21] Bonhoeffer, in other words, resonates with the concerns of Søren Kierkegaard, his fellow Lutheran from almost a century earlier:

> Lutheranism [with its rhetorically strong emphasis on grace] is a corrective—but a corrective made into the norm, the whole, is *eo ipso* [by that very fact] confusing in the next generation (when that for which it was meant to correct no longer exists). And as long as this continues things get worse with every generation, until in the end the corrective produces the exact opposite of what was originally intended. And such, moreover, is the case. Taken by itself, as the whole of Christianity, the Lutheran corrective produces the most subtle type of worldliness and paganism.[22]

As Brian Hook and R. R. Reno have put it, "For Bonhoeffer, the Christianity of the twentieth-century Germany tends toward two errors, both of which undermine Christian resistance to evil. The first temptation affirms the sole sufficiency of grace as the foundation and basis of the Christian life, but transforms Jesus' call into spiritual platitudes that have no weight and consequence in ordinary life. This leads to the error of cheap grace."[23] In other words "the gospel becomes a purely 'spiritual truth' that leaves the world unchanged."[24] As a Lutheran, Bonhoeffer was well aware of this danger. For he had been challenged to reckon with it in his own approach to the Christian faith.

---

21. This is captured succinctly in Sorum, "Cheap Grace, Costly Grace." For his full argument, see Sorum, *Following Jesus*.

22. Kierkegaard, *Journals of Kierkegaard*, 232–33.

23. Hook and Reno, *Heroism and Christian Life*, 197.

24. Hook and Reno, *Heroism and Christian Life*, 197.

In July 1931 Bonhoeffer met Karl Barth for the first time. He loved Barth's lectures. But he relished their informal dinner conversation even more. After their encounter, Bonhoeffer confided in a letter to his friend Erwin Sutz that Barth challenged him by saying that he "was making grace into a principle and was bludgeoning everything else to death with it."[25] It may be that Bonhoeffer also remembered the stinging critique of Reinhold Niebuhr in response to one of his papers at Union Seminary: "In making grace as transcendent as you do I don't see how you can ascribe any ethical significance to it. Obedience to God's will may be a religious experience, but it is not an ethical one until it issues in actions which can be socially valued."[26] As Bethge rightly says, after Bonhoeffer's return from the United States he was concentrating "on the terrifying proximity of an actively intervening God," in a way that would "preserve the majesty of God from being cheapened in the pulpit, and sought to proclaim him in the concreteness of grace-filled command."[27]

By the time Bonhoeffer was lecturing on discipleship, in 1935, he had become clear that "Christians must assume that God's grace is effective in the world, effective in space and time. Justification of the ungodly, then, is not 'acceptance of the unacceptable.' It is transformation of the sinner into a servant of righteousness. The grace is costly. It cost Jesus his life, and it may well cost the same of any who would follow him."[28]

According to Hook and Reno, the second temptation that Bonhoeffer was reacting against "seeks to make the call of Jesus effective by carefully coordinating human achievement with the power of God's grace. This yields the error of domesticated grace."[29] In other words, "as Christians try to combat the temptation to spiritualize the gospel, they too easily fall back into the second error, a tacit dependence on human and worldly patterns of power and effectiveness. To show the reality of grace, one carefully coordinates the divine power of Jesus with the subordinate, but real, powers of the faithful person."[30]

Hook and Reno note that "Bonhoeffer combats the errors of cheap grace and domesticated grace at every turn." According to Bonhoeffer, "The believer possesses nothing and has no basis on which to stand other than Jesus' call." In other words, "The combination—effective opposition and the

---

25. Bonhoeffer, DBWE 11, 38.
26. Bonhoeffer, DBWE 10, 451n13.
27. Bethge, *Dietrich Bonhoeffer*, 185.
28. Hook and Reno, *Heroism and Christian Life*, 197.
29. Hook and Reno, *Heroism and Christian Life*, 197.
30. Hook and Reno, *Heroism and Christian Life*, 197–98.

rejection of any human basis for opposition—is manifest in Bonhoeffer's careful combination of the visible and hidden character of discipleship."[31]

Bonhoeffer is convinced that a holistic grasp of the Scriptures—with Jesus at the center—helps prevent these destructive errors. Thus, the opening sentences of the preface to *Discipleship*: "In times of church renewal Holy Scripture naturally becomes richer in content for us. Behind the daily catchwords and battle cries needed in the Church Struggle, a more intense, questioning search arises for the one who is our sole concern, for Jesus himself. What did Jesus want to say to us? What does he want from us today? How does he help us to be faithful Christians today?" (37)

Bonhoeffer clarifies the first claim regarding the whole of Scriptures in his book *Life Together*, which draws lessons from the community life of the Finkenwalde Seminary. "The Holy Scriptures do not consist of individual sayings, but are a whole and can be used most effectively as such. The Scriptures are God's revealed Word as a whole. The full witness to Jesus Christ the Lord can be clearly heard only in its immeasurable inner relationships, in the connection of Old and New Testaments, of promise and fulfillment, sacrifice and law, Law and Gospel, cross and resurrection, faith and obedience, having and hoping."[32] But of course Bonhoeffer wants to be clear that the word of God spoken through Scriptures is for us in our daily, "worldly" lives. In reading the Scriptures, he says,

> we are uprooted from our own existence and are taken back to the holy history of God on earth. There God has dealt with us, and there God still deals with us today, with our needs and our sins, by means of the divine wrath and grace. What is important is not that God is a spectator and participant in our life today, but that we are attentive listeners and participants in God's action in the sacred story, the story of Christ on earth. God is with us today only as long as we are there. A complete reversal occurs here.... Our salvation is "from outside ourselves" (*extra nos*). I find salvation not in my life story, but only in the story of Jesus Christ. Only those who allow themselves to be found in Jesus Christ—in the incarnation, cross and resurrection—are with God and God with them.[33]

Thus, the challenge: if the church is to have dynamic spiritual life, then the Scriptures as a whole must become rich and vitally important. However, the book *Discipleship*, and most of what he would write for the rest of his

---

31. Hook and Reno, *Heroism and Christian Life*, 198.
32. Bonhoeffer, DBWE 5, 60.
33. Bonhoeffer, DBWE 5, 62.

life, was also centered in what Bonhoeffer names as "our sole concern" in his opening sentences of *Discipleship*—"Jesus himself." This is reiterated in numerous ways throughout *Discipleship*.

In introducing "The Call to Discipleship" in chapter 2, Bonhoeffer seeks to clarify the authority and power of the person of Jesus as conveyed through the Gospels.[34] "Because Jesus is the Christ, he has authority to call and to demand obedience to his word. Jesus calls to discipleship, not as a teacher and a role model, but as the Christ, the Son of God" (57). Discipleship, in fact, "is nothing other than being bound to Jesus Christ alone. This means completely breaking through anything pre-programmed, idealistic, or legalistic. No further content is possible because Jesus is the only content. There is no other content besides Jesus. He himself is it" (58–59). Or put differently: "Christianity without the living Jesus Christ remains necessarily a Christianity without discipleship; and a Christianity without discipleship is always a Christianity without Jesus Christ. It is an idea, a myth. . . . Discipleship is bound to the mediator, and wherever discipleship is rightly spoken of, there the mediator, Jesus Christ, the Son of God, is intended. Only the mediator, the God-human, can call to discipleship" (59).

John Webster has well captured what Bonhoeffer intends in this chapter. "Discipleship," says Webster, "is a matter of following Jesus as personal absolute, the absolute in person. It is not a command to take upon oneself a commitment to some cause, principle or truth beyond or behind Jesus, as if Jesus were the symbol or highest instance of something other than himself. The name of Jesus cannot be eliminated without losing everything. As Bonhoeffer puts it, in the matter of discipleship 'Jesus is the only content.'" Webster continues,

> This point is particularly important to register because there exists a permanent temptation, theological and practical, to substitute something else for the offensively particular name of Jesus, to search for something more generic, something which does not bring with it the affront of Jesus' implausible and singular direction: "Follow me." It is a temptation to which the church has often succumbed and continues to do so: contemporary substitutes for the name of Jesus include: justice; spirituality; inclusiveness; orthodoxy; moral truth. However valuable some of these generic realities may appear to be, however much gospel resonance they may bring with them, they run the risk of abstracting from the pure singularity of Jesus and his command.

---

34. Barth's influence can be detected in many ways throughout *Discipleship*. It helps to see the influence, beginning already in this chapter of *Discipleship*, if one reads Neder, *Participation in Christ*.

His name—his non-transferrable identity as *this* one—is the one reality in which salvation is to be found. And his name is to be filled out, not by reference to some principle which he illustrates or which may even be drawn from him. He is the divine self-declaration in person.[35]

Anyone who cares about what Bonhoeffer and Barth care about should pause here and slowly reread this profound summary from John Webster. This concern regarding the irreplaceable singularity of Jesus is precisely what animated the specific framing of portions of Bonhoeffer's public lectures on peace. It underlies Bonhoeffer's theological disagreements with the social gospel as taught at Union Theological Seminary as well as Niebuhrian realism and the typical Lutheran two-kingdom theology. And it is what serves as the theological substructure of his critique of a principled approach to ethics. The bulk of the remaining portions of part 1 of *Discipleship* is on the Sermon on the Mount. However, because of his theological concerns, Bonhoeffer must prepare the ground for a theological engagement with the Sermon on the Mount. Put differently, in order to subvert this "permanent temptation," Bonhoeffer of necessity names other preliminary matters (in three brief but vitally important chapters).

In the first of these chapters, "Simple Obedience," Bonhoeffer wants to make it clear that obedience expressive of true faith *in* and faithfulness *to* Jesus must be reflective of a "simple obedience," a single-mindedness, an unqualified allegiance to Jesus (77–83). Otherwise, it is simply one more form of cheap grace. This chapter likely reflects Bonhoeffer's ongoing indebtedness to Kierkegaard.[36] Discipleship—the Christian life, if it has integrity—begins with the stark, Abrahamic decision of faith. Will we trust in God or not? Will we be obedient or not? However, Bonhoeffer frames this chapter not by referencing Abraham but rather by focusing on the story of the rich young ruler (Matt 19:16–30). In his commentary on Matthew, theologian Frederick Dale Bruner, who is deeply influenced by Luther and Barth, helps us see why Bonhoeffer frames the chapter on "Simple Obedience" with this story.[37] Jesus agrees with the rich young ruler that the "*road to life is the road of God's Commandments.* This truth unites both testaments."[38] When the young man asks what commandments he must

35. Webster, "Discipleship and Calling," 141–42.

36. Charles Marsh mentions that during the writing of *Discipleship*, Bonhoeffer sometimes carried *Fear and Trembling* by Kierkegaard around with him (Marsh, *Strange Glory*, 244). *Fear and Trembling* is framed around the story of Abraham being asked to sacrifice Isaac.

37. Bruner, *Matthew*, 2:285–315.

38. Bruner, *Matthew*, 2:290; emphasis his.

keep, Jesus answers by naming several of the commands from the second table of the Ten Commandments (and the summary, "you shall love your neighbor as yourself"). As Bruner says, "These human Commandments are at the heart of Jesus' way of *salvation*. . . . Murderers, adulterers, thieves, liars, dishonorers of parents, and all violators of persons will not inherit the kingdom of God—Jesus here says this as seriously as Paul does repeatedly in his Epistles (e.g., 1 Cor 6:9–10; Gal 5:19–21; Eph 5:5). There is no immoral way to the kingdom."[39] After Jesus has named these commandments, the young man says: "I have kept all these; what do I still lack?" (Matt 19:20). This provides the perfect opening for Jesus's clarifying statement. "If you wish to be perfect [perfectly mature or complete], go, sell your possessions, and give the money to the poor, and you will have treasure in heaven: then come, follow me" (Matt 19:21). Again, Bruner helps us to see why Jesus makes this move. It is "because, while devotion to the first table of the law (and its Godward commands) can be *claimed*, devotion to the second table of the law (and its otherward commands) can be *seen*. 'Because hypocrites often seem to be keeping the first table, the second table proves better for making examination.'"[40] In other words, Jesus is pressing this rich young man to be honest about the fact that he is not singularly devoted to the Lord. "'*Keep the Commandments!*' then, is many things, but it is at least a ministry of the law, to drive the hearer to the gospel."[41] That is to say, "this keeping will require a continual kneeling ('come to me'); this road of Commandments will require many nourishing beatitudes along the way ('Blessed are the poor in spirit'); *and this way of good works cannot be walked without a faith that does not trust in good works*. But the truth of the Gospel of Matthew is that the one who says, 'come to me for rest' is the same one who immediately equips with his yoke of Commands (11:28–30). Jesus' Commands *are* the way to life in Matthew."[42]

Bonhoeffer acknowledges in this chapter on "Simple Obedience" that obedience will sometimes be embodied in circumstances that are fraught with conflicting goods and apparent paradoxes. This means that living the Christian faith in daily life will require wisdom and discernment. Two cautions must be remembered as such discernment is employed. First, "obedience to Jesus' call is never an autonomous human deed. Thus, not even something like actually giving away one's wealth is the obedience required" (83). And, second, "wherever simple obedience is fundamentally

---

39. Bruner, *Matthew*, 2:293; emphasis his.
40. Bruner, *Matthew*, 2:293; emphases his.
41. Bruner, *Matthew*, 2:290; emphasis his.
42. Bruner, *Matthew*, 2:291; emphases his.

eliminated, there again the costly grace of Jesus' call has become the cheap grace of self-justification" (81). In other words, as Bonhoeffer says later in a prison letter, the Christian life is not about trying to be a saint; it is about having faith, a lifetime of daily, active faith.[43]

Bonhoeffer might have been well served at the end of this chapter to have returned to Jesus's teaching to his disciples about what they were to learn regarding the call to the rich young ruler—and the man's rejection of the call. "'Truly I tell you,' says Jesus, 'it will be hard for a rich person to enter the kingdom of heaven'" (Matt 19:23). "When the disciples heard this, they were greatly astounded and said, 'Then who can be saved?' But Jesus looked at them and said, 'For mortals it is impossible, but for God all things are possible'" (Matt 19:5-26). Bruner's comments on this sound so much like what Bonhoeffer will later say when commenting on loving enemies, that I quote them at length:

> Commandment-keeping (with its under side of faith and its flip side of self-sacrifice) is the road to the kingdom. But Jesus now teaches that getting *on* this road requires a transforming miracle, a hoisting, possible only to God, impossible for humans. Our v. 26 does not cancel the preceding vv. 16-25; it enables them. Too much evangelical exposition has said that the miracle of regeneration is *the alternative* to obedience rather than *the way* to obedience, an escape clause rather than an entry qualification, a way to be saved without having to abandon one's quest for wealth rather than the way that saves one *from* the quest for wealth.
>
> What Jesus does *not* mean by "this is impossible for human beings" is the interpretation that says, "If you will just be born again and experience miraculous conversion, you can then continue seeking money, honor, and success, for conversion does not replace all these earthly goods; it actually assists their acquisition." In this way, success seminars often prostitute God to prosperity and make what they call "faith" a way to be a winner. This using of God is a contemporary Antichrist that the church must combat with all the resources of Jesus' teaching.
>
> What Jesus *does* mean by this verse is that God can work the miracle of putting God instead of gain on the throne of the human heart (cf. Ps 119:36). No *human* power can displace the desire for "more" as the reigning human drive. Only God's power can. Unless this miracle of dethronement-enthronement

---

43. Helpful in grasping how Bonhoeffer may have seen this is Westphal, *Kierkegaard's Concept of Faith*, esp. 1-120. Also see Kirkpatrick, *Attacks on Christendom*, esp. 139-74.

occurs again and again, there is no hope of salvation. That is the sober meaning of v. 26.[44]

And that is truly the sober meaning of Bonhoeffer's chapter on "Simple Obedience."[45]

The next chapter is on "Discipleship and the Cross" (84–91). In this chapter Bonhoeffer wants to make it clear that suffering comes with being a follower of Jesus. Hearing these words from their teacher was likely encouraging to Bonhoeffer's students. For some of them had suffered; many pastors had been arrested. His words reassured them that they were being followers of Jesus. And all of them knew that their future was uncertain, undergoing training in an illegal seminary in the midst of Nazi Germany. But Bonhoeffer also wants them to grasp the specifics of the suffering flowing from the gospel and its ongoing nature. Thus, he distinguishes the forms of suffering entailed by following Jesus from "random suffering" that of course is simply a part of normal human existence. They need to know that in its essence "discipleship is being bound to the suffering Christ" (89). And those who are bound to Jesus, yoked with him, therefore by definition bear the cross—entering into the suffering of the world. "Bearing," says Bonhoeffer, "constitutes being a Christian" (91).

The last of these short chapters that lead into Bonhoeffer's lengthy treatment of the Sermon on the Mount is on "Discipleship and the Individual" (92–99). The central, and vitally important, point of this chapter is to say that our individual lives as followers of Jesus are redefined by Jesus becoming the mediator between each of us and all of our relationships. Our way of living in the world is transformed through the mediation of our Lord through the person of Jesus. Bonhoeffer puts it this way:

> So people called by Jesus learn that they had lived an illusion in their relationship to the world. The illusion is immediacy. It has blocked faith and obedience. Now they know that there can be no unmediated relationships, even in the most intimate ties of their lives, in the blood ties to father and mother, to children, brothers and sisters, in marital love, in historical responsibilities. Ever since Jesus called, there are no longer natural, historical or experiential unmediated relationships for his disciples. Christ the mediator stands between son and father, between husband and wife, between individual and nation, whether they

---

44. Bruner, *Matthew*, 2:308; emphases his.

45. Keeping in mind John Webster's cautions about over-theorizing Bonhoeffer, it is nonetheless helpful to surface interesting questions regarding "simple obedience" by reading Kaiser, *Becoming Simple and Wise*, and Phillips, *Human Subjectivity 'in Christ'*.

can recognize him or not. There is no way from us to others than the path through Christ, his word, and our following him. Immediacy is a delusion. (95)[46]

Now we come to chapter 6. At eighty-three pages, this chapter on the Sermon on the Mount is by far the longest in the book. Section by section Bonhoeffer offers theological reflections on the claims of these three chapters from Matthew's Gospel. These pages cannot be properly understood without having grasped the preceding, theologically framing chapters. Put differently, Bonhoeffer seeks to make a way for the living voice of our Lord to address us as an evangelical invitation to follow him, even as we allow him, the living Lord, to mediate between us and our relationships in the world.

Bonhoeffer launches into the Sermon on the Mount by acknowledging the extraordinary nature of what Jesus calls his disciples to do. The "extraordinary" discipleship asked of them only makes sense because Jesus—the Word of God made flesh—is present with them, pronouncing his blessing upon their lives, upon our lives.[47] Jesus makes these disciples into a distinct, visible community, separate from the *Volkskirche*—the people's church that is broadly inclusive but defined by figures and forces other than Christ.[48]

There are many things one could say about Bonhoeffer's engagement with the Sermon on the Mount. It is simultaneously inspiring and challenging—just as the original words from Jesus are. But to illustrate his general approach, I will simply focus on Bonhoeffer's reflections on retribution and love of enemies—the longest discussion of any specific topic in the book. His words are clear, challenging, and almost unheard of in 1937 Germany. One of his clearest and most challenging summaries is given toward the end of his section on "The Enemy":

> It is the great mistake of a false Protestant ethic to assume that loving Christ can be the same as loving one's native country, or friendship or profession, that the better righteousness [called for by Jesus] and *Justitia civilis* [civil justice] are the same. Jesus does not talk that way. What is Christian depends on the "extraordinary." That is why Christians cannot conform to the world, because their concern is the περισσόν [extraordinary]. What does the περισσόν, the extraordinary, consist of? It is the existence of those blessed in the Beatitudes, the life of the

---

46. This will be very important in understanding portions of *Ethics*. (See our ch. 5.)

47. Again, very helpful to grasp Bonhoeffer's intent is Bruner, in his *Matthew*, 1:154–94.

48. Very helpful in seeing this is Bergen, *Twisted Cross*, 1–20, 44–60.

disciples. It is the shining light, the city on the hill. It is the way of self-denial, perfect love, perfect purity, perfect truthfulness, perfect nonviolence. Here is undivided love for one's enemies, loving those who love no one and whom no one loves. It is love for one's religious, political, or personal enemy. In all of this is the way which found its fulfillment in the cross of Jesus Christ. What is the περισσόν? It is the love of Jesus Christ himself, who goes to the cross in suffering and obedience. It is the cross. . . . [This is what] allows Christians to step beyond the world in order to receive victory over the world. (144–45)

In calling his followers to love their enemies, Jesus, says Bonhoeffer, is asking them to "renounce their own rights for his sake" (132). He continues, "Our voluntary renunciation of counter-violence confirms and proclaims our unconditional allegiance to Jesus as his followers, our freedom, our detachment from our own egos. And it is only in the exclusivity of this adherence that evil can be overcome" (133). "Indeed," Bonhoeffer says, "in giving witness to their sole allegiance to Jesus, they create the only solid foundation for community and place sinners into the hands of Jesus" (133). Bonhoeffer underscores this call several times within these fourteen pages. However, he also wants to make sure he is not misunderstood. Therefore, he addresses related, important subjects.

One of these is the subject of evil. A commitment to nonviolence for Christians does not require a naïveté about evil. "Our concern here is not only with evil," Bonhoeffer says, "it is with the person who is evil. Jesus calls the evil person evil. My behavior should not give excuses and justification for those who indulge in violence or who oppress me. Nor do I intend to express my understanding for the rights of an evil person by my patient suffering. Jesus has nothing to do with such sentimental considerations. The humiliating blow, the violent deed, and the act of exploitation remain evil. Disciples are to know this and to give witness to it just as Jesus did, because otherwise the evil person will not be engaged and overcome." But having made this clear, Bonhoeffer also says: "There is no thinkable deed in which evil is so large and strong that it would require a different response from a Christian. The more terrible the evil, the more willing the disciple should be to suffer. Evil persons must be delivered into the hands of Jesus. Not I but Jesus must deal with them" (134).

The next paragraph is crucially important if we are not to distort the teaching of Bonhoeffer, the Lutheran theologian. For he is rather directly, self-consciously challenging Lutheran ethics. In fact, as is obvious in this passage, he sees himself in alignment with a central passion of Luther, thus subverting one Lutheran idea by reaffirming another Lutheran conviction—*sola Scriptura*:

> At this point, the Reformation interpretation introduced a decisively new concept, namely, that we should differentiate between harm done to me personally, and harm done to me as a bearer of my office, that is, in the responsibility given me by God. In the former case I am to act as Jesus commands, but in the latter case I am released from doing so. Indeed for the sake of true love, I am even obligated to behave in the opposite way, to answer violence with violence in order to resist the inroads of evil. This is what justifies the Reformation position on war, and on any use of public legal means to repel evil. But this distinction between private person and bearer of an office as normative for my behavior is foreign to Jesus. He does not say a word about it. He addresses his disciples as people who have left everything behind to follow him. "Private" and "official" spheres are all completely subject to Jesus' command. The word of Jesus claimed them undividedly. He demands undivided obedience. In fact, the distinction between private and official is vulnerable to an insoluble dilemma. Where in real life am I really only a private person and where only the bearer of my office? Wherever I am attacked, am I simultaneously the father of my children, the pastor of my congregation, the statesman of my people? For this reason, am I not required to fight back against any attack, just because of my responsibility for my office? Am I not always myself in my office, too, who stands alone before Jesus? Should this distinction cause us to forget that followers of Jesus are always completely alone, single individuals who can act and make decisions finally only by themselves and that the most serious responsibility for those entrusted to me takes place precisely in *these* acts? (134–35; emphasis his)

As he writes about this, Bonhoeffer is aware that Jesus is not prescribing a "general ethical program" regarding the love of enemies. As he says, "Nonresistance as a principle for secular life is godless destruction of the order of the world which God graciously preserves. But it is not a programmatic thinker who is speaking here. Rather, the one speaking here about overcoming evil with suffering is he who himself was overcome by evil on the cross and who emerged from that defeat as the conqueror and victor" (136).

Thus, in distinguishing the visible Christian community from the *Volkskirche*, the people's church, Bonhoeffer has redefined our life in Christ as it relates to the world. Our commitment is to loving enemies, not retaliating against them. In calling us to do this, Bonhoeffer says, "Jesus releases his community from the political and legal order, from the national form of the people of Israel, and makes it into what it truly is, namely the community of the faithful that is not bound by political or national ties.... For the community of discipleship, which makes no national or legal claims for itself, retribution means patiently bearing the blow, so that evil is not added to evil." In this way the Christian community "is giving witness to their sole allegiance to Jesus" (132–33).

After his discussion of the Sermon on the Mount, Bonhoeffer concludes part 1 of *Discipleship* with a chapter on Matthew 10, discussing the missional call and activities of the first disciples (183–98). This chapter will—in the context of reflecting on witnessing to the larger world—reiterate some themes that have already been named, while adding a new emphasis or two. Anyone who has read widely in the Bonhoeffer corpus knows that Bonhoeffer was understandably disheartened and sometimes disgusted by the way in which most of the German Protestant Church—especially its leaders—had abandoned the gospel for Nazi ideology. But as he reflects on Matthew 10, he reminds himself and his readers that if our work is truly shaped by the call of Jesus, then we, like him, feel sadness, weep for the brokenness of those co-opted by Nazi lies, and do acts of mercy out of love—for those sheep without a shepherd. As he puts it at the beginning of his discussion: "The gaze of the Savior falls in pity on his people, on God's people" (183). He also knows that truly witnessing to the gospel will entail suffering for the messengers who bring the good news. And the temptation will be great to avoid the work to which we are called, out of fear. Thus, he says: "Anyone who is still afraid of people is not afraid of God. Anyone who fears God is no longer afraid of people. Daily reminders of this statement are valuable for preachers of the gospel" (196). And, finally, Bonhoeffer reminds his readers that those who toil in the work of the gospel must trust that such labor will produce fruit, as promised by Jesus.

Bonhoeffer is aware that the specific language of discipleship belongs to the world of the Gospels. It is related to the physical reality of being literally called to follow Jesus as he travels the roads of Palestine. Thus, as he moves into part 2 on the subject of "The Church of Jesus Christ and Discipleship," he must name what he sees as the continuities and discontinuities between the Gospels and the Pauline epistles. He begins by identifying an obvious difference: after Jesus is dead, risen, and ascended he is not physically leading his followers as they walk through their days and weeks.

Nonetheless, if we make too much of this, says Bonhoeffer, something has gone wrong; we have not truly grasped our present reality in the church.

In other words, we are placing "ourselves outside the living presence of the Christ. Our reflections on the discontinuities should take seriously that Jesus Christ is not dead but alive and still ... present with us today, in bodily form and with his word. If we want to hear his call to discipleship, we need to hear it where Christ himself is present. It is within the church that Jesus Christ calls through his word and sacrament" (201–2) Repeating what he has said in relation to the Gospels, he now reiterates, "Discipleship in essence never consists in a decision for this or that specific action; it is always a decision for or against Jesus Christ." And lest we imagine differently, Bonhoeffer wants to make it clear: "Christ speaks to us exactly as he spoke to [the original disciples as portrayed in the Gospels]" (202). In other words, "the synoptic Christ is neither more nor less distant from us than the Christ of Paul," says Bonhoeffer. "The Christ who is present with us is the Christ to whom the whole of scripture testifies. He is the incarnate, crucified, risen, and glorified Christ; and he encounters us in his word" (206).

Because his book is on discipleship, and that is the language of the Gospels and not the language of Paul, Bonhoeffer still must discern the parallel in Paul's writings.

> What the Synoptics describe as hearing and following the call to discipleship, Paul expresses with the concept of *baptism*. Baptism is not something we offer to God. It is, rather, something *Jesus Christ offers to us*. It is grounded solely in the will of Jesus Christ, as expressed in his gracious call. Baptism is essentially a paradoxically passive action; it means being baptized, suffering Christ's call. In baptism we become Christ's possession. The name of Jesus Christ is spoken over baptismal candidates, they gain a share in that name; they are baptized "into Jesus Christ." ... They now belong to Jesus Christ. Having been rescued from the rule of this world, they now have become Christ's own. (207; emphases his)

What Bonhoeffer has just said is to him vitally important theologically. It centers our Christian identity in the prior, redemptive work of God in Christ. What he then proceeds to say is equally important theologically—and is what makes this book, and his views, radical. It begins with the following claim. "Baptism implies a *break*.... [Through this break] I am deprived of my immediate relationship to the given realities of the world, since Christ the mediator and Lord has stepped in between me and the world. Those who are baptized no longer belong to the world, no longer serve the world, and are no longer subject to it. They belong to Christ alone, and relate to the world only through Christ" (207; emphasis his).[49]

Reflecting on the significance of baptism is one way that Bonhoeffer expresses his opposition to an over-spiritualizing of faith and the vital importance of the visibility of the church—a very important theme in his understanding of ecclesiology.[50] "The initiation into faith, baptism, is 'a public event,'" writes Bonhoeffer. Baptism marks citizenship in a new kingdom, governed by Christ. It signals a change of loyalty and requires us "to stand visibly in the fellowship of Jesus Christ."[51] "The visible mark of baptism is more than initiatory. One is called to stand visibly with a community of teaching and worship that is continuous through time, and which, moreover, is a public reality, a church with its own order and discipline."[52]

To convey this claim, contextually, Bonhoeffer again employs a well-known political term as a way to be theologically subversive. *Lebensraum* was a common military term used before World War I that continued to be employed during the Nazi era, often linked to imperialistic ambitions.[53] In fact, Bonhoeffer himself had said in a 1932 lecture on "The Right to Self-Assertion" that "war originates from the era when the European thought that only by killing the other could one create living space [*Lebensraum*] for oneself."[54] Bonhoeffer knew that Nazism was literally lethal in its intentions, but he also knew it intended to kill the identity of the church through disallowing it *Lebensraum*. Thus, the church must be bold in its response.

> We must now ask whether spaces of proclamation and order are already sufficient to describe the visible form of the community of the body of Christ, or whether this community claims yet another space in the world. The answer of the New Testament is unambiguous. It holds that the church-community claims a physical space here on earth not only for its worship and its order, but also for the daily life of its members. That is why we

---

49. This was also the subject of "Discipleship and the Individual," DBWE 4, 92–99; on which, see discussion above.

50. On the visibility of the church, see especially Bonhoeffer, DBWE 4, 48, 110–14; 225–52; 261ff.; 296ff.; cf. DBWE 14, 393–412; 815–42; 434ff. and of course *Sanctorum Communio* and *Life Together*. Bergen helps us to see how this emphasis on visibility is counter to the emphases within German Christianity (*Twisted Cross*, esp. 1–20, 44–60, and 191).

51. Hook and Reno, *Heroism and Christian Life*, 198–99.

52. Hook and Reno, *Heroism and Christian Life*, 199.

53. See Snyder, *Encyclopedia of Third Reich*, s.v.; and Barth, *Unique Time of God*, 39.

54. Bonhoeffer, DBWE 11, 255.

must now speak of the *living space [Lebensraum]* of the visible-church community.

Jesus' community with his disciples was all-encompassing, extending to all areas of life. The individual's entire life was lived within this community of disciples. And this community is a living witness to the bodily humanity of the Son of God. The bodily presence of the Son of God demands the bodily commitment to him and with him throughout one's daily life. With all our bodily living, existence, we belong to him who took on a human body for our sake. In following him, the disciple is inseparably linked to the body of Jesus. (232)

In other words, as Hook and Reno remind us, Bonhoeffer knows that "'the church needs *Lebensraum*. [For] in its worship and discipline, the church makes a claim over the entire life of the baptized, and with the claim, 'the Church invades the life of the world and conquers territory for Christ.'"[55]

According to the Nazis, in their understanding, "this *Lebensraum* . . . must be purified of contaminating races, especially Jews, in order to allow for the full flowering of Aryan greatness."[56] Bonhoeffer of course challenged such evil intentions. However, in *Discipleship*, where he is attempting to name the basics of a theological and spiritual foundation for faithfulness and resistance, as Hook and Reno suggest, "Bonhoeffer does not offer liberal criticisms of this aggressive desire for a visible community of Aryan purity. He does not insist on a principle of tolerance. He does not preach the virtues of diversity. He does not defend the rights of the individual. Instead, he depicts the church as a public reality, a polis, that 'takes up space in the world.'"[57] Rather, Bonhoeffer responds by saying

the church not only needs space for living but also must purge and purify. . . . The church must expel heresy; it must renounce compromises and complicity with worldly powers. There can be no question of Christian nations, Christian races, as some German theologians had speculated during the 1930s in hopes of baptizing Nazism. Territory must be taken, Bonhoeffer argues, and that territory must be sanctified through service and turned

---

55. Hook and Reno, *Heroism and Christian Life*, 199.

56. Hook and Reno, *Heroism and Christian Life*, 199. To get a sense of how deep and pervasive this was, see Kühne, *Belonging and Genocide*.

57. Bonhoeffer actually uses the word *polis* to describe the Christian community in DBWE 4, 261. Also see Bonhoeffer, DBWE 14, 272; and Zimmermann, *I Knew Dietrich Bonhoeffer*, 63.

to the purposes of worship. By these means, he writes, the church "makes a deep invasion into the sphere of secular life."[58]

Particularly with Jews in mind, Bonhoeffer proceeds to offer specific admonitions. "To allow other baptized Christians to participate in worship but to refuse to have community with them in everyday life, and to abuse them and treat them with contempt, is to become guilty against the body of Christ itself. To acknowledge that other baptized Christians have received the gifts of salvation, and then to deny them the provisions necessary for this earthly life, or to leave them knowingly in affliction and distress, is to make a mockery of the gift of salvation and to behave like a liar" (234). He continues:

> Where the world despises other members of the Christian family, Christians will love and serve them. If the world does violence to them, Christians will help them and provide them with relief. Where the world subjects them to dishonor and insult, Christians will sacrifice their own honor in exchange for their disgrace. Where the world . . . oppresses, they will stoop down and lift up the oppressed; where it hides behind lies, they will speak out for those who cannot speak, and testify for the truth. For the sake of brothers or sisters—be they Jew or Greek, slave or free, strong or weak, of noble or of common birth— Christians will renounce all community with the world, for they serve the community of the body of Jesus Christ. (237)[59]

However, he also wants to make it clear that Christian discipleship is not only about responding to the mistreatment of fellow (Jewish) Christians. "The church-community can never consent to any restrictions of its service of love and compassion toward other human beings" (236). Or, as he put it earlier in *Discipleship*, "the protection of God's community extends not only to brothers and sisters who belong to the church community but beyond" (121).

Bonhoeffer is also clear that if aggressive, apparently militaristic language, such as *Lebensraum*, is to be employed, it must be redefined by Jesus. For this is not the language of heroism. Rather, it is a reminder that the Christian community lives and acts in ways expressive of Christian convictions within the public spaces. And lest Christians think otherwise, this living, this decisive acting, may well involve suffering. In other words, "this invasion is as saturated with blood, sacrifice, and suffering as anything

---

58. Hook and Reno, *Heroism and Christian Life*, 199.

59. To see how this is directly counter to German Christian teaching, see Bergen, *Twisted Cross*, 85–88.

imagined by the Nazi propagandists."[60] In fact, this may be what Bonhoeffer had in mind, already in 1933, when he said that speaking up for the Jews might mean that the church would need to throw itself into the spokes of the wheel, offering the ultimate sacrifice, in order to stop what was being done.[61]

These last few pages have been devoted to reflections on Bonhoeffer's strong emphasis on the visibility of the Christian community. In fact, it is hard to overstate the vital importance of this for Bonhoeffer. Not only is there a substantive chapter on the subject of "The Visible Church-Community" in the second part of the book, but there was already a substantial discussion within his treatment of the Sermon on the Mount. And for Bonhoeffer this was connected very practically to life in the Confessing Church. And in dramatic ways. While working on this book he wrote a couple of provocative essays regarding the importance of the church faithfully, visibly being the body of Christ.[62] His famous (or infamous) line that captures the life-and-death nature, the utter seriousness of this for him is: "Whoever knowingly separates himself from the Confessing Church in Germany separates himself from salvation."[63] This was, in the mid-1930s, a deliberately provocative statement. However, the basic sentiment was nothing new. It was why he and Franz Hildebrandt had earlier considered starting a new, free church, separated cleanly from a German Protestantism that was so compromised that it was more German than Christian.[64] It was why, in a letter to his grandmother, on August 20, 1933, he said: "It is becoming increasingly clear to me that what we are going to get is a big, *völkisch* national church that in its essence can no longer be reconciled with Christianity, and that we must make up our minds to take entirely new paths and follow where they lead. The issue is really Germanism or Christianity, and the sooner the conflict comes out in the open, the better. The greatest danger of all would be in trying to conceal this."[65] He put it more simply in a letter to his friend Helmut Rössler in October 1931: "Invisibility is ruining us." We need to see that Christ "has been here"—and indeed is among us now.[66]

60. Hook and Reno, *Heroism and Christian Life*, 199.

61. See my discussion of Bonhoeffer's essay on "The Church and the Jewish Question" in ch. 3.

62. Bonhoeffer, "The Confessing Church and the Ecumenical Movement," DBWE 14, 393–412; Bonhoeffer, "On the Question of Church Communion," DBWE 14, 656–78 (and discussion, 678–97).

63. Bonhoeffer, DBWE 14, 675.

64. Bethge, *Dietrich Bonhoeffer*, 292.

65. Bonhoeffer, DBWE 12, 159.

66. Bonhoeffer, DBWE 11, 55. The plural "us" and "among us now" are my additions

(Thus, he enacted his experiment in serious Christian life together within his Finkenwalde seminary community.)

Life Together

The final chapter of *Discipleship*, "The Image of Christ," provides the clearest, albeit brief, summary of Bonhoeffer's understanding of what it means to be formed as disciples within this book.[67] "To become 'like Christ'—that is what disciples are ultimately destined to become. The image of Jesus Christ, which is always before the disciples' eyes—and before which all other images fade away—enters, permeates, and transforms them, so that the disciples resemble, indeed become like their master. The image of Jesus Christ shapes the image of the disciples in daily community" (281).[68]

This was precisely what Bonhoeffer was after in the way he constructed the seminary community at Finkenwalde, as summarized in his book *Life Together*.[69] Bonhoeffer had expressed his hope for such a community to his friend Erwin Sutz in 1934: "The next generation of pastors, these days, ought to be trained entirely in church-monastic schools, where pure doctrine, the Sermon on the Mount, and worship are taken seriously."[70] And Bonhoeffer had later clarified to his brother Karl-Friedrich that by "monasticism" he meant a "new kind of monasticism" or, in other words, "a life of uncompromising discipleship."[71] Bonhoeffer would structure the days for his students at Finkenwalde to fit with these commitments. Of course, a good portion of each weekday was simply given to the normal pastor-training curriculum. Integrated into this curriculum were his unique lectures on discipleship. The days were enveloped by worship—at the beginning and conclusion of each day. There were also a weekly sermon and monthly celebration of the Lord's Supper together. In addition to Bonhoeffer's profound way of articulating life-transforming biblical theology through his lectures on discipleship, there were long readings from Scripture each day. A half hour was set aside just after breakfast each day; a single passage was chosen for the

---

in light of developments in his theology by the time of *Discipleship*.

67. Two recent, very helpful book-length treatments of formation according to Bonhoeffer are McGarry, *Christ among Band of People*, and Huber, *Dietrich Bonhoeffer's Ethics of Formation*.

68. Translation amended slightly. The meaning in the second sentence seems clearer if the one phrase is set apart by dashes.

69. Very helpful for seeing the connections between *Discipleship* and seminary life is House, *Bonhoeffer's Seminary Vision*.

70. Bonhoeffer, DBWE 13, 217.

71. Bonhoeffer, DBWE 13, 285.

week to serve as the focus for this time of meditation. A half hour of singing preceded lunch each day. Clearly, Bonhoeffer wanted his students—future pastors—to be encountered by the word of God through these serious engagements with Scripture. Bonhoeffer had become convinced, along with Barth, that those trained in theology needed to move beyond the "surface" readings of Scripture that are made possible by the various forms of biblical criticism. Here is how he put it to his brother-in-law Rüdiger Schleicher in a letter on April 8, 1936:

> Let me first admit quite simply: I believe that the Bible alone is the answer to all our questions, and that we merely need ask perpetually and with a bit of humility in order to get the answer from it. One cannot simply *read* the Bible like other books. One must be prepared genuinely to query it. . . . Just as you grasp the words of someone dear to you not by first analyzing them but merely by accepting them, and just as they may then resonate in your ears for days, simply as the words of this particular person whom we love, and just as in these words the person who spoke them is increasingly disclosed to us the more we "ponder them in our heart" as Mary did, so also should we deal with the word of the Bible. Only if we finally dare come to the Bible assuming that the one speaking to us here really is the God who loves us and has no intention of abandoning us with our questions will we come to rejoice in the Bible.[72]

Lest we misconstrue these provocative words as the sentiments of an anti-intellectual (and thus forget who Bonhoeffer was), we should also note his comment to Barth, in a letter in September 1936: "It is perfectly clear to me that none of these things has any legitimacy if not accompanied—simultaneously!—by genuinely serious, rigorous theological, exegetical, and dogmatic work."[73]

The basic structure of the seminary community life was an expression of a vision Bonhoeffer had before any students showed up to be trained. However, he also responded to the needs he saw in his students. As he reported to Barth in the letter mentioned above: "One simply cannot imagine how empty and indeed utterly burned out most of the brothers come to the seminary. Empty both with regard to theological knowledge and certainly with regard to familiarity with the Bible, as well as with regard to their personal lives."[74] Thus, these spiritual practices were intended to address the

---

72. Bonhoeffer, DBWE 14, 167; emphasis his.
73. Bonhoeffer, DBWE 14, 254.
74. Bonhoeffer, DBWE 14, 253.

needs among them. As were other practices, such as listening to African American spirituals that Bonhoeffer had brought with him from the United States. And practicing confessing to one another—asking, in effect, "How are things with your soul?"[75] Additionally, time was allotted for games and music in the evenings (along with occasional trips together).

We began this chapter by mentioning that *Discipleship* was truly a socio-theological tract for its times. How does this relate to the life together of the seminary community at Finkenwalde? In his proposal for the House of Brothers that he sent to the Old Prussian Union on September 6, 1935, Bonhoeffer said:

> A group of completely free, committed pastors is needed in order to preach the word of God for the sake of decision and discernment of the Spirit in the present and future struggles of the church, a group prepared for immediate service and proclamation whenever new emergency situations might arise. They must be prepared to make themselves available wherever their services are needed, under any circumstances and without consideration of any financial or other privileges otherwise associated with the ministry. . . . The goal is not monastic isolation but rather the most intensive concentration for ministry to the world.[76]

Bonhoeffer elaborates on this last sentence in this passage from *Life Together*:

> Every day brings the Christian many hours of being alone in an unchristian environment. These are times of *testing*. This is the proving ground of a genuine time of meditation and genuine Christian community. Has the community served to make individuals free, strong, and mature, or has it made them insecure and dependent? Has it taken them by the hand for a while so that they would learn again to walk by themselves, or has it made them anxious and unsure? This is one of the toughest and most serious questions that can be put to any form of everyday Christian life in community [*Lebensgemeinschaft*]. Moreover, we will see at this point whether Christians' time of meditation has led them into an unreal world from which they awaken with a fright when they step out into the workaday world, or whether it has led them into the real world of God from which they enter into the day's activities strengthened and purified. Has it transported them for a few short moments into a spiritual ecstasy that vanishes when everyday life returns, or has it planted the

75. Bonhoeffer, DBWE 14, 254.
76. Bonhoeffer, DBWE 14, 96.

> Word of God so soberly and so deeply in their heart that it holds and strengthens them all day long, leading them to active love, to obedience, to good works?[77]

Indeed, formation for obedience, active love, and good works was always Bonhoeffer's intention. It's not as if directing the seminary or creating this community as a new kind of monasticism was, so far as Bonhoeffer was concerned, the alternative to publicly speaking out for the Jews or speaking out against war. This is why one evening per week at Finkenwalde was devoted to discussions of unfolding events in the Third Reich. It is why, in a sermon in July 1937, Bonhoeffer not only speaks about how Christians are not to take vengeance into their own hands, but also says that "it is an evil age when the world silently allows wrong to be done."[78]

Bonhoeffer still believed—and taught—that Christians should speak out for and act on behalf of those who cannot speak or act for themselves. He still believed what he said in a letter to his brother in early 1936 as he reflected on his vision for a new form of monasticism: "Things do exist that are worth standing up for without compromise. To me it seems that peace and social justice are such things, as is Christ himself."[79]

In the last few pages, we have discussed how Bonhoeffer not only presented lectures that became a book on discipleship, but how he created a Christian community that was intended to form disciples among those receiving pastoral training at Finkenwalde. However, we dare not conclude this chapter without returning to the centrally animating question for Bonhoeffer in the book *Discipleship*: "What did Jesus want to say to us? What does he want from us today? How does he help us to be faithful Christians today?" (37) And perhaps after we have finished this journey with Bonhoeffer in our attempt to grasp what he means by discipleship, we can appreciate more fully the wonderfully rich language in several key paragraphs from his provocative chapter on "Costly Grace," where he mixes images from various books of the New Testament.

> Costly grace is the gospel which must be sought again and again, the gift which has to be asked for, the door at which one has to knock.
>
> It is costly, because it calls to discipleship; it is grace, because it calls us to follow *Jesus Christ*. It is costly, because it costs people their lives; it is grace, because it thereby makes them live. It is costly, because it condemns sin; it is grace, because

---

77. Bonhoeffer, DBWE 5, 91–92.
78. Bonhoeffer, DBWE 14, 965.
79. Bonhoeffer, DBWE 13, 285.

it justifies the sinner. Above all, grace is costly, because it was costly to God, because it costs God the life of God's Son—'you were bought with a price'—and because nothing can be cheap to us which is costly to God. Above all, it is grace because the life of God's Son was not too costly for God to give in order to make us live. God did, indeed, give him up for us. Costly grace is the incarnation of God.

Costly grace . . . comes to us as a gracious call to follow Jesus; it comes as a forgiving word to the fearful spirit and the broken heart. Grace is costly, because it forces people under the yoke of following Jesus Christ; it is grace when Jesus says, "My yoke is easy, and my burden is light." (45)[80]

I began this chapter by naming how the book *Discipleship* was surprisingly—subversively—theo-political, just like the gospel it is rooted in. As I finish it, I am quite conscious of the challenge to keep both elements of this awareness alive, refusing to collapse one dimension into the other. Bonhoeffer was convinced that what he articulated in this book was truly "doing theology and only theology"—which is never reducible to a merely usable gospel. However, he also truly believed that theology is "never merely ideation. It is always and inherently a total way of life."[81] And therefore, convictions about Jesus, about the church, always entail a particular way of life—such as loving enemies—in the midst of the culture in which we live, including "a world full of Nazis."

---

80. It would be worthwhile to compare the present chapter with Nation et al., *Bonhoeffer the Assassin?*, 125–60. The spirit of the book *Discipleship* is conveyed in some significant ways by Ziegler, *Militant Grace* (as well as his "Christ for Us Today" and "Dietrich Bonhoeffer"). I also believe it would be fruitful to compare the discussion in this chapter with Taylor, *Reading Scripture as the Church*.

81. Rowe, *World Upside Down*, 17.

5

"A Blanket License to Commit Evil Acts"?[1]

Introduction

Dietrich Bonhoeffer's central convictions are, in some ways, obvious. However, his nuanced elaboration on the meaning of these convictions for envisioning and living life is often anything but transparent. For years now I have been aware of this. I have also known that this is true partly because in all of his theological work—from *Communio Sanctorum* to *Discipleship* to certain letters in *Letters and Papers from Prison*—Bonhoeffer was challenging traditional formulations of theology. He was attempting to reframe theology and theological ethics in fresh and creative ways. This dual reality of the clarity of central convictions and the complexity of nuanced explanation is on full display in Bonhoeffer's book *Ethics*.

Given the original nature of *Ethics*, combined with the fact that this set of manuscripts was in the form of working drafts when Bonhoeffer was arrested in April 1943, it seems understandable that there are disagreements about the meanings of these texts. This should lead us all to be humble and recognize the need for tentativeness in our conclusions. At the same time, many of us recognize Bonhoeffer as a brilliant and important theologian. We are sure, therefore, that we have much to learn from this outstanding theologian and disciple of Christ. Thus, too much tentativeness seems irresponsible. A determination to know what he might say to us in our time seems much more fitting with the seriousness of his life and writings in the

---

1. It would be worthwhile for the reader to compare the present chapter with the two chapters on *Ethics* in Nation et al., *Bonhoeffer the Assassin?*, 161–220.

context of the dangerous world of the Nazi regime. So, I, like most Bonhoeffer interpreters, strive to wrench meaning from Bonhoeffer's works.

This chapter will mostly focus on what were perhaps intended to be the first four chapters in *Ethics*, culminating in the essay on "History and Good."[2] It is within this essay that Bonhoeffer offers his most extensive reflections on what have become key terms for the reception of *Ethics*: responsibility, vicarious representation, a willingness to become guilty, and freedom. These expressions take on a particular poignancy within the context of Bonhoeffer's life situation. For as the earliest of these texts were being written, in the summer of 1940, Bonhoeffer was about to become an agent for the Abwehr, the military intelligence agency for Nazi Germany. And the text on "History and the Good" is given even more gravity because of references within the essay, albeit oblique ones, to extraordinary situations and what he refers to as borderline cases. In the context of Bonhoeffer's life within Nazi Germany early in World War II, this essay has assumed a key role in discerning whether Bonhoeffer abandoned certain convictions articulated most clearly in *Discipleship*. Put more pointedly, is Eberhard Bethge correct in suggesting that expressions like vicarious representation and taking on the guilt of others became by 1940 centrally defining terms for Bonhoeffer, terms reflective of his active involvement in attempts to kill Hitler? And did correlative terms such as responsibility and realism supersede the need to discuss the differences between violence and nonviolence, as Bonhoeffer now simply embraced the violent demands brought on by the destructive necessities of life?

Given the influence of Bethge's interpretations of Bonhoeffer, these are questions that beg to be answered as we read the difficult and complex essays contained in the unfinished manuscripts we call *Ethics*, especially the essay "History and the Good."

I realized recently that it is Clifford Green, the editor of the English translation of the critical edition of *Ethics*, who has helped me to be clearer about the meaning of *Ethics* as a whole. How has he done this? So far as I know, Green has worked as hard as any Bonhoeffer scholar not only to date the various manuscripts that comprise what we refer to as *Ethics* but, more importantly, to make educated guesses as to the (theo-)logical ordering of the manuscripts so as to clarify Bonhoeffer's conception of this book

---

2 I am assuming the order of the chapters proposed by the German editors and Clifford Green. (See Tödt et al., "Editors' Afterword to the German Edition," in DBWE 6, 440–49, esp. 447–48.) The argument regarding the centrality of Jesus would remain if this order were challenged; the details of the argument, of course, would have to be revised.

project.³ Thus Green, and his German co-editors, helps us to see that we cannot truly understand subsequent chapters (including "History and the Good") without understanding the first three chapters that set the stage theologically for understanding the rest of these unfinished manuscripts. More specifically, Green argues that we will not truly understand *Ethics* without grasping "the Christological center" of this work.⁴ That Christ is central to Bonhoeffer's approach to ethics should come as no surprise to anyone who truly knows his theology. The editors simply made this centrality more transparent by determining the priority of the first three chapters and thus showing how Bonhoeffer established this theological framework for his approach to ethics in the many subjects discussed in succeeding chapters. Furthermore, Green is one of the few Bonhoeffer scholars who has signaled the great importance of peace to Bonhoeffer's theology. Green's essay on Bonhoeffer's understanding of peace is well summarized in the following paragraph:

> Bonhoeffer's peace ethic is intrinsic to his whole theology. It cannot be separated from his Christology, his understanding of discipleship and the Sermon on the Mount, his way of reading the Bible, and his understanding of the gospel and of the church. It belongs to the heart of his faith. Accordingly, it cannot be reduced to a principle. It is not a discrete option on a menu of ethical "positions." It is not a separate interchangeable part that can be removed from his theology and replaced by something else called, perhaps, "realism," or even "responsibility." His peace ethic is woven throughout his theology and discipleship as a whole. It can't be removed without shredding the whole cloth.⁵

This paragraph, if true, has profound implications. It means that the Bonhoeffer who wrote *Ethics* continued to hold to the same views of peace he had named so clearly in the mid-1930s (*unless* his theology as a whole had been substantially altered).⁶ When we add to this the way in which he defines everything in relation to the centrality of Christ, then it also requires

---

3. Green, "Text of Bonhoeffer's *Ethics*," 3–66, along with his co-authored "Editors' Afterword to the German Edition" in the English translation of *Ethics* (DBWE 6), 409–49, esp. 440–48.

4. Green, "Editor's Introduction." On the profound importance of this point, see Ziegler, "'Completely within God's Doing.'"

5. Green, "Pacifism and Tyrannicide," 45.

6. Green also seems to agree with this claim. However, he refuses to accept Bonhoeffer's claim to be a pacifist, even in 1936. Thus, in the essay I quoted above, Green refers to Bonhoeffer's "peace ethic." In his most recent essay on the subject he refers to Bonhoeffer's "conditional pacifism." See Green, "Bonhoeffer's Christian Peace Ethic."

the redefining of key terms such as responsibility in light of this centrality (and thus not assuming the meaning such terms have typically had within the field of ethics).

The First Three Chapters: Establishing the Framework for a Truly Christian Ethic

Bonhoeffer could hardly be bolder—or clearer—in the way he opens chapter 1, "God's Love and the Disintegration of the World": "The knowledge of good and evil appears to be the goal of all ethical reflection. The first task of Christian ethics is to supersede that knowledge" (299).[7] He is well aware of the dramatic implications of the claim he has just made. It means that if Christians are to continue to use the term *Christian ethics* at all, then what needs to be understood is that "Christian ethics claims to articulate the origin of the whole ethical enterprise, and thus to be considered an ethic only as the critique of all ethics" (299–300). That is to say, Bonhoeffer wants to make clear that humans cannot on our own truly know good and evil. In fact, to suggest we can is a sign of our broken unity with God, our failure to trust in God, our grasping at an (ungodly) independence. He is convinced that if we do not grasp this then we are not offering a truly Christian approach to ethics at all. Thus he devotes the opening substantial portion of the essay to clarifying this fundamental point.

He follows this deconstructive move by pointing Christians to our true source of knowledge. Those who are in Christ, he says, "are filled with a new knowledge in which the knowledge of good and evil has been overcome. They are filled with the knowledge of God, yet no longer as those who have become like God, but those who bear the image of God. They now no longer know anything but 'Jesus Christ the crucified' (1 Cor. 2:2); and in Christ they know all things" (317). Having established this point, he spends the rest of the chapter discussing what it means to do the will of God. For our knowledge of God in Christ is, after all, for the purpose of living, says Bonhoeffer. Quoting Ephesians 5:9, he says, we are to "walk as children of light—discerning what is pleasing to the Lord." Such discernment, he continues, involves the whole of our being. For walking as children of light requires having our lives transformed and our minds renewed "'so that [we] may discern what is the will of God' (Rom. 12:2)" (320). And lest we imagine otherwise, Bonhoeffer reminds us that "discerning the will of God is possible only on the basis of knowing the will of God in Jesus Christ" (323). The last eight pages or so of this chapter are devoted to helping the

---

7. This and subsequent parenthetical references in this chapter cite *Ethics*, DBWE 6.

reader move toward specifics regarding what it means to discern God's will, by knowing the *living* God among us and being *in* Jesus Christ. In naming this Bonhoeffer specifically references the Sermon on the Mount (326). The last six pages, following this textual reference, are given to reflections on the centrality of love for our discerning and living the will of God. He makes it clear that we do not know what love is apart from the embodiment of love in Jesus Christ (332–38).[8]

Bonhoeffer begins chapter 2 by continuing to unfold the necessary deconstructive work. Just as he had said in chapter 1 that we must give up our ideas of good and evil, so in chapter 2, "Christ, Reality, and Good," he says that we must give up our notions of being good or doing something good. What is truly important, says Bonhoeffer, "is not that I become good, or that the condition of the world be improved by my efforts, but that the reality of God show itself everywhere to be the ultimate reality. Where God is known by faith to be the ultimate reality, the source of my ethical concern will be that God be known as the good [*das Gute*], even at the risk that I and the world are revealed as not good, but as bad through and through" (48).

If we are truly to grasp this, says Bonhoeffer, then we must see that "the source of a Christian ethic is not the reality of one's own self, not the reality of the world, nor is it the reality of norms and values. It is the reality of God that is revealed in Jesus Christ" (49). Put pointedly, "all concepts of reality that ignore Jesus Christ are abstractions" (54). As we can see, Bonhoeffer is continuing to establish a fundamental framework for approaching ethics in a truly Christian way. His claims here, as in the first chapter, must be seen as the basis for everything he will say in subsequent chapters.

The rest of the chapter attempts to move the reader beyond traditional understandings of two realms that would cordon off the reality of Jesus Christ into some separate compartment distinct from daily "secular" life. Bonhoeffer's nuanced discussion of these complex issues is clearly intended to avoid the granting of an independence to the secular world that happens too often in traditional Lutheran social ethics, as well as the withdrawal from the world that too often happens in monasticism and those traditions labeled as "enthusiastic" or "spiritualist." Thus, in his own way, he is calling his readers to understand a "unity of the reality of God and the reality of

---

8. It would not be difficult to establish how Bonhoeffer is, throughout these first three chapters of *Ethics*, simply reestablishing the grounds for our life in Christ that he articulated in his book *Discipleship*. First and foremost is simply the centrality of Christ, including the inseparability of his life and teaching. I specifically identify some links to *Discipleship* below; the editor of *Ethics*, Clifford Green, also notes some connections through footnotes within that book. Also see Schmitz, "Reading *Discipleship* and *Ethics* Together."

the world established in Christ." However, so that we do not misunderstand what he means by unity, he provides this further explanation: "That which is Christian is not identical with the worldly, the natural with the supernatural, the revelational with the rational. Rather, the unity that exists between them is given only in the Christ-reality, and that means only as accepted by faith in this ultimate reality" (59). That is to say, he reaffirms the concept of "the visibility of the church," something he went to great lengths to clarify in *Discipleship*.[9] As he says, "the church of Jesus Christ is the place [*Ort*]—that is, the space [*Raum*]—in the world where the reign of Jesus Christ over the whole world is to be demonstrated and proclaimed" (63). He goes on to say that "of course, it is presupposed that such a witness to the world can only happen in the right way when it comes out of sanctified life in God's church-community" (64).[10] After this discussion of the visibility of the church, followed by a comment on responsibility, Bonhoeffer briefly discusses several specific mandates given in Scripture: work, marriage, government, and the church.[11] He concludes the chapter by returning to the subject of the last part of chapter 1, namely the will of God. Again, he makes the same point: "The will of God, as it was revealed and fulfilled in Jesus Christ, embraces the whole of reality." Put differently, he wants to underscore his central claim: "Faith in this Jesus Christ is the single source of all good" (75).

"Today we have villains and saints again, in full public view. The gray on gray of a sultry, rainy day has turned into the black cloud and bright lightning flash of a thunderstorm. The contours are sharply drawn. Reality is laid bare. Shakespeare's characters are among us" (76). This is Bonhoeffer's evocative way of signaling the theme of his third chapter, "Ethics as Formation."[12] Put more prosaically: "We experience and recognize ethical reality not by craftiness, not by knowing all the tricks, but only by standing straightforwardly in the truth of God and by looking to that truth with eyes that it makes simple [*einfältig*] and wise" (78). Bonhoeffer will return to the constructive theme of formation in the last ten pages. But first, he needs to name how true simplicity and wisdom should not be confused with our normal ways of categorizing moral existence.

Bonhoeffer thus offers several pages of reflection on the failures of the reasonable, the fanatics, the dutiful, those trusting in their own conscience

---

9. This is most obviously true in DBWE 4, 110–15, 225–52.

10. One might again note the larger discussion in DBWE 4, 253–80.

11. Bonhoeffer gives more sustained attention to this subject in his discussion of vocation in "History and Good [2]," 289–97, as well as in the essay "The Concrete Commandment and the Divine Mandates," DBWE 6, 388–408.

12. Jennifer Moberly has written a fine book on the profound implications of this chapter. See Moberly, *Virtue of Bonhoeffer's Ethics*, especially ch. 4.

or freedom, and those who avoid public controversy by escaping into their own private virtuousness (78–80). Even the heroic Don Quixote-type figures of the past are not sufficient for the present. Moral weapons of the past simply will not do, says Bonhoeffer; "we must replace rusty weapons with bright steel" (81). The central—and defining—weapon in our arsenal is "the living, creating God" (81). In fact, if we are grounded "in the reality of the world reconciled with God in Jesus Christ, the command of Jesus gains meaning and reality" (82). Then we will realize:

> The world will be overcome not by destruction but by reconciliation. Not ideals or programs, not conscience, duty, responsibility or virtue, but only the consummate love of God can meet and overcome reality. Again, this is accomplished not by a general idea of love, but by the love of God really lived in Jesus Christ. This love of God for the world does not withdraw from reality into noble souls detached from the world, but experiences and suffers the reality of the world at its worst. The world exhausts its rage on the body of Jesus Christ. But the martyred one forgives the world its sins. Thus reconciliation takes place. *Ecco homo.* (83)

If we can grasp this, says Bonhoeffer, then we can also know what it means that God takes on the guilt of the world (83–84, 88). Thus being relieved of this burden ourselves, we as members of the body of Christ can enter into the sufferings of the world, even in the midst of a tyrannical ruler:

> The message of God's becoming human attacks the heart of an era when contempt for humanity or idolization of humanity is the height of all wisdom, among bad people as well as good. The weaknesses of human nature appear more clearly in a storm than in the quiet flow of calmer times. Among the overwhelming majority of people, anxiety, greed, lack of independence, and brutality show themselves to be the mainspring of behavior in the face of unsuspected chance and threats. At such a time the tyrannical despiser of humanity easily makes use of the meanness of the human heart by nourishing it and giving it other names. Anxiety is called responsibility; greed is called industriousness; lack of independence becomes solidarity; brutality becomes masterfulness. By this ingratiating treatment of human weaknesses, what is base and mean is generated and increased ever anew. The basest contempt for humanity carries on its sinister business under the most holy assertions of love for humanity. (85–86)

Much of what Bonhoeffer is alluding to in this discussion is the idolization of Hitler—and the obvious contempt for humanity that follows such idolatry. However, he is also reminding his readers that it is not enough simply to name the obvious. For there is "also a sincerely intended love for humanity that amounts to the same thing as contempt for humanity. It rests on evaluating human beings according to their dormant values—the health, reasonableness, and goodness deep beneath the surface." In other words, "one loves a self-made picture of human beings that has little similarity to reality, and one ends up despising the real human being whom God has loved and whose being God has taken on" (87). Considering the destructive oppression of the Third Reich, Bonhoeffer returns to a practical—but radical, almost unthinkable—outcome of having our lives centered in the living God. "Only because God became human is it possible to know and not despise real human beings. Real human beings may live before God and we may let these real people live beside us and before God without either despising or idolizing them. This is not because of the real human being's inherent value, but because God has loved and taken on the real human being" (87).

Bonhoeffer turns next to a discussion of success. "The figure of the judged and crucified one remains alien, and at best pitiable, to a world where success is the measure and justification of all things" (88). For those of us who worship this crucified one, we can see that success is often idolized. When this happens, people "become blind to right and wrong, truth and lie, decency and malice. They see only the deed, the success" (89). Bonhoeffer continues:

> The statement that success is the good is challenged by an opposing one that looks at the conditions of lasting success, namely, that only the good is successful. Here the capacity for judgment is retained in the face of success. Here right remains right and wrong remains wrong. Here one does not close one's eyes at the decisive moment, only to open them after the deed has been done. And here, consciously or unconsciously, a law of the world is acknowledged according to which justice, truth, and order are, in the long view, more stable than violence. (89)

Most importantly, "The form of the crucified disarms all thinking aimed at success, for it is a denial of judgment" (90). "Over against the successful, God sanctifies pain, lowliness, failure, poverty, loneliness, and despair in the cross of Christ. Not that all this has value in itself; it is made holy by the love of God, who takes it all and bears it as judgment" (90). Bonhoeffer is well aware that what he is saying at best seems counterintuitive. Thus, he adds:

"It is a mystery of God's reign over the world that this very cross, the sign of Christ's failure in the world, can in turn lead to historical success; this cannot be made into a rule, though in the suffering of God's church-community it repeats itself here and there" (90–91).

Finally, in the last ten pages, Bonhoeffer returns directly to the announced theme of this chapter—formation. Needless to say, he once again centers his approach in Christ. "The form of Jesus Christ alone victoriously encounters the world. From this form proceeds all the formation of a world reconciled with God" (92). In other words, this formation does not occur merely by embracing some teachings or principles derived from Jesus. "Formation occurs only by being drawn into the form of Jesus Christ" (93). To be clear, however, even those drawn toward Christ should not imagine that formation happens "as we strive 'to become like Jesus,' as we customarily say, but as the form of Jesus Christ himself so works on us that it molds us, conforming our form to Christ's own (Gal. 4:9). Christ remains the only one who forms" (93).[13] "Transfigured into the form of the risen one, [Christians] bear here only the sign of the cross and judgment. In bearing them willingly, they show themselves as those who have received the Holy Spirit and are united with Jesus Christ in incomparable love and community" (95). All of this is to say that "the starting point of Christian ethics is the body of Christ, the form of Christ in the form of the church, the formation of the church according to the form of Christ" (97). Because God loves the whole world, the church experientially anticipates the reconciliation of God with the world. "The church now bears the form that in truth is meant for all people. The image according to which it is being formed is the image of humanity. What takes place in the church happens vicariously and representatively as a model for all human beings" (97). "The church is nothing but that piece of humanity where Christ really has taken form" (97). "Therefore essentially its first concern is not with the so-called religious functions of human beings, but with the existence in the world of whole human beings in all their relationships. The church's concern is not religion, but the form of Christ and its taking form among a band of people" (97).

The formation being spoken of here gives specific shape to our lives; it is not abstract. It forms us for obedience, for specific faithful lives lived within the context of the world God loves. "Here we must risk making concrete judgments and decisions. Here decision and deed can no longer be shifted onto the individual's personal conscience. Here concrete commandments and guidance are given, for which obedience will be demanded"

---

13. Much of what Bonhoeffer writes in this chapter echoes sections of the second half of *Discipleship*. But here, especially see DBWE 4, 281–88.

(102). Early in this chapter Bonhoeffer had signaled that he is truly speaking of formation, a development of a stability of character across time, through acknowledging that at times one might act out of character. It is worse, he says, to be a liar than to tell a lie, worse to be evil than to commit an act of evil. It is also worse, Bonhoeffer says, to fall away than to fall down. "The most brilliant virtues of the apostates are as dark as night compared with the darkest weaknesses of the faithful" (77). Yet the larger framing context for the chapter is knowing reality in Jesus Christ and being formed by that reality—with reminders that we might fail, but that we nonetheless are called to witness to the God who alone is good.

History and Good: To Act Responsibly in Accord with Reality

Now we come to chapter 4, "History and Good," or what are two different versions of the chapter, "History and Good [1]" and "History and Good [2]."[14] In both versions, Bonhoeffer discusses responsibility, vicarious representation, taking on human guilt, and freedom. Some of his language in both versions echoes what he has named in earlier chapters. At other points he seems to assume what he has said earlier. The shape and particulars of each version are unique. What is obvious in both is Bonhoeffer's strong emphasis on the centrality of Jesus Christ.

Responsibility is a topic that Bonhoeffer addresses from the outset of this chapter and that arises repeatedly throughout the essay.[15] To acknowledge a sense of responsibility, suggests Bonhoeffer, is to realize that one lives in relation to other persons. One encounters other people "and this encounter entails being charged, in ever so many ways, with responsibility [*Verantwortung*] for the other human being. History arises out of accepting this responsibility for other human beings or for entire communities or groups of communities" (220).

Once again, in the midst of his reflections on responsibility, Bonhoeffer challenges the Kantian notion of universal principles. In specific situations, norms for behavior are not derived from "a clearly recognized good

---

14. I have decided not to reference the chapters separately, partly because of the awkwardness of doing this and partly because it appears that these two drafts both represent content Bonhoeffer wanted to include in a finished chapter. We can't pretend to know how he would have made them into a single chapter. However, so the reader can know which version I am referencing, let me identify the page numbers for each. Version 1 is 219–45; version 2 is 246–98.

15. One of the influential writers on responsibility at the time was Max Weber. See Weber, *Politics as a Vocation*, esp. 43–49. The essay I have found most helpful on the subject of responsibility in *Ethics* is Wannenwetsch, "'Responsible Living' or 'Responsible Self.'"

and a clearly recognized evil." Rather they are known in the encounter with "the concrete neighbor, as given to me by God." Choices for behaviors are "risked in faith while being aware that good and evil are hidden in the concrete historical situation" (221). Bonhoeffer continues: "Those who act responsibly take the given situation or context into account in their acting, not merely as raw material to be shaped by their ideas, but as contributing to forming the act itself. It is not some foreign law that is imposed on reality. Instead, the action of the responsible person is most profoundly in accord with reality" (222).

We will return later to discuss what historical situations in early 1940s Germany and in his life Bonhoeffer might be alluding to. For now, I want to suggest that we will not understand these apparently radically contextualist statements unless we both pay attention to subtle clues within a couple of the statements and, even more, attend to the christologically defining context of the chapter (conforming with the christological framing of the book as a whole).

The subtle clues are "the concrete neighbor, *as given to me by God*" and "risked *in faith*." For Bonhoeffer these are not trivial modifiers, but rather defining ones. However, we need not depend simply on such hints. For his framing of these comments is anything but subtle. For all of the key terms for understanding Bonhoeffer's evocative (and often misunderstood) language—responsibility, vicarious representation, taking on guilt and freedom—are given their meaning in reference to Jesus Christ.[16]

Take responsibility as a prime example.[17] The responsible person, says Bonhoeffer, is to "act in accord with reality." But what is reality? What does it mean to live in alignment with it? For Bonhoeffer this is clear. "In Jesus Christ, the Real One, all reality is taken on and summed up; Christ is its origin, essence, and goal. That is why it is only in and from Christ that it is possible to act in a way that is in accord with reality" (263). Or again: "Good is the action that is in accordance with the reality of Jesus Christ; *action in accordance with Christ is action in accord with reality*" (228-29; emphasis

---

16. I agree with Jennifer Moberly that Clifford Green has not adequately justified the addition of the word *action* when translating the German word *Stellvertretung*, which normally means simply representation or substitution. Given its importance to Bonhoeffer for naming the relationship of Christ or the body of Christ to the world, especially in relation to its suffering, then the more emphatic "vicarious representation" seems appropriate. But not "vicarious representative action," unless action is specified. See Moberly, "Felicity to the Original Text," 350. Thus I translate *Stellvertretung* as vicarious representation.

17. After reading what Bonhoeffer says in *Ethics* on responsibility, it is interesting to notice what he said on responsibility in a public lecture on "The Right to Self-Assertion" to students in a technical college in Feb. 1932: Bonhoeffer, DBWE, 11, 246-57.

his). "Jesus Christ is the very embodiment of the person who lives responsibly." In fact, "his entire life, action, and suffering is vicarious representation [*Stellvertretung*]" (231). Bonhoeffer elaborates:

> The sayings of Jesus, for example, those in the Sermon on the Mount, can then only be understood as words of the one who lives in concrete responsibility for all human beings, really standing in their place and acting on their behalf (and not confronting them with ideals that they cannot fulfill), as words of the one whose responsibility consists in freely given love for the real human being (and not in the realization of some kind of idea of the human), as words of one whose pure love manifests itself by entering into the guilt of human beings (and not by isolating itself from this guilt). The sayings of Jesus, for example, in the Sermon on the Mount, are the interpretation of his existence, and thus the interpretation of that reality in which history finds its fulfillment in God's becoming human, in the reconciliation of the world with God. They are divine commandments for our action in history insofar as they are the reality of history that has been fulfilled in Christ. (235–36)

Bonhoeffer follows these extraordinary claims by offering ten pages of argument for why the Sermon on the Mount is crucial for understanding our Christian actions within real human history. Toward the end of these reflections—written in 1942 Germany—he says: "The Sermon on the Mount is either valid as the word of God's world-reconciling love everywhere and at all times, or it is not really relevant for us at all" (243). "The responsibility of Jesus Christ for all human beings has love as its content and freedom as its form. . . . The commandments of God's righteousness are fulfilled in vicarious representation, which means in concrete, responsible action of love for all human beings" (232). Very specifically he says, "by grounding responsible action in Jesus Christ we reaffirm precisely the limits of such action" (224). We must keep such comments in mind when he says that "the essence of responsible action intrinsically involves the sinless becoming guilty." For he begins this sentence by saying: "Because of Jesus Christ . . ." Moreover, he follows it by saying, "It is a sacrilege and an outrageous perversion to extrapolate from this statement a blanket license to commit evil acts. Only where a person becomes guilty out of love and responsibility does their action have a part in the justification pertaining to Jesus Christ's sinless guilt-bearing" (234–35). "The Sermon on the Mount as the proclamation of the incarnate love of God calls people to love one another, and thus to reject everything that hinders fulfilling this task—in short, it calls them to self-denial. In renouncing one's own happiness, one's own rights, one's own righteousness, one's own dignity, in renouncing violence and success, in renouncing one's own life, a person is prepared to love the neighbor" (242). Toward the end of a substantial discussion of pseudo-realism, Bonhoeffer says: "Furthermore, the foundations of this so-called realism are false insofar as they fail to understand the meaning of the Christian concept of love and thus of the concepts of self-denial, forgiveness, suffering, renunciation, love of enemies, and innocence [*Unschuld*]" (240–41).[18]

I said at the outset of this chapter that some of Bonhoeffer's detailed expositions of what it means to live with these convictions are not transparent. One of those opaque places is a portion of his section on "The Structure of Responsible Life," sixteen pages within "History and Good [2]" (272–89). It is in this section that Bonhoeffer seems to have specific situations in mind within his context in 1942 Germany. These could have included German militarism, World War II, the persecution and attempted annihilation of the Jews, the persecution of the Confessing Church, the too-frequent collusion of the Confessing Church with Nazism, attempts to kill Hitler, and so on. Yet he gives us no clues as to what situations he has in mind. When he names specifics, they seem more like possibilities for academic reflection than the particulars he is thinking of when he mentions taking on guilt or living responsibly. But is that truly the case? He was more aware than the average German at the time of what was going on at the highest levels of the regime and in the resistance movement. He was from a well-connected family. His brother-in-law, Hans von Dohnanyi, with whom he was close friends, had been on the inside of the government since early in Hitler's reign. Since the end of October 1940, Bonhoeffer himself had worked with the military intelligence agency, the Abwehr. In that capacity he had traveled with some regularity throughout Western Europe. These travels included meetings with friends from a number of European countries.

So, in connection with all of this, Bonhoeffer offers sixteen pages of reflections on acting in the midst of extreme circumstances that he refers to as borderline cases and "extraordinary situations of ultimate necessity" (273). In this world erected by Nazism, what does it mean to act responsibly? To live in accordance with reality? And therefore freely, willingly to embody vicarious representation, which includes assuming the guilt of humanity—and thus living only by the hope of divine grace and forgiveness?

Many interpreters of Bonhoeffer assume that we *know* what he is alluding to by these questions. He is, of course, referencing his own involvement in plots to kill Hitler (probably connected, many assume, to his work

---

18. Needless to say, the sentences here echo what Bonhoeffer says regarding the Sermon on the Mount in *Discipleship*, esp. 105–10, 131–45.

in the Abwehr). Thus, he is providing a moral rationale to warrant assassinating a duly appointed leader or, more precisely, to warrant tyrannicide. For certainly, long before 1942, Bonhoeffer sees Adolf Hitler as a ruthless tyrant with grand, violent ambitions.

There are, however, several problems with this hypothesis—and that is what it is—for understanding these pages and these questions. First, as should be obvious, it ignores the particulars of the christological framing that permeates the essay—including the call to love enemies and renounce violence. Second, there is no textual evidence for such a claim. That is to say, there is nothing in this chapter that seems, even vaguely, to refer to killing a ruler. One could argue that this is understandable. Nonetheless, it needs to be stated. For, third, it is assumed that we "know" what he is alluding to, even with vague references, because we "know" he was involved in attempts on Hitler's life. And therefore, of course, that is what he is referring to by extraordinary situations, necessities, and so forth.

As I argued in chapter 1, unless we believe that Bonhoeffer's efforts in 1942 through his friend Bishop George Bell to get Britain not to take advantage of Germany if Hitler is removed from power counts as "involvement in attempts to kill Hitler," then there is no evidence he was so involved.

However, let me offer a different hypothesis for what Bonhoeffer might have had in mind by his references to "extraordinary situations of ultimate necessity" and so on. If I were to look for a particular situation that was quite personal and difficult for Bonhoeffer, there is a fairly obvious one that comes to mind. And that is the fact that most of his former seminary students were serving on the front lines in Hitler's army. In fact, by September 1942 at least twenty-one of his former students had died on the front lines.[19] By this time, he was regularly writing circular letters to former students, naming those who have died. He often wrote personal letters to family members regarding their husbands or sons. His letters are always full of sensitivity. However, is it possible that Bonhoeffer in these pages of *Ethics* has in mind *not* the fact that many of his former students *are dying* in military service but rather that most of them *are killing* as soldiers on the front lines?[20] Occasionally, he received candid letters from former students relating the brutality they were ordered to participate in, such as the cold-blooded murder of civilians and surrendered soldiers.[21] A number of times in this section of "History

---

19. Bonhoeffer, DBWE 16, 358–59.

20. It is instructive to read the thoughts of Joachim Kanitz, one of Bonhoeffer's former seminary students, as he reflects on his discussion with his former teacher in the summer of 1942 while he is still a soldier. (See Nation et al., *Bonhoeffer the Assassin?*, 11.)

21. See, e.g., Erwin Sander, DBWE 16, 251–53. And we should not imagine that

and Good [2]" Bonhoeffer references war and soldiers (273, 281, 285, 287). Might it be this extreme situation that he has in mind? Is it possible that he—effectively living out his life as a conscientious objector—is attempting to reflect on the moral character of his former students who, in this extreme circumstance, are doing something he clearly thinks is immoral? Might he have been thinking of their letters when he wrote that it was worse to be evil than to do an act of evil?

So, in the midst of extremely difficult circumstances, Bonhoeffer is quite sensitive toward his former students who either were not convinced by his teaching on nonviolence or who couldn't face the consequences of formally claiming to be a conscientious objector, which was a capital offense. But it's not as if Bonhoeffer had been unclear about this dimension of discipleship in his teaching at Finkenwalde. We have the testimony of Joachim Kanitz, a former student, who, on leave from the military, met with Bonhoeffer in the summer of 1942. He reports that in simply meeting with his teacher—who himself showed sensitivity—Kanitz himself felt shame. He remembered the pacifism that Bonhoeffer had taught them at Finkenwalde. And because of this, he says, "These seven years as a soldier were utter hell for me. Sometimes I was close to insanity because of it. At any rate, the only thing I could conclude for the rest of my life was: never again."[22]

I certainly think my hypothesis is more likely than any notion that he is writing reflections to justify his "involvement" in any attempts on Hitler's life. Apart from anything else, why should we assume that he is offering reflections on his own behavior? He is, after all, not keeping a personal diary in these pages. He is writing a book on ethics for Christians.

As stated before, we need to be humble. I think we can't really know what specific situations he had in mind. Having read a number of books on daily life in the Third Reich, I am aware of the incredible challenges any Christian wanting to live a life of Christian integrity faced within that context. Bonhoeffer's honest and moving reflections in his essay on "Guilt, Justification, Renewal" make it obvious that he was aware of many issues of moral failure on the part of the church that needed to be confronted (134–45).

Conclusion

I want to end with a challenge. Show me one other author who offers an argument for the legitimation of violence—or more specifically

such behavior was unusual. See, e.g., Neitzel and Welzer, *Soldaten*.
22. Nation et al., *Bonhoeffer the Assassin?*, 11.

tyrannicide—who makes Jesus Christ central in the way Bonhoeffer does within *Ethics*. When I say "in the way Bonhoeffer does," that includes lengthy defenses of the relevance of the Sermon on the Mount, along with specific references to love of enemies and renouncing violence as integral to our understanding Jesus Christ, "the lord and law of the real," who "is the very embodiment of the person who lives responsibly." (All of this echoes his even fuller arguments for renouncing violence in the book *Discipleship*.) I don't believe such an author exists. Nor do I believe Bonhoeffer is such an author.

When we look at the argument of the first four chapters of *Ethics* as a whole, rather than lifting intriguing phrases out of context, it seems obvious that Bonhoeffer was still in the early 1940s, as he was in 1937 in *Discipleship*, calling on his readers to embrace costly discipleship.[23] This means that we allow our minds to be transformed in Christ, that we allow our embodied existence, individually and communally, to be formed by Christ. This means that we love our enemies and renounce violence. We might, with the Bonhoeffer of 1932 or 1936, say that we should not shy away from using the word "pacifist" to describe ourselves—without ever forgetting that our life is not rooted in abstract principles but rather in Jesus Christ.

Having been clear about the costliness of this discipleship, we might also, out of an awareness of the extremity of the situation in Nazi Germany and an empathy formed by our loving Lord—in the midst of what seem like situations of "necessity"—reflect on how our former students, who have killed in the name of Hitler, finally must simply place their trust in God and thus "live only by divine grace and forgiveness."[24] Yet nothing that has been said should cause us to forget Bonhoeffer's admonition to remember that borderline cases should never become norms and that "breaking the law must be *recognized* in all its gravity" (297; emphasis his). Furthermore, we remember his admonition that being willing to take on guilt "out of love and responsibility" does not mean that our actions are defined by what appear to be the necessities of the situation. For, "it is a sacrilege and an outrageous perversion to extrapolate from this statement a blanket license to commit

---

23. We should also remember that Bonhoeffer continued to train pastors in his seminary-in-exile until the spring of 1940, continuing, I assume, to use *Discipleship* as a part of the curriculum.

24. Bonhoeffer, DBWE 6, 274. This sentence, in light of Bonhoeffer's own costly choices and sensitive reflections on his former students who have killed in Hitler's army, remind me of comments by theologian Kathryn Greene-McCreight, who suffers from bipolar disorder. On one hand, she says quite clearly that committing suicide is wrong. On the other hand, in regard to those who have suffered severe depression and have killed themselves, she says: "I feel nothing for them except compassion, pity, and sorrow" (Greene-McCreight, *Darkness Is My Only Companion*, 45, 47.)

evil acts" (234).²⁵ "The responsibility of Jesus Christ for all human beings has love as its content and freedom as its form" (232). For it is in Jesus Christ that our lives are formed and limits for our actions defined.

****

As I was making some final revisions to this manuscript, I, for the umpteenth time, reread Bonhoeffer's substantial and complicated reflections on "The Structure of Responsible Life" (257–89). I asked myself if I believe that these reflections truly fit with what I have argued in this book and in this chapter. And my answer was again: yes! And precisely for the reasons given in this chapter. Laced quite deliberately throughout this long discussion are assertions of the central role of the living Christ for defining reality, for defining a truly Christian sense of responsibility—with the centrality of Jesus linked to teachings of Jesus, including the Sermon on the Mount. It continues to strike me that only someone who doesn't know *Discipleship* and the fact that Bonhoeffer specifically stated in 1944 that he still stood by what he wrote in that book could misunderstand these references. For he has already made clear what the centrality of Jesus entails.

However, I didn't decide to add these few paragraphs because of what I said in the previous one. Rather, there was something else I noticed. First, a little context. I was astounded when I first read the following statement from Ferdinand Schlingensiepen, the son of a Confessing Church pastor. Toward the end of his biography of Bonhoeffer, Schlingensiepen basically says that after 1940 Bonhoeffer did not need to use the word "decision" any more. Why? Because after he decided to become involved in attempts to kill Hitler—"the central decision of his life, to which everything else had been leading, had finally been taken"—no other decisions were really necessary.²⁶ Along with this, he says that Bonhoeffer, having made this decision, had basically returned to the ethics he articulated in Barcelona in 1929: "'There are no acts that are bad in and of themselves, even murder can be sanctified.'" Schlingensiepen continues, "These were dubious words, out of the mouth of a pastoral assistant, but now they had become appallingly true and had to be put into action."²⁷ I also well remember my experience of sending drafts of the first three (biographical) chapters of *Bonhoeffer the Assassin?*

25. Bonhoeffer, DBWE 6, 234. For those who don't know, Bonhoeffer's alleged involvement in attempts to kill Hitler has been used to justify the Allied involvement in World War II, the killing of doctors who perform abortions, the killing of alleged dictators in Latin America, and (by some Bonhoeffer scholars) the wars in Iraq and Afghanistan.

26. Schlingensiepen, *Dietrich Bonhoeffer*, 285.

27. Schlingensiepen, *Dietrich Bonhoeffer*, 286.

to a Christian author that I knew was both a pacifist and had a reasonable knowledge of Bonhoeffer's life and thought, in order to get his response. He responded with a very critical email, saying that he did not believe the Bonhoeffer I portrayed was a pacifist.

What does this have to do with my rereading of Bonhoeffer on "the structure of the responsible life"? On the one hand, Bonhoeffer is very clear. "Where Christ, true God and true human being, has become the unifying center of my existence, conscience in the formal sense still remains the call, coming from my true self, into unity with my self" (278). And whatever he may mean by embracing responsibility—joined to a free conscience—he makes it clear that "acceptance of responsibility must not destroy this unity" (281). A central way for Bonhoeffer to name this is to say that "the origin and goal of my conscience is not a law but the living God and the living human being as I encounter them in Jesus Christ" (278). However, in the midst of these reflections, he mentions that Jesus "ate with sinners and outcasts." "As one who loved without sin, he became guilty, seeking to stand within the community of human guilt" (279). As I reread this, I realized something. Bonhoeffer, in the midst of seeking to live out of "the unifying center of his existence"—namely, Jesus Christ—had truly been freed, like Jesus, to be at peace with being misunderstood by others.

6

Discipleship amidst the Rubble

Introduction

The following eyewitness account of Bonhoeffer's execution was provided by the doctor at Flossenbürg concentration camp, where Bonhoeffer was hanged on April 9, 1945:

> Through the half-open door in one room of the huts I saw Pastor Bonhoeffer, before taking off his prison garb, kneeling on the floor praying fervently to his God. I was most deeply moved by the way this lovable man prayed, so devout and so certain that God heard his prayer. . . . In the almost fifty years that I worked as a doctor, I have hardly ever seen a man die so entirely submissive to the will of God.[1]

Fabian von Schlabrendorff, Bonhoeffer's fellow prison inmate, offered his own reflections on the daily life of Bonhoeffer the prisoner.

> Dietrich Bonhoeffer told me of his interrogations. . . . He characterized [them] with one short word: disgusting. His noble

---

1. Fischer-Hüllstrung, "A Report from Flossenbürg," in Zimmerman and Smith, *I Knew Dietrich Bonhoeffer*, 232. I have read the challenge to this account by Jørgen L. F. Mogensen (Mogensen, "Ein Zeuge aus dem KZ-Flossenbürg"). Mogensen may be right that it is inaccurate. However, the portrait by the prison doctor does seem to fit the picture that others have offered of Bonhoeffer during this time. (See, e.g., Payne Best's descriptions of Bonhoeffer in his last days, in Bethge, *Dietrich Bonhoeffer*, 907, 920, 921–26, summarized toward the end of the present chapter.) Thus I have, with Bethge, simply stayed with the account as offered by the doctor (Bethge, *Dietrich Bonhoeffer*, 927–28).

and pure soul must have suffered deeply. But he betrayed no sign of it. He was always good-tempered, always of the same kindliness and politeness towards everybody, so that to my surprise within a short time, he had won over his warders, who were not always kindly disposed. . . . Many little notes he slipped into my hands on which he had written biblical words of comfort and hope. . . .

Each Wednesday he received his laundry parcel which also contained cigars, apples or bread, and he never omitted to share them with me the same evening when we were not watched; it delighted him that even in prison you were able to help your neighbor, and let him share in what you had. . . .

On 7th of February 1945 in the morning I spoke to him for the last time. . . . At that time when the Nazi rule was in a state of collapse and the prisons so crowded that it was no longer possible to keep the prisoners apart, Dietrich Bonhoeffer again acted as the appointed servant to the Word of Jesus Christ. He held devotional meetings, comforted those in despair, tried to raise their courage, and in his imperturbability was an example for many. . . .

When after several months I returned to my home, which had been destroyed by bombs, I at first saw nothing but rubble. Anything which the bombs had spared had been stolen. Only one book lay undamaged among the bricks and mortar: Dietrich Bonhoeffer's *Nachfolge* [*Discipleship*].[2]

Apparently various fellow prisoners as well as prison guards complimented Bonhoeffer to his face in ways similar to what Schlabrendorff described.[3] Most likely, this is what led Bonhoeffer to write his now justly famous, self-critical poem entitled "Who Am I?"

> Who am I? They often tell me
> I step out from my cell
> calm and cheerful and poised, like a squire from his manor.
> Who am I? They often tell me
> I speak with the guards freely, friendly and clear,
> as though I were the one in charge.
>
> Who am I? They also tell me

---

2. Fabian von Schlabrendorff, "In Prison with Dietrich Bonhoeffer," in Zimmermann and Smith, *I Knew Dietrich Bonhoeffer*, 227–31. Schlabrendorff was personally involved in the attempt to kill Hitler on Mar. 13, 1943.

3. The Tegel prison chaplain, Harold Poelchau, says as much in "The Freedom of the Prisoner," in Zimmermann and Smith, *I Knew Dietrich Bonhoeffer*, 222.

> I bear days of calamity
> serenely, smiling and proud,
> like one accustomed to victory.
>
> Am I really what others say of me?
> Or am I only what I know of myself?
> Restless, yearning, sick, like a caged bird,
> struggling for breath, as though hands were compressing my throat,
> yearning for colors, for flowers, for birdsong,
> thirsting for kind words, human closeness,
> shaking with rage at despotisms and pettiest insult,
> tossed about, waiting for great things to happen,
> helplessly fearing for friends so far away,
> too tired and empty to pray, to think, to work,
> weary and ready to take my leave of it all?
>
> Who am I? This one or the other?
> Am I this one today and tomorrow another?
> Am I both at once? Before others a hypocrite
> And in my own eyes a pitiful, whimpering weakling?
> Or is what remains in me like a defeated army,
> fleeing in disarray from victory already won?
>
> Who am I? They mock me, these lonely questions of mine.
> Whoever I am, you know me, O God, I am yours.[4]

What seems obvious is that by the summer of 1944, when Bonhoeffer composed this poem, he was a man of deep humility and prayer, seeking the face of God, yearning to be faithful to God in the way he lived. Given this, he therefore offered honest, prayerful reflections on the perceptions of others *and* on his own sense of a poverty of spirit and failings in the midst of the suffocating and death-dealing environment of a Nazi prison.

The Language of the Heart, a Life of Integrity in Community

In reflecting on the poem "Who Am I?" Michael Northcott rightly pushes back against interpretations of Bonhoeffer's life that would eliminate or even understate the personal dimensions of his faith—elements so well expressed

---

4. Bonhoeffer, DBWE 8, 459–60, amended, borrowing from the translation in Wannenwetsch, *Who Am I?*, 12–13 (especially regarding a line in the fourth stanza, missing from the translation in the collected works). I have also altered the last line. I know of no good reason to use King James English to translate this line; it makes it seem old fashioned and "churchy" in a way that isn't connected to daily life in the 1940s or early twenty-first century—in other words, not in keeping with the spirit of Bonhoeffer.

in this poem. As Northcott puts it, "Bonhoeffer's distinctive accounts of the self in community and of spiritual discipline, and his practices of communal and private devotions, all of them reflected in this poem, present us with a portrait of the authentic self that is by no means dismissive of the language of the heart and narratives of inwardness."[5] As Bonhoeffer said in reflections on Psalm 119, "Because [God's] commandments are supposed to remind us daily and witness to us that God is the Lord, a purely external fulfillment of the commandments is not enough. Not only lips and hands but the entire undivided heart must be involved."[6] However, we should also hear Bonhoeffer's own cautions, expressed in a letter on July 8, 1944. There he says that "the Bible does not know the distinction that we make between the outward and the inward life. . . . The 'heart' in the biblical sense," says Bonhoeffer, "is not the inner life but rather the whole person before God."[7]

What seems clear is that as early as 1927, when Bonhoeffer wrote his doctoral thesis, *Sanctorum Communio*, he was seeking to speak of the whole person before God by bridging the frequent division between individual and community, showing instead their inherent inseparability for Christians. Thus on the one hand Bonhoeffer had distanced himself from "Hegel's over-identification of the individual with society," an identification which simply subsumes the individual into society.[8] The alternative, for Bonhoeffer, was certainly not individualism or an undue focus on one's own experiences.[9] Rather, for Bonhoeffer, a Christian's individual life, always embedded within a Christian community and embodied through daily life in the world, was to be lived honestly, authentically, in the presence of God—laying open "the whole person before God."

By the early 1940s Bonhoeffer had for years regularly read and meditated on the Psalms. Living with the Psalms in this way, he knew that faithfulness entailed personal trust in God and that such trust included cultivating "the language of the heart." At the same time Bonhoeffer developed a rich social account of life in Christian community. For he also believed that "the individual apart from the Christian community is unthinkable."[10] By the mid-1930s Bonhoeffer would name this quite

5. Northcott, "Who Am I?," in Wannenwetsch, *Who Am I?*, 17.

6. Bonhoeffer, "Meditations on Psalm 119, 1939–1940," DBWE 15, 496–528, here 503.

7. Bonhoeffer, DBWE 8, 456; also see 457. He also specifically criticizes pietism (DBWE 8, 500), while still affirming an emphasis on individual faith (DBWE 8, 502).

8. Northcott, "Who Am I?," in Wannenwetsch, *Who Am I?*, 18.

9. "'But for goodness sake, let's turn our eyes away from ourselves!' he once wrote to Bethge" (quoted in Gracie, *Meditating on the Word*, 104).

10. Northcott, "Who Am I?," in Wannenwetsch, *Who Am I?*, 19.

powerfully through his forceful articulations of the need for understanding the "visibility"—that is, the particular and often distinctive identity—of the Christian community. But for Bonhoeffer a community of the faithful was also importantly composed of individuals. Thus, seeing our life under the reign of God does not preclude the nurturing of hearts turned toward God. In fact, in order for authentic submission to God's reign to be sustained such cultivation is required. We—each of us and all of us within the body of Christ—should *know* God, that is, have an active faith in a living God. Northcott captures this well by reflecting on the similarities of the poem "Who Am I?" with a certain genre of Psalms:

> The poem is indeed much like an individual Psalm of Lament in form. For Bonhoeffer, resolution of the putative conflict between inner and outer, desire and agency, intention and act, public and private, is found by analogy with the Psalmist who when he dwells on the desires of the heart apart from God is driven to despair. [When t]he Psalmist recalls the joy of God's presence in the Temple (Psalm 40), and that God's knowledge of him is greater than his own (Psalm 139), his tendency to despair is replaced with praise and wonder at the glory of God. Like the Psalmist, Bonhoeffer acknowledges his own inner sense of divisions and of struggle and like the Psalmist also he sets this struggle in the context of his relations, or deprivations of relations, with other creatures.[11]

Over the years I have often been moved by the poem "Who Am I?" But it was only after reading a 2009 collection of essays on Bonhoeffer's prison poetry that I realized the wisdom of the following reflections by Eugene Peterson as pertinent to Bonhoeffer's poetry:

> *Poetry* is language used with personal intensity. It is not, as so many suppose, decorative speech. Poets tell us what our eyes, blurred with too much gawking, and our ears, dulled with too much chatter, miss around and within us. Poets use words to drag us into the depth of reality itself. They do it not by reporting on how life is, but by pushing-pulling us into the middle of it. Poetry grabs for the jugular. Far from cosmetic language, it is intestinal. It is root language. Poetry doesn't so much tell us something we never knew as bring into recognition what is latent, forgotten, overlooked, or suppressed.[12]

---

11. Northcott, "Who Am I?," in Wannenwetsch, *Who Am I?*, 16. Northcott then quotes portions of the fourth stanza of "Who Am I?" to display the congruency of what he has just said and Bonhoeffer's poem.

12. Peterson, *Answering God*, 11–12.

In fact, some of Peterson's further comments may help us to see why Bonhoeffer sometimes chose the medium of poetry while in prison. And why some of his poetry, like "Who Am I?," becomes prayer. "The poetry," says Peterson, "requires that we deal with our actual humanity—these words dive beneath the surfaces of prose and pretense, straight into the depths. We are more comfortable with prose, the laid-back language of our arms-length discourse. The prayer requires that we deal with God—this God who is determined on nothing less than the total renovation of our lives."[13]

Brian Brock is quite right to suggest that "Bonhoeffer is an example of how the Psalter trains Christians to put on a persona before God which is not theirs, an 'alien self,' to embolden them to live before and for others in novel ways."[14] This regular reading, this training of the self, was not something new Bonhoeffer did in prison simply because he had spare time on his hands. Rather, as he reported to his parents on May 15, 1943, a little more than a month after he was arrested, he was reading the Psalms daily "as I have done for years. There is no other book I know and love as much."[15] In fact, as Brock suggests, Bonhoeffer seems to have followed Luther in seeing the Psalms as *the* book in the Bible "devoted to training our speech and affections toward God," the God known through Jesus Christ.[16]

But it had not always been so. If we are to take Bonhoeffer's 1936 confession to Elizabeth Zinn seriously, both his inner life and his outer life—which is to say, his whole life lived before God—began to change at the beginning of the 1930s. Up to that time, Bonhoeffer says, his academic involvement in "the cause of Jesus Christ" was simply an expression of his "crazy vanity." The church was not particularly important to him. Nor had he "ever prayed, or had done so only very rarely," Bonhoeffer admitted. "I was not yet a Christian, but rather in an utterly wild and uncontrolled fashion my own master.... The Bible, especially the Sermon on the Mount, freed me from all this. Since then everything has changed."[17] By the time he was arrested in April 1943 he had been seeking to live this transformed life for more than a decade.

Northcott, in his essay, is attempting to distinguish Bonhoeffer from liberal theological streams of his day, as well as from tendencies in certain current theologies that minimize the importance of attending to individual

---

13. Peterson, *Answering God*, 12.
14. Brock, "Success and Failure," in Wannenwetsch, *Who Am I?*, 62.
15. Bonhoeffer, DBWE 8, 81.
16. Brock, *Singing Ethos of God*, 73.
17. Bonhoeffer, DBWE 14, 134.

spiritual disciplines.[18] As Northcott put it, "Confession, the recitation of Psalms, and the reading of Scripture, private meditation, the prayer of the heart: these are the therapies prescribed by the Christian tradition for the reorientation of the disordered self to the original order of creation."[19] And these are indeed the therapies that Bonhoeffer prescribed for his seminary students—and sought to live out himself. In a letter to Karl Barth, for instance, Bonhoeffer not only reflects on how important it is to teach his students to meditate on the Scriptures and to pray daily but also at times to ask a student, "How are things with your soul?"[20] It was also obvious to his students at the time that these "therapeutic" practices were *not only* for individual edification. As Bonhoeffer said in his proposal for establishing a "House of Brethren" within the Finkenwalde seminary: "The goal is not monastic isolation but rather the most intensive concentration for ministry in the world."[21] In fact the spiritual practices encouraged at the seminary were precisely expressions of how "he sought to build a counter-politics and counter-Church in the heart of Nazi Germany at Finkenwalde."[22]

In prison his context had changed. But one of the first things Bonhoeffer did after he was arrested was to "establish a strict daily routine from which he did not depart: physical exercise, his long-accustomed meditation [and prayer], and after his Bible was returned to him on the third day, the memorizing and reading the Scriptures."[23] Such regular spiritual practices continued to shape Bonhoeffer's life lived before God—and sustained his ongoing witness to the gospel of Jesus Christ. Through his acts of generosity and comfort, he sought to create as much community as was possible even in the bleak, individualistic world he was forced to endure in prison.

But we also should not underestimate how difficult imprisonment was for Bonhoeffer. Eberhard Bethge describes his first night. "The night of 5 April 1943 was cold in the reception cell in Tegel. Bonhoeffer could not bring himself to use the blankets of the wood bed; he could not stand their stench. Someone wept loudly in the next cell. The next morning dry bread was tossed through a crack in the door. The staff had been instructed not to speak to the new arrival. The warden called him a 'scoundrel.'"[24] Bethge comments that the experience of imprisonment was more difficult

---

18. Northcott, "Who Am I?," in Wannenwetsch, *Who Am I?*, 15–24.
19. Northcott, "Who Am I?," in Wannenwetsch, *Who Am I?*, 23.
20. Bonhoeffer, "To Karl Barth, September, 1936," DBWE 14, 252–55, here 254.
21. Bonhoeffer, DBWE 14, 96.
22. Northcott, "Who Am I?," in Wannenwetsch, *Who Am I?*, 23.
23. Bethge, *Dietrich Bonhoeffer*, 831; prayer is added to the list later (852–53).
24. Bethge, *Dietrich Bonhoeffer*, 799.

for Bonhoeffer than he was willing to admit.[25] There was the humiliation of wearing handcuffs, the filth, and the wardens who often acted like thugs. And then there were the multiple separations: from respect, work, the past, the future, and especially from friends and family. This latter separation was probably the most difficult. Bonhoeffer came from a very close-knit family. Along with this, he deeply valued friendships and had only recently become engaged to Maria von Wedemeyer. All of these separations—on top of the harshness of the prison environment—undoubtedly were emotionally quite difficult for him. In fact, in the beginning he struggled with whether to fight for his life or to kill himself. The temptation to suicide was likely related to his realization that he might very well undergo interrogation and torture, during which he would be tempted to give information that would lead to the arrest and execution of people he knew who were involved in treasonous activities.

It may be that the warden initially referred to Bonhoeffer as a "scoundrel," but this dismissive label did not serve long to define such an affable, social disciple. Bonhoeffer was soon making friends both with fellow inmates and guards. He was found to be a good conversationalist and someone to whom individuals could take their troubles. Because his father was a physician, he had useful medical knowledge. He was perceived to be wise and prudent. And during air raids he was sometimes called upon to offer comfort and prayer for those who were fearful and anxious.

In the beginning, Bonhoeffer was allowed to communicate to the outside world only by writing a one-page letter to his parents every ten days. However, because of friendships he developed with guards, the guards supplied him with writing materials and he was soon permitted to send and receive letters frequently. Bethge is undoubtedly right that "letters became Bonhoeffer's elixir of life in Tegel. He lived through them."[26] He was also allowed to receive parcels from family members. By this means he received some extra food (which he often shared), as well as books. He managed to secure the latest part volume of Barth's *Church Dogmatics*, as well as volumes by Søren Kierkegaard. But most of his reading, other than the Bible, was non-theological. Reading and composing reflections allowed Bonhoeffer to have a structure to his days. And these activities provided meaning, making it possible to live out his vocation as a theologian in the suffocating confines of his cell.

During Bonhoeffer's imprisonment, in addition to poetry, he wrote the beginnings of a novel and a play. These creative writings have much to

25. Bethge, *Dietrich Bonhoeffer*, 831–34.
26. Bethge, *Dietrich Bonhoeffer*, 838.

offer us in assessing who he was. I have already quoted and commented on one poem. But for the rest of this chapter, I want to focus mainly on the texts that began making Bonhoeffer famous when they were first published, namely some of his more theologically oriented letters, written in the months between April and August of 1944.

"Who Is Christ for Us Today?"

Anyone who has been studying theology as long as I have—that is, for some five decades—knows that Bonhoeffer was hailed as a trailblazer for theologians who in the 1960s were celebrating their discovery of the secular city and "the death of God." Phrases from Bonhoeffer's 1944 prison writings were seen as hopeful signposts pointing the way to a new liberation from religion. Intriguing phrases such as "the world has come of age," a "worldly and nonreligious" interpretation of Christianity, and "living before God without God" became lenses through which to view Bonhoeffer's life and theology, especially because an early compilation of the prison letters was one of his first books to be translated into English.

But if we are truly to understand his theology as articulated in prison—including some of these provocative phrases—we must see them in connection with his earlier theology.[27] For after all, as he himself said in a letter on April 22, 1944, there is much more continuity than discontinuity in his life and thought, especially after his time abroad (in 1930–1931).[28] Importantly for my argument, Bonhoeffer specifically says in a letter on July 21, 1944, that he still stands by what he wrote in the book *Discipleship*.[29] Eberhard Bethge says that we can see that the book *Discipleship* and *Letters and Papers from Prison* end in similar ways—"with the motif of *imitatio*."[30] The most straightforward way to name the continuity is to point to the centrality of Jesus Christ for Bonhoeffer's life and theology. But it is also not to ignore dramatic changes that have occurred. In 1937, as he opened his book *Discipleship*, he was intent on examining "the daily catchwords and battle cries needed in the Church Struggle." And he was sure that what was needed was "a more intense, questioning search . . . for the one who is our sole concern, for Jesus himself. What did Jesus want to say to us? What

---

27. Of the many writings on Bonhoeffer's theological writings in prison the following are the ones that have most influenced my discussion below: Matthews, *Anxious Souls Will Ask*; Wüstenberg, *Theology of Life*; and Wüstenberg, "Religionless Christianity."

28. Bonhoeffer, DBWE 8, 357–58; 352–53.

29. Bonhoeffer, DBWE 8, 486.

30. Bethge, *Dietrich Bonhoeffer*, 860.

does he want from us today? How does he help us to be faithful Christians today?"[31] In a sense that is still his concern. But, lying in prison, he now is reflecting not on what is needed in the midst of an intense church struggle, but rather how do we reflect on the reasons for massive failure on the part of the Protestant Church? And for Bonhoeffer, his initial probing questions circle around this central one: "What keeps gnawing at me is the question, what is Christianity, or who is Christ actually for us today?"[32]

Let me make a few other comments before turning directly to some of his prison writings in the late spring and summer of 1944. We need to remember that these are private, vulnerable, theological letters sent to a trusted friend (Eberhard Bethge). And, written over the course of only a few months, these are simply initial reflections from a theologian who would have had much more to say had he lived longer. What we have are creative, initial thoughts from someone grieving deeply the failure of his church and seeking ways to imagine a more faithful future for the body of Christ. To give readers who are unfamiliar with these letters a sense of what they are like, here is a sample of Bonhoeffer's provocative thought, taken from correspondence in April 1944.

> We are approaching a completely religionless age; people as they are now simply cannot be religious anymore.... "Christianity" has always been a form (perhaps the true form) of "religion." Yet, if it becomes obvious one day that this "a priori" doesn't exist, that it has been a historically conditioned and transitory form of human expression, then people really will become radically religionless—and I believe this is already more or less the case.... The foundations are being pulled out from under all that "Christianity" has previously been for us, and the only people among whom we might end up in terms of "religion" are "the last of the knights" or a few intellectually dishonest people.... How can Christ become Lord of the religionless as well? Is there such a thing as a religionless Christian? If religion is only the garb in which Christianity is clothed—and this garb has looked very different in different ages—what then is religionless Christianity? Barth, who is the only one to have begun thinking along these lines, nevertheless did not pursue these thoughts all the way, did not think them through.... The question to be answered would be: What does a church, a congregation, a sermon, a liturgy, a Christian life, mean in a religionless world? How do we talk about God—without religion, that is, without

---

31. Bonhoeffer, DBWE 4, 37.
32. Bonhoeffer, DBWE 8, 362.

the temporally conditioned presuppositions of metaphysics, the inner life, and so on? How do we speak (or perhaps we can no longer even "speak" the way we used to) in a "worldly" way about "God"? How do we go about being "religionless-worldly" Christians, how can we be [êk-klesía], those who are called out, without understanding ourselves religiously as privileged, but instead seeing ourselves as belonging wholly to the world? Christ would then no longer be the object of religion, but something else entirely, truly Lord of the world.[33]

And now let me attempt to enter into the detail of Bonhoeffer's theological letters from 1944, in which reflections such as these dominate. He continues to be deeply influenced by Karl Barth and draws insights from philosopher Wilhelm Dilthey. What is Bonhoeffer doing as he seeks to understand what went wrong with previous understandings of Christianity, while he looks toward the future for life in Christ?[34]

First, we can see that Bonhoeffer speaks quite critically of the way in which a focus on metaphysics—a distant, transcendent God—has allowed Christians to ignore the reality of God in our midst. In a letter on April 30, 1944, Bonhoeffer observes that religious people often speak of their need for God only at the end of their own knowledge or strength—at human boundaries, such as death. "I'd like to speak of God not at the boundaries but in the center," Bonhoeffer says, "not in weakness but in strength, thus not in death and guilt but in human life and human goodness.... God is the beyond in the midst of our lives. The church stands not at the point where human powers fail, at the boundaries, but in the center of the village. That's the way it is in the Old Testament, and in this sense we don't read the New Testament nearly enough in the light of the Old."[35] A few months later, in an outline for a book, Bonhoeffer writes, "Jesus's 'being-for-others' is the experience of transcendence! . . . [and] our relationship to God is a new life in 'being there for others,' through participation in the being of Jesus."[36]

A second critique Bonhoeffer offers of typical religion is its individualism. The alternative for Christians is to be meaningfully and actively involved in the body of Christ. In the conclusion to his outline for a book, he importantly adds:

---

33. Bonhoeffer, DBWE 8, 362–64.

34. On Bonhoeffer's reflections on Barth, see DBWE 8, 428–30. On Barth and Dilthey's influence, see Wüstenberg, *Theology of Life*.

35. Bonhoeffer, DBWE 8, 366–67.

36. Bonhoeffer, DBWE 8, 501.

The church is church only when it is there for others. As a first step it must give away all its property to those in need. The clergy must live solely on the freewill offerings of the congregations and perhaps be engaged in some secular vocation. The church must participate in the worldly tasks of life in the community—not dominating but helping and serving. It must tell people in every calling what a life with Christ is, what it means "to be there for others." In particular, *our* church will have to confront the vices of hubris, the worship of power, envy and illusionism as the roots of all evil. It will have to speak of moderation, authenticity, trust, faithfulness, steadfastness, patience, discipline, humility, modesty, contentment. It will have to see that it does not underestimate the significance of the human "example" (which has its origin in the humanity of Jesus and is so important in Paul's writings!); the church's word gains weight and power not through concepts but by example.[37]

Third, Bonhoeffer emphasizes in several letters "the profound this-worldliness of Christianity." So as not to be misunderstood, Bonhoeffer also says, "I do not mean the shallow and banal this-worldliness of the enlightened, the bustling, the comfortable, or the lascivious, but the profound this-worldliness that shows discipline and includes the ever-present knowledge of death and resurrection. I think Luther lived in this kind of this-worldliness."[38] Bonhoeffer named some of the specifics he had in mind when he offered reflections from prison for the baptism of Eberhard and Renate Bethge's newborn son, Dietrich:

> What reconciliation and redemption mean, rebirth and Holy Spirit, love for one's enemies, cross and resurrection, what it means to live in Christ and follow Christ, all that is so difficult and remote that we hardly dare speak of it anymore. In these words and actions handed down to us, we sense something totally new and revolutionary, but we cannot yet grasp it and express it. This is our own fault. Our church has been fighting during these years only for its self-preservation, as if that were an end in itself. It has become incapable of bringing the word of reconciliation and redemption to humankind and to the world.[39]

---

37. Bonhoeffer, DBWE 8, 503–4.
38. Bonhoeffer, DBWE 8, 485.
39. Bonhoeffer, "Thoughts on the Day of Baptism for D. W. R.," DBWE 8, 389.

If we are to recover these ways of understanding and living out the Christian faith, said Bonhoeffer in 1944, speaking of the next generation, then it must begin with the realization that "all Christian thinking, talking, and organizing must be born anew, out of . . . prayer and action."[40]

Bonhoeffer also says, fourth, that in a secular world that does not assume the existence of God and in which the church will be forced to give up its privileged place, we as Christians are freed to see how God acts and is present in the world. Thus, on July 16, he says:

> God consents to be pushed out of the world and onto the cross; God is weak and powerless in the world and in precisely this way, and only so, is at our side and helps us. Matt. 8:17 makes it quite clear that Christ helps us not by virtue of his omnipotence but rather by virtue of his weakness and suffering! This is the crucial distinction between Christianity and all religions. Human religiosity directs people in need to the power of God in the world. . . . The Bible directs people toward the powerlessness and the suffering of God; only the suffering of God can help.[41]

Two days later Bonhoeffer reflects on how Christians, knowing this about the God they know and serve, also enter into the suffering of the world with God.[42]

Finally, in these letters, Bonhoeffer refers to modern people as those who have come of age. They can see, he said, through the immaturity, the inauthenticity of an overdependence on God that led to an unhealthy passivity of the Protestant Church in Germany. Pietism, Bonhoeffer claimed was "a final attempt to preserve Protestant Christianity as religion; [and] orthodoxy, the attempt to save the church as an institution of salvation." But he saw "little [true, authentic] faith in Christ. 'Jesus' disappears from view."[43] Bonhoeffer noted that "The 'religious act' is always something partial; 'faith'. . . is involving the whole of one's life."[44]

We have now come full circle. We can see that, in the midst of some new theological language, drawn from reading in prison, Bonhoeffer is asking afresh how Christians—the body of Christ—can embrace the call to costly discipleship in the midst of daily life, a discipleship made possible by the costly grace of the God made flesh in Jesus Christ.

40. Bonhoeffer, DBWE 8, 389.
41. Bonhoeffer, DBWE 8, 479.
42. Bonhoeffer, DBWE 8, 480.
43. Bonhoeffer, DBWE 8, 500.
44. Wüstenberg, "Religionless Christianity," 67. Bonhoeffer originally noted this when he observed Muslims on his visit to Tripoli in 1924.

After August 1944 the only letters we have from Dietrich are a few short notes to his parents (the last one on January 17, 1945). On October 8 Bonhoeffer was transferred from Tegel to the guarded cellar at the Reich Central Security Office; he was there four months and was interrogated repeatedly. Following this, he was in the concentration camp at Buchenwald for seven weeks. Finally, he was part of a prison transport traveling through southern Germany for a week, landing eventually in the camp in Flossenbürg, where he was executed.

Conclusion: In the Midst of the Polyphony of Life, the Cantus Firmus Continues

But I will end similarly to the way I began this chapter, lest we misunderstand what Bonhoeffer meant by religionless Christianity. Captain Payne Best, a British Secret Intelligence Service (MI6) agent, was in Buchenwald with Bonhoeffer.[45] Best offered the following reflections: "Bonhoeffer was all humility and sweetness; he always seemed to diffuse an atmosphere of happiness, of joy in every smallest event in life, and of deep gratitude for the mere fact that he was alive. . . . He was one of the very few men I have ever met to whom his God was real and ever close to him." Best continues: Bonhoeffer's "soul really shone in the dark desperation of our prison . . . [we were] in complete agreement that our warders and guards needed pity far more than we and that it was absurd to blame them for their actions." On April 3 both Bonhoeffer and Best left Buchenwald on a transport truck. They arrived at Schönberg on Friday, April 6. At the request of others, Bonhoeffer conducted a worship service on Sunday morning, April 8, the Sunday after Easter. He offered reflections on Isaiah 53:5 ("With his wounds we are healed") and 1 Peter 1:3 ("Blessed be the God and Father of our Lord Jesus Christ! By his great mercy we have been born anew to a living hope though the resurrection of Jesus Christ from the dead"). Not long after the service ended, he heard the words: "'Prisoner Bonhoeffer, get ready and come with us!'" As he was leaving for Flossenbürg, "he asked Payne Best to remember him to [his long-time friend, George Bell,] the bishop of Chichester if he should ever reach his home. [Tell him,] 'this is the end—for me the beginning of life.'"

However, I cannot end with an honoring of Bonhoeffer and how he seemed to have faith to the end. As valuable and encouraging as this witness is, it is, finally, testimony to the God who was the center of his life. In

---

45. The account in this paragraph is drawn from Bethge, *Dietrich Bonhoeffer*, 920–26.

May 1944, in several different letters to Bethge, Bonhoeffer played with the image of "the polyphony of life." On May 20 he wrote to Eberhard about the challenges his friend was facing (separation from his wife, Renate; the difficulties of military life; and constant reminders of the destructiveness of war). Dietrich sought to encourage his trusted friend in the faith.

> There is a danger, in any passionate erotic love, that through it you may lose what I'd like to call the polyphony of life. What I mean is that God, the Eternal, wants to be loved with our whole heart, not to the detriment of earthly love or to diminish it, but as a sort of cantus firmus [fixed melody] to which the other voices of life resound in counterpoint. One of these contrapuntal themes, which keep their *full independence* but are still related to the cantus firmus, is earthly love.... Where the cantus firmus is clear and distinct, a counterpoint can develop as mightily as it wants. The two are "undivided and yet distinct," as the Definition of Chalcedon says, like the divine and human natures of Christ. Is that perhaps why we are so at home with polyphony in music, why it is important to us, because it is the musical image of this Christological fact and thus also our *vita christiana* [Christian life].... Only this polyphony gives your life its wholeness, and you know that no disaster can befall you as long as the cantus firmus continues.[46]

Indeed!

This single word was the way I initially ended this chapter, following the evocative quote from Bonhoeffer. And for me the central point of the quote is to be clear about the cantus firmus.

I still believe that it is important to hear Bonhoeffer's clear affirmation of the cantus firmus—the fixed and enduring melody revealed through Jesus Christ. And within that, it is important to know, in light of our identity in Christ, that (to borrow from Augustine) we have rightly ordered loves. However, as I was revising this chapter, I began reading the recently translated book by Andreas Pangritz, *The Polyphony of Life*.[47] Pangritz reminded me of who Bonhoeffer was apart from resisting the Nazis, of the evenings and weekends and holidays he organized for his students at Finkenwalde— to celebrate the joys of the life God has given to us. In other words, Bonhoeffer's knowledge and love of music—and thus, his creative use of musical imagery—are reminders that this earthly life we have is to be cherished, celebrated, and enjoyed. Loving God with the whole of our being, in other

---

46. Bonhoeffer, DBWE 8, 393–94.
47. Pangritz, *Polyphony of Life*.

words, is not to be to the detriment of other loves, but rather forms them and enhances them—for the full flourishing of humanity as well as for the glorifying of God. We dare not forget this, even as discipleship is tough, even in the midst of the rubble. Amen and amen.

Epilogue

"Invisibility Is Ruining Us!"

We Need to See That Christ Has Been Here.[1]

There are various events in Bonhoeffer's youth that anticipate his future. One such incident involved the response of his family to his announcement at age fourteen that he was planning to be a theologian. Coming from a non-churched family, his siblings discouraged him. They and his father thought he would be wasting his time. As Bethge reports it, they saw the church as "a poor, feeble, boring, petty, and bourgeois institution." Young Dietrich didn't disagree, "but he confidently replied: 'In that case I shall reform it!'"[2]

Four years later, between April and June 1924, Dietrich travelled to Italy, Sicily, and Libya, with his brother, Klaus. For young Dietrich this trip contained a number of transformative experiences. He was in many ways quite impressed with the Catholic Church he experienced in Rome. "The universality of the church was illustrated in a marvelously effective manner. White, black, yellow members of religious orders—everyone was in clerical robes united under the church. It truly seems ideal."[3] On a Sunday evening he experienced a worship service in which forty young women were becoming nuns. In his diary Bonhoeffer wrote: "The ritual was truly no longer merely ritual. Instead, it was worship in the true sense. The whole thing gave one an unparalleled impression of profound, guileless piety. . . . It was the first

---

1. Based on a letter Bonhoeffer sent in Oct. 1931 (Bonhoeffer, DBWE 11, 55).
2. Bethge, *Dietrich Bonhoeffer*, 36.
3. Bonhoeffer, DBWE 9, 88.

day on which something of the reality of Catholicism began to dawn on me—nothing romantic, etc.—but I think I'm beginning to understand the concept of 'church.'"[4]

As he reflected on the universal—the catholic—nature of the church he was observing in Rome, he turned to reflections on Protestantism in Germany. He spoke critically of the fact that it was the "established church," the state church. If it were not that, says Bonhoeffer, it might then "represent an unusual phenomenon of religious life and serious thoughtful piety. It would therefore be the ideal form of religion, which is sought after in so many ways today." He continues, "It is not the content of the gospel of the Reformation that repels people so much as the form of the gospel, which one still tries to tie to the state. If it had remained a sect it would have become the church the Reformers intended."[5]

Tripoli taught Bonhoeffer other important lessons. He commented on how Arabs "who have such a well-developed sense of tradition and culture are to be transformed into slaves. When one sees that the Arabs are treated with great brutality and vulgarity by the Italian soldiers, one can understand their bitterness and callous fear."[6] He also contrasted the Christianity he knew from what he observed in Islamic life. "In general, it seems to me that there is an immense similarity between Islam and the lifestyle and piety recorded in the Old Testament. In Islam, everyday life and religion are not separated at all. Even in the Catholic Church they are separated, for the most part. At home one just goes to church. When one returns a completely different life begins. It is thoroughly different for the Muslims."[7]

The following winter, 1924–1925, Bonhoeffer discovered the writings of Karl Barth. From that point forward, his theology (including theological ethics) would reflect the profound influence of Barth. However, the lessons he learned from his trip with his brother Klaus would also remain with him as he developed his understanding of the church.[8] His first substantial attempt to formulate his understanding of the church was through his 1927 doctoral thesis, *Sanctorum Communio*. In this work he provides a social account of the body of Christ that is decisively framed by a Christian theology very much indebted to Barth. Soon after he received the first copies of the published version of this work, in early September 1930, he boarded a

4. Bonhoeffer, DBWE 9, 89.
5. Bonhoeffer, DBWE 9, 106.
6. Bonhoeffer, DBWE 9, 116.
7. Bonhoeffer, DBWE 9, 118. A downside: "So war is also a service to Mohammed and Allah" (DBWE 9, 118).
8. Bethge also sees his experiences on this trip as permanently influential (Bethge, *Dietrich Bonhoeffer*, 60–65).

ship for New York City. He could not have anticipated the transformation he would undergo during his ten months abroad. His own reflections suggest that during this time he, for the first time, truly became a Christian.

Clifford Green is helpful in framing Bonhoeffer's hope for his new foreign adventure. "As he experienced a new country, a different theological culture, the churches of the New World, a nation on the rise, and a country riven by race, Bonhoeffer was looking for 'a cloud of witnesses.'"[9] And he would find it—in an unexpected place! Bonhoeffer would, in some ways, have a parallel experience to Barth, only more than a decade later and in a different cultural context. Barth had been very attracted to the European version of the social gospel movement, through Swiss Reformed theologians like Leonard Ragaz and Hermann Kutter.[10] He entered into this rather fully for a short time. Then he would have his own spiritual awakening through a fresh, eye-opening encounter with the Scriptures in the midst of World War I.[11] Following this, he would reframe his understanding of the gospel, including its social dimensions, partly because of his encounter with Christoph Blumhardt.[12] From that time forward, his new awareness of the crisis provoked by the word of God would distinguish his approach from Christian socialism, but he would in his own way always understand the gospel to have social dimensions.

Similarly, Bonhoeffer, at the beginning of the 1930s in New York City, would encounter the social gospel both through his teachers at Union Theological Seminary and through Abyssinian Baptist Church, a Black church led by its dynamic pastor, Adam Clayton Powell Sr. Bonhoeffer had serious theological questions about the white versions of the social gospel as mediated by his professors at Union.[13] However, he deeply resonated with the more spiritually dynamic, gospel-centered, practical social gospel as experienced through Abyssinian Baptist.[14] In fact, like Barth, this understanding of the social dimensions of the gospel would remain with him for the rest of his life. Having returned from these experiences in the US, in October 1931

9. Green, "Editor's Introduction," 17.

10. See Dorrien, *Social Democracy in Making*, 217–310.

11. See Busch, *Karl Barth*, 60–125; and Dorrien, *Social Democracy in Making*, 218–69.

12. Dorrien comments that "Barth owed more to his friendship with the younger Blumhardt than he owed to Kierkegaard, Dostoyevsky, or Overbeck." (Dorrien, *Social Democracy in Making*, 246). See Collins Winn, *"Jesus Is Victor!"*; cf. Ward, *Theology, Sociology and Politics*, 123–88; and Correll, *Shepherds of the Empire*, 141–81.

13. Bonhoeffer, DBWE 12, 236–43.

14. To get a sense of what he might have resonated with, see McNeill et al., *Witness*, 78–151; and Dorrien, *New Abolition*, 425–47.

Bonhoeffer wrote a letter to theologian and friend Helmut Rössler. In it he mourned the state of the church of Luther's Germany. "Invisibility is ruining us," he said. We need to see "that Christ has been here."[15]

Bonhoeffer's clearest theological reflections on the importance of the visibility of the church—and thus the social dimensions of the gospel—were given expression in his book *Discipleship*. I have summarized that in chapter 4. However, I think it might be helpful in this epilogue to offer a more conceptual account of these concerns, expressed throughout Bonhoeffer's writings. To do this, I will utilize a little-known essay, "The Church as Witnessing Community," by the late theologian and widely respected Barth scholar, John Webster, because this essay sounds so much like Bonhoeffer.[16] The framing question is: "How do the judgment and mercy of God manifest in the Christian gospel shape the social and cultural testimony of the Christian community?" (21) "We should be clear from the outset," says Webster, "that the primary issues are as much theological as they are moral, political and social" (21). More specifically,

> Cultural testimony must emerge from the church's constant and singular preoccupation, which is to give attention to God's self-declaration in the gospel, and to allow its thought, speech and action to be broken and remade through its hearing. The community of Jesus Christ is a community which is brought into being by the gospel, sustained in life by the gospel and summoned to bear witness to the gospel; and because that is true, the church can only be what it is if its entire life and activity emerges out of the event of starting again with the gospel. For the community of Jesus Christ, there is simply nowhere else to begin. (21)

This sort of affirmation is at the root of Bonhoeffer's opposition to a principled approach to ethics (which leaves the gospel behind) and an articulation of what in his earlier writings sounded like a radically contextual approach to ethics (wanting to make room for a fresh hearing of the gospel each day). These root concerns would remain with Bonhoeffer. However, he came to have confidence not only in the ongoing revelation of God through Jesus Christ but also in its ongoing consistency (known through Jesus, the biblical witness, and Christ existing as community). But he also realized the need

---

15. Bonhoeffer, DBWE 11, 55.

16. Webster, "Church as Witnessing Community," 21–33. In the following few paragraphs, page numbers for this essay will be given in the text. Also see Webster, "Christ, Church, and Reconciliation" in *Word and Church* and "Visible Attests the Invisible." Cf. the engagement with Webster in Taylor, *Reading Scripture as the Church*, 25–91.

for vigilance in sustaining the Christian community's ongoing dependence on the God known through Jesus Christ.

If one is to urge Christian involvement in the world, as did Bonhoeffer, *and* sustain theological integrity in doing so, then theological attention must be given to how the gospel relates to public witness. This is true, "first, in order to resist the moralism which so easily afflicts the church's social and cultural testimony. By 'moralism' I mean the fatal turn by which the church's human responsibility and action become the centre of gravity in its dealings with its context. When that happens, then gospel, church and witness all are distorted. 'Gospel' is instrumentalized" (22). In the context of Nazi Germany—but really in any context, where there are elements of violence, injustice, and unrighteousness that need to be countered—Christians must address public issues. However, we must also strenuously avoid aligning the church with any non-Christian ideology or being overly focused on specific policies. For, if the Christian witness is "to be protected from moralism, it can only be by being faced with the gospel as something which *resists* us, which cannot just be harnessed to whatever social and cultural projects we consider it ought to pull in its train. And the task of theology is just that: to exemplify the church facing the resistance of the gospel" (22).

"We need to give theological attention to the gospel, second, in order to ensure the Christianness of our social and cultural testimony" (22). Among other things, this means the church should not feel compelled to speak publicly to every issue that arises. "There are many issues on which the church will have little to say of direct relevance; indeed it will always be the case that its witness will have a necessarily strange and tangential character, simply because it persists in talking of God. The church's witness is *witness*—testimony to something laid upon it from outside; it is not the church casting around for something to say" (23). This was certainly true for Bonhoeffer. On the one hand, he did fight strenuously against the coordination of the Protestant Church with Nazism. And this was because he knew that such coordination would fundamentally distort the nature of the church, its understanding of the gospel and its witness. Otherwise, however, he spoke to few public issues. He felt compelled to speak publicly about war multiple times because he saw the issue of violence as being close to the heart of the gospel. He also felt similarly about the issue of anti-Semitism, both in relation to ethnic Jews who were Christians and Jews who were outside of the Christian community.

"We need to give theological attention to the gospel, third, because Christian witness in the social and cultural sphere rests upon a Christian understanding of reality. To put the point technically: Christian witness presupposes Christian ontology. More straightforwardly: Christian witness rests upon a 'reading' of reality, a given sense of how the world really is, and therefore of how humankind should act in the world" (23). In other words, Webster says, "close to the heart of Christian social and cultural witness is thus the command to testify to the truth" (23). There are at least three ways in which Bonhoeffer echoes this concern. The first is with his concept of the order of preservation. Second, with his claim, both in *Discipleship* and *Ethics*, that reality is only truly known through Jesus Christ. And third with his notion that the church is meant to be what the world will ultimately be.

But, of course, all of these reflections beg the question: what is the gospel? For either Webster or Bonhoeffer, answering that question with any adequacy requires reading a considerable amount of their writing. For Bonhoeffer the central answer is given in *Discipleship*. But to hint at a response, I will continue to borrow from Webster in order to offer some brief conceptual reflections that seem apt. "When we try to define the gospel, we need to resist the temptation to make it into a manageable and relatively tame message, something which can perform useful functions in our religious cultural worlds, and which we can make our own by annexing it to our own viewpoints or projects of social transformation" (24). In other words, the gospel is not something merely "usable" but rather "the gospel concerns God and God's actions, and so is known only in the miracle of revelation and faith, and present among us after the manner of God, that is, spiritually, and not as some kind of religious or ecclesiastical possession" (24). If "we lose sight of this, and convert the gospel into just another Christian cultural commodity, then it very rapidly becomes 'something which would survive as Good News apart from faith and without God" (25). Put most simply, "the gospel is 'the gospel of Christ.' Jesus himself, the proclaimer and embodiment of God's good news *is* the gospel" (25; emphasis his).

It is important to remind ourselves that the gospel is indeed *good* news. It is such because "in it we encounter God's gracious work for us and our salvation" (25). This good news originates "in God himself, it concerns his presence and action, and points human life to its true fulfillment in fellowship with God" (25). Though ultimate redemption lies in the future, "the gospel is the presence of salvation, the freeing of all things from disorder and confinement and the gift of life in fellowship with God. The gospel is the active reality of God's grace, God taking up the cause of those whose sin has eaten away at their humanity" (26). And the gospel is good news "because it is comprehensively true. All human reality is what it is in the light of the gospel" (27). This means that the gospel is "*particular* because it is stubbornly tied to the career and name of Jesus." However, the gospel is also "universal in reach, since it is the good news of the one in whom God gathers up all things (*cf.* Eph. 1:11)" (27; emphasis his).

Radical implications follow from these claims. We need to realize that this means "the gospel is always against the grain of our expectations" (26). It is "a great deal less serene than we may be tempted to believe" (27). "More than anything else," therefore, this gospel entails "a matter of disorientation."

> There is an immediate consequence to be drawn here for the church's social and cultural witness: that witness must not proceed by transmuting the gospel into a stable, measurable, quantifiable social or cultural value. We can no more do that than we can channel a volcano into a domestic heating system. The gospel is no mere "principle" which can then be "applied" to issues about forms of common life or political economy. The gospel is about death and resurrection, new creation, and it is that new order of reality, rather than any immediate social applicability, which is the burden of the church's testimony. (27)

All of this has implications for how we think about the church. "Most fundamentally, it means that the church is what it is because of the gospel" (27). If this is to have any meaning then we must be "very strict to allow the gospel to exercise in an immediate way a controlling and critical influence" within our Christian communities (28). "'Church' is the event of gathering around the magnetic centre of the good news of Jesus Christ" (28). But since the church is possessed by rather than itself possessing the gospel, then "it will be most basically characterized by astonishment at the good news of Jesus" (29). The church is church both in its activities of gathering together *and* being dispersed into its daily life beyond the gathered community.

> The acts of the church in gathering are those acts by which the church is drawn towards the source of its life, and reinvested in the truth and goodness of the gospel. The acts of the church in dispersal are those acts in which the church follows the external impulse of its source of life, and is pushed beyond itself in testimony and service. It is crucial that neither the acts of gathering nor the acts of dispersal are somehow to be considered as independent, free-standing operations which we may talk about without reference to the action of God. The gospel is not inert; it does not merely furnish the occasion for the church to get busy. Whatever the church does about the gospel is always response to the fact that God has already taken matters into his own hands. (29–30)

It is important to remember, as 1 Peter puts it, that the church "is 'a chosen race . . . a holy nation, God's own people . . . that you may declare the wonderful deeds of him who called you out of darkness into his wonderful light'

(1 Pet. 2:9)" (30). This is a reminder that God acts and speaks before and apart from the life of the church. But it also reminds the church that it "is authentically the church in so far as it engages in witness" (30). The church is chosen for vocation—for witnessing, for serving—not for removing itself from the larger world. As Bonhoeffer said, "the church is church only when it exists for others." As it discerns the particulars of its witness and service, the church (and Christians within it) should keep several things in mind. First, "that Christian witness will be concerned to explain that the world has a given nature" (32). Second, given that there is a given nature, then this approach to witness is teleological. This means "that Christian witness will be concerned to explain that the world as new creation has given ends. Its trajectory is not wholly indeterminate, a matter merely for human deliberation; its end is, rather, in accord with its nature. Without an account of ends, there is little barrier against the secularised eschatology of modernity, whose sheer human vulgarity is once again to be unfurled before us as we prepare to elect our government taskmasters" (32). All of this means that, third, "Christian witness will be concerned to explain that human social and cultural activity are truthful insofar as they are in accordance with the nature and end as determined by the purposes of God. Christian witness will have a particular interest in urging that good action is truthful action" (32).

I have drawn largely from Webster's words. However, I am convinced that I could find "chapter and verse" in Bonhoeffer's writings in order to establish that Bonhoeffer's views largely coincide with Webster's. For Bonhoeffer, as for Webster, these theological convictions are fundamental. However, it is also the case that Bonhoeffer very much wanted to see these convictions embodied—made visible—in the context of daily life. He wanted the Christian community to make known that Christ had been among them.

Therefore, I end this epilogue with the extraordinary story of one Christian community that did exactly what Bonhoeffer hoped for. These Christians gave witness to the power of the gospel among them in the midst of Nazi-occupied France.

During the time Bonhoeffer was at Union Seminary and Abyssinian Baptist Church, in the winter of 1930–1931, Pastor André Trocmé was undergoing a similar "spiritual awakening" in Sin-le-Noble, a northern French community near the Belgian border.[17] What apparently sparked this spiritual awakening was a particular meeting of a group that Trocmé regularly led, a small group of men who were poor and struggling with alcoholism. One evening Trocmé was leading a discussion of a recently published book that sought to prove that Jesus was simply a myth invented by the apostle

---

17. Chalamet, *Revivalism and Social Christianity*, 102–4.

Paul. Trocmé found himself posing a question. "If Jesus really walked upon this earth, why do we keep treating him as if he were a disembodied, impossibly idealistic ethical theory? If he was a real man, then the Sermon on the Mount was made for people on this earth; and if he existed, God has shown us in flesh and blood what goodness is for flesh-and-blood people."[18] Philip Hallie reports:

> All of this he said calmly to the ten men who were present. He had not planned to say these things, nor had he planned to take any particular action after their talk, but suddenly they found themselves on their knees together. Each made a confession to God of his own weaknesses, as the young people in Saint-Quentin had done, and they all stood up. They found themselves looking at each other with new eyes, without defensiveness, shyness, or pride. They all felt the spirit of God in them, and decided to go right home to bring that extraordinary new awareness to their wives and children. This was the beginning of what came to be called the "awakening at Sin-le-Noble." In its full intensity it lasted for more than three months, and in the course of it, all the divisions and disputes in the parish disappeared. People became as dear to each other as Jesus was to them.[19]

Trocmé himself underwent a spiritual transformation through these experiences. As he put it, it was "'a spiritual springtime. All those things that had formerly been vague, colorless, seen from the outside . . . became suddenly for me living, interesting, inspiring. Each man became inestimably precious in my eyes.'"[20] Interestingly, about five years before Bonhoeffer, Trocmé was also exposed to the (white) social gospel during a year at Union Theological Seminary. But he found it too secular for his taste.[21] He had also been involved in Christian organizations that emphasized the social dimensions of the gospel in France.[22] His sense of the social dimensions of the gospel would also never leave him, although reframed by his experiences of a "spiritual springtime."

In 1934 Pastor Trocmé moved to a different parish, the remote community of Le Chambon-sur-Lignon, in southern France. Almost two thirds of the 5,000 Chambonnais were Reformed, descendants of a religious

---

18. Hallie, *Lest Innocent Blood Be Shed*, 68. There are also now several more book-length accounts of this story.
19. Hallie, *Lest Innocent Blood Be Shed*, 68.
20. Hallie, *Lest Innocent Blood Be Shed*, 68.
21. Hallie, *Lest Innocent Blood Be Shed*, 62.
22. Chalamet, *Revivalism and Social Christianity*, 46–124.

minority, the Huguenots, who had experienced persecution, perseverance, and faithfulness in the midst of hardships.[23] Into the 1980s, this community still knew hymns that recalled the willingness of many of their spiritual ancestors, generations earlier, to become martyrs for their faith. This is not at all insignificant. As Bonhoeffer noted in his visit to Rome in 1924, being a minority—especially a persecuted minority—rather than a state church can help the church be clearer in its Christian identity. But it is also true that this does not happen automatically. As Jaroslav Pelikan has famously said, we need to know the distinction between *traditionalism*, which is the dead faith of the living, and *tradition*, which is the living faith of the dead.[24] In fact, soon after he arrived, "Trocme summarized the spirit of Le Chambon in his autobiographical notes as a village that seemed to be moving toward 'death, death, death, and the pastor was entrusted with helping the village die.'"[25] But Trocmé saw it as his task to transform this parish. For Trocmé's passion and vision for the gospel—and living in faithfulness to it—were still very much with him as he was moved to Le Chambon. Thus, he was determined from the outset of his new ministry to bring spiritual life into this sleepy rural parish. To enliven the faith of the Christians of Le Chambon, Pastor Trocmé organized a network of thirteen Bible studies in homes throughout the parish to connect the parishioners with each other and to deepen the call to discipleship (beginning soon after his arrival in 1934). Observing them after the enlivening of their faith, Philip Hallie perceived that "centuries of persecution had given the Huguenots, and Trocmé in particular, what [might be called] 'a sturdy quality.' Being a minority had helped make them clear-cut in their thinking and firm in their convictions. Having been tested by adversity, they had kept themselves alive by remaining lucid and unshakable. The Psalmist in Psalm 26 has said to God: 'Prove me, O Lord, and try me; test my heart and mind.' History had done this for the Huguenots."[26] All of this is to say, it is not insignificant that most of these Christians were from this heritage, with a long, known tradition of sacrifice, suffering—and even martyrdom. However, it was vitally important that their pastors regularly called them to a renewed faith, which included embodying serious discipleship—and the parishioners responded.

When Philip Hallie, a Jewish philosopher, did research for his book on Le Chambon by interviewing individuals there, Pastor Trocmé had already

---

23. Most of the remaining one-third were what we in the US would refer to as Plymouth Brethren. A tiny minority were Catholic.
24. Pelikan, *Vindication of Tradition*, 65.
25. Hallie, *Lest Innocent Blood Be Shed*, 78.
26. Hallie, *Lest Innocent Blood Be Shed*, 132–33.

died. And Trocmé's widow, Magda, downplayed the significance of her husband for what took place in this parish. However, Hallie realized, after having lived in Le Chambon for about two years, that he still couldn't quite put his finger on what made what happened at Le Chambon happen. And then it occurred to him: "the most obvious answer was Pastor Trocmé himself. His powerful sermons in the boxy granite temple inspired the people of the village to follow in the footprints of Jesus, loving all humankind and willing to suffer, even to die, for others. He was part and parcel of the great tradition of imitating Jesus the Christ."[27] Despite Magda's disclaimers, it was impossible to imagine that what happened in this community during World War II would have happened without Trocmé, "the spiritual center of Le Chambon," a man referred to by his wife as a "turbulent stream, thrusting its way with great speed and force through and around obstacles."[28] He and his wife, in very different ways, were dynamic leaders within this parish. And his co-pastor Eduard Theiss served as a stable counterpart to Trocmé's turbulence.

Trocmé's passion and clarity took on a specific urgency in certain sermons. Perhaps none more so than in his sermon preached on June 23, 1940, the day after the Armistice was signed with Nazi Germany. Because it is such a key document, I quote it at length:

> Let us hang our heads in shame before God, each one of us, as individuals, as leaders or members of a family, as citizens and as Christians, as pastors and church elders, as youth leaders, as members of youth groups, as Church worshippers. We beg God to forgive us for our own sins and for the sins of our people, for the sins of humanity today and of the Church today. In this we are united. It is to God alone that we must look for relief from our suffering. However, we must guard against some forms of humility that would be disobedience of God.
>
> First, let us be on our guard against confusing humility with hopelessness, and from believing and spreading the word that all is lost. It is not true that all is lost. Gospel truth is not lost, and it will be proclaimed loud and clear in our church from this pulpit, and during our pastoral visits. The word of God is not lost, and that is where you will find all the promises and possibilities of a recovery for all of us, for our people, and for the Church. Faith is not lost; real humility doesn't weaken faith; it leads to a deeper faith in God, a more powerful desire to serve.

---

27. Hallie, *Lest Innocent Blood Be Shed*, 35.
28. Hallie, *Lest Innocent Blood Be Shed*, 80, 47.

Second, we must guard against humbling ourselves not for our own sins but for the sins of others, in a spirit of bitterness and rancor....

Third, in our shame, let us not lose our faith and our convictions based on the Gospel. We may not have made proper use of the freedom that was given to us, but let us not give up that freedom, under the cover of humility, and turn ourselves into slaves; let us not give in without a struggle to the new ideologies. Have no illusions: the events of recent days mean that the totalitarian doctrine of violence now enjoys formidable prestige in the eyes of the world because it has, from the human point of view, been impressively successful.

It is by giving our lives to Jesus Christ, according to his Gospel, to his universal Church, that we keep our faith and show true humility.

Finally, understand that the return to obedience obliges us to make some breaks: breaks with the world, and breaks with ways of living that we have accepted so far. We face powerful heathen pressures on ourselves and on our families, pressures to force us to cave in to this totalitarian ideology. If this ideology cannot immediately subjugate our souls, it will try, at the very least, to make us cave in with our bodies. The duty of Christians is to resist the violence directed at our consciences with the weapons of the spirit. We appeal to all our brothers in Christ to refuse to agree with or cooperate in violence, especially in the coming days when that violence is directed against the English people.

To love, to forgive, to show kindness to our enemies, that is our duty. But we must do our duty without conceding defeat, without servility, without cowardice. We will resist when our enemies demand that we act in ways that go against the teachings of the Gospel. We will resist without fear, without pride, and without hatred. But this moral resistance is not possible without a clean break from the selfishness that, for a long time, has ruled our lives. We face a period of suffering, perhaps even shortages of food. We have all more or less worshipped Mammon; we have all basked in the selfish comforts of our close family, in easy pleasure, in idle drinking. We will now be made to do without many things. We will be tempted to play our own selfish game, to cling on to what we have, to be better off than our brothers. Let us abandon, brothers and sisters, our pride and our egotism, our love of money and our faith in material possessions, and learn to trust God in Heaven, both today and tomorrow, to bring our daily bread, and to share that bread with our brothers and sisters.

May God free us from both worry and complacency. May he give us his peace, which nothing and nobody can take away from his children. May he comfort us in our sorrows and in all our trials. May he see fit to make each of us humble and faithful members of the Church of Jesus Christ, of the body of Christ, waiting for his kingdom of justice and love, where his will shall be done on earth as it is in heaven.[29]

Before the year was out, in the winter of 1940–1941, refugees started coming to Le Chambon. Philip Hallie refers to what happened at Le Chambon as a "kitchen struggle," because the struggle against Nazism and anti-Semitism and *for* embodied love for neighbors, enemies, and refugees who showed up on their doorsteps happened largely through the intimate interconnections of the lives of the parishioners of Le Chambon—connections sustained in their kitchens and living rooms. A network of Bible studies blossomed into lifelines of compassion and generosity for refugees fleeing for their lives. Many within this parish of 5,000 responded generously, at great sacrifice, with an awareness of the danger, in order to express the practical comfort and service called for by the gospel. Once they started welcoming refugees into their lives—living lives of sacrifice, generosity, and compassion—they developed habits. These habits formed who they were—thus forming their character within a community of character. Therefore, it is not surprising that decades later when film director Pierre Sauvage asked them why they did what they did, they simply said things like "I don't know"; "We were used to it"; "It happened quite naturally"; "When there were no beds, we simply gave up ours"; there was "no choice." In other words, it seemed "natural" to them because it had become second nature; it was who they were.[30] However, within the film, *Weapons of the Spirit*, there are other key quotes that indicate it was not simply doing what came naturally. When co-pastor Eduard Theiss was asked to summarize the Christian faith in a sentence, he said Jesus had done it himself: "You shall love the Lord your God with all your heart, your soul, your mind; and love your neighbor as yourself." The interviewer asked: "It just had to be applied?" Theiss's response: "Yes." Madame Barraud, when asked why the

---

29 Trocmé, "Appendix: The Weapons of the Spirit," in Grose, *Good Place to Hide*, 304–8. For Trocmé's much later, more fully developed views see Trocmé, *Jesus and Nonviolent Revolution*.

30. See Philip Hallie's reflections on the habits that formed the "great virtues" of compassion and generosity within the Chambonnais in "Magda and the Great Virtues," in Hallie, *In Eye of Hurricane*, 21–46.

Chambonnaise did what they did, said: "People still believed in something." "The Bible says to feed the hungry, to visit the sick. It's a normal thing to do." Marie Brottes, in explaining why she did what she did, summarized the story of the good Samaritan, ending by saying, "Clearly the Jews had fallen among thieves." She added, "Faith is nothing if not expressed through works." Pierre Sauvage, whose life was saved as an infant by the Chambonaise, said: "The holocaust would not have been possible without the apathy or complicity of Christians." And what this film shows—what Philip Hallie's book shows—is that these Christians in Le Chambon were not apathetic or complicit: they embodied, at great cost to themselves, "the weapons of the Spirt" to fight against fear and hate and to fight, in Christ, for the lives of those in great need who came to them.[31] In fact, by the end of the war, this life-giving parish had saved the lives of somewhere between 3,500 and 5,000 (mostly Jewish) refugees.

Philip Hallie discovered the story of Le Chambon in the midst of doing research on the problem of cruelty in the world. One day he came across a very brief account of the story of what happened in Le Chambon during World War II. He found himself deeply moved, with tears falling onto his cheeks. He knew then that he had to know more about this story, which led him to travel to southern France, do research and interviews and, eventually, produce the moving book *Lest Innocent Blood Be Shed*. In the 1994 paperback edition of the book, Hallie offered further reflections on this story, partly related to responses he had to his book, partly in order to express his appreciation as a World War II veteran of the extraordinary story of how a Christian pacifist pastor daringly led his parish to provide such a clear witness to the gospel (sacrificially welcoming refugees even while loving enemies).

Hallie tells about one experience he had after he had given a lecture in Minneapolis to a group of women. One woman in the back of the audience stood up after his talk and proceeded to ask for clarity regarding the specific village he was speaking about in France (there was more than one named Le Chambon). Once this was clarified, she said: "Well, you have been speaking about the village that saved the lives of all three of my children." Needless to say, this caught the attention of everyone in the room. She asked if she might say a little more; she did so from the front of the room. "The Holocaust was storm, lightning, thunder, wind, rain, yes. And Le Chambon was the rainbow." Some people in the room gasped. Hallie repeated the word "rainbow." Hallie comments: "We understood each other. We understood that the rainbow is one of the richest images in the Bible. . . . The rainbow

---

31. Sauvage, *Weapons of the Spirit*.

reminds God and man that life is precious to God, that God offers not only sentimental hope, but a promise that living will have the last word, not killing."[32] Hallie follows this by saying:

> Ever since the woman from Minneapolis witnessed to that hope, I realized that for me too the little story of Le Chambon is grander and more beautiful than the bloody war that stopped Hitler. I do not regret fighting in that war—Hitler had to be stopped, and he had to be stopped by killing many people. The war was necessary. But my memories of it give me only a sullied joy because in the course of the three major battles I participated in, I saw the detached arms and legs and heads of young men lying on blood-stained snow. The story of Le Chambon gives me unsullied joy.[33]

He continues, "The reason the rainbow is closer to my heart than the Flood that was World War II is that the people of Le Chambon helped without harming, saved lives without torturing and destroying other lives. This is why the rainbow gives me unsullied joy and necessary and useful killing does not."[34] As this Jewish philosopher ends these reflections, he feels compelled to say, after living with this story for almost twenty years, that he knew with "all certainty that Trocmé's belief in God was at the center of the rescue efforts of the village."[35] And what is obvious as one reads this story is that God is known centrally to Trocmé and these parishioners through Jesus Christ. It was in his name that they sacrificed; it was to his name that they gave witness.[36]

---

32. Hallie, *Lest Innocent Blood Be Shed*, xvii.
33. Hallie, *Lest Innocent Blood Be Shed*, xviii.
34. Hallie, *Lest Innocent Blood Be Shed*, xix.
35. Hallie, *Lest Innocent Blood Be Shed*, xxi.
36. It is striking to note the contrast between two film documentary accounts of this story: *Weapons of the Spirit*, directed by Pierre Sauvage, and *Heroes: Saving Jewish Lives from the Nazis*, directed by Marc Villiger. The former film presents the story in a way that largely coincides with the story as told by Philip Hallie. The latter film mostly strips out the specifically Christian dimensions of the story, reframing it mostly in secular terms.

Appendix 1

Whose Bonhoeffer? Which Hermeneutic?
Toward Preserving the "Whole Cloth"

It is ironic that Clifford Green more or less dismisses my current understanding of Bonhoeffer out of hand because, as he sees it, mine is "an attempt to force Bonhoeffer into a Mennonite framework."[1] Put differently, he asserts that I read Bonhoeffer through "an Anabaptist/ Mennonite hermeneutic."[2] This claim is ironic on several levels. Let me explain.

In some significant ways my journey to pacifism is similar to Bonhoeffer's.[3] My father, along with the fathers of most of my friends, was a World War II veteran. Thus, I grew up as a typical patriot. I fondly remember, e.g., selling poppies as a child, to raise money for the VFW. I would as a little boy pretend to be a soldier, imagining myself as Sergeant Saunders in the World War II TV series *Combat*, killing as many Germans as I could while I made my way along our local creek, which happened to be called the Rhine. I was raised in a non-churched family, in my case, a decidedly non-Christian family. I became a Christian in November of 1970, during

---

1. Green, "Hauerwas and Nation," 7. I say he has dismissed my views out of hand because in his most recent essay, none of my writings are mentioned in his bibliography, despite the fact that I have written more on the subject than anyone else (Green, "Bonhoeffer's Conditional Peace Ethic.")

2. Green, "Hauerwas and Nation," 7.

3. Of course, there are differences, but both of us were affected by the previous war; we were brought up to be patriots; we were from unchurched homes; we came to see pacifism as self-evident through an encounter with the living God known through Jesus Christ, with the specific words to love enemies being brought to us through the Sermon on the Mount; we later spoke publicly against war in our specific cultural contexts and taught discipleship to seminary students.

the Vietnam War. I turned eighteen in October 1971; every young man at the time knew what it meant to approach his eighteenth birthday. Between the time I became a Christian and registered for the draft I had become a conscientious objector. Why? For the same reason Bonhoeffer did. Through the Sermon on the Mount, I came to see pacifism as self-evident. And this happened through being encountered by the living God known through Jesus Christ in the context of the dynamic worship services and Christian life of a Baptist church.

I read *The Cost of Discipleship* before I read any writings by either sixteenth-century Anabaptists or twentieth-century neo-Anabaptists/Mennonites—or even knew who Mennonites were. Though I was a theological novice, this book deepened my understanding of discipleship (including a strong call to love enemies). And it may have prepared the way for my reception of the writings of John Howard Yoder when I encountered these writings several years later. It was also in the mid-1970s when I first became acquainted with broad ecumenical, inter-faith, and secular peace and social justice networks (both locally, in Louisville, Kentucky, and more broadly, through reading). At the time, in addition to theological issues, I focused on the death penalty, human rights, child abuse and neglect, feminism, creation care, and the nuclear arms race.

During the first half of the 1980s, I founded and directed an ecumenical peace and social justice organization, the Champaign-Urbana Peace Initiative. Even as I spoke about the nuclear arms race and US involvement in Latin America, I continued to wrestle with theological issues. Like Bonhoeffer, I could see that I needed to distinguish my own theological, Christ-centered pacifism not only from non-pacifist views but also from humanist and liberal pacifist views. As I worked at this, the writings of John Howard Yoder and Stanley Hauerwas (and those they pointed me toward, including Karl Barth) were very helpful.

I appreciate it that in his 2015 essay in which he critiques the views of Hauerwas and me, Clifford Green acknowledged in a footnote that I have been writing about Christians in Nazi Germany since 1980.[4] In the summer and fall of 1980 I in fact did a tremendous amount of reading on the Confessing Church (and German Christians) and about resistance within Nazi Germany on the issues of ideology, anti-Semitism, euthanasia, and war—culminating in a 110-page master's thesis and a 70-page research paper (the latter on the Confessing Church). And though I didn't write in detail on Bonhoeffer, I carefully read and outlined Bethge's biography of Bonhoeffer (because of its value for my research). In the summer of 1989,

---

4. Green, "Hauerwas and Nation," 6n20.

at Christian Theological Seminary, I wrote a 47-page essay on Bonhoeffer and pacifism, under the direction of a visiting Czech Bonhoeffer scholar, Ján Ligŭs. Green mentions the abbreviated version of this essay published in 1991 in *The Journal of Theology for Southern Africa*.[5] Sometime around the year 2000, while I was living in London, via email, Green asked me for a copy of the original essay so he could deposit it in the Bonhoeffer collection at Union Theological Seminary. My memory is that after he received it, he sent me an email echoing the words of John Godsey, who referred to my paper as "outstanding."[6] However, what Green has not acknowledged in either his review of my 2013 book or his literature review of 2015, is that my interpretation in this 1989 essay (and the abbreviated published version) is fundamentally in agreement with Green. At the time, I assumed the truth of Eberhard Bethge's claim that Bonhoeffer was never a pacifist, while anticipating Green's later writings that emphasize Bonhoeffer's strong peace ethic (and consistency in this ethic from 1931 to the end of his life). After a new round of research in 1994, under the direction of Ray Anderson at Fuller Theological Seminary, I wrote another essay on Bonhoeffer and pacifism, published in 1999.[7] Though I still accepted Bethge's view that Bonhoeffer was never a pacifist, in rereading this essay today I can sense my uneasiness. It wasn't clear to me how Bethge's claim fit with many of Bonhoeffer's writings. Nonetheless, quite understandably, I thought: who was I to challenge the authoritative views of Eberhard Bethge?

So, what am I saying? Green is apparently not remembering what he had read in my earlier work. For, if one traces my views through these essays one can see that I have not "forced" Bonhoeffer to fit my Mennonite/pacifist hermeneutic. If that were the case, then why for thirty years would I agree with Bethge in regards to Bonhoeffer not being a pacifist, while anticipating Green's views regarding the continuity of Bonhoeffer's theology and his strong peace ethic? Rather than forcing Bonhoeffer into my framework, what has actually happened is that I have been willing, through deeper and broader research, over several decades, to have my mind changed. Clarity began to emerge during my sabbatical, 2009–2010. During this year, I read Bonhoeffer more carefully than I ever had.[8] I also read several accounts

---

5. Nation, "Pacifist and Enemy of the State."

6. *International Bonhoeffer Society Newsletter, English Language Section* 42 (Oct. 1989) 5. I assume the comment was made by Godsey. It is unsigned; Godsey was the editor.

7. Nation, "Discipleship in a World Full of Nazis."

8. Also by 2010 I had gone deeper in my knowledge of Barth's theological ethics and generally had a broader and deeper knowledge of theology and ethics, including teaching seminary courses in both areas.

of the conspiracies against Hitler, including the recently published book by Sabine Dramm, *Dietrich Bonhoeffer and the Resistance*. The more I read the more I became aware of the problems in Bethge's portrayal of Bonhoeffer's shifts in ethics in tandem with his vague account of Bonhoeffer's "involvement" in the conspiracy.

It is true that I have been a pacifist since 1971. It is also true that I am an expert on the writings of John Howard Yoder and, to a lesser extent, the writings of Stanley Hauerwas. However, I have never imagined, because of that, that I was free to try to "make" Bonhoeffer into a pacifist—and precisely the sort of pacifist I wanted him to be. The trajectory of my scholarship on Bonhoeffer reflects my attempt to take Bonhoeffer's life and writings seriously within their own contexts.

So, actually, the reality is the opposite of what Green claims. It is not that I have tried to make Bonhoeffer into a neo-Anabaptist, but rather Bonhoeffer, then Yoder and Hauerwas made me into a Mennonite. Just as Bonhoeffer and Franz Hildebrandt were considering breaking completely with the established Protestant Church in Germany, so I decided by the 1990s that I should probably join a denomination that (theoretically) did not confuse being American (liberally or conservatively) with being Christian. Thus, I became a Mennonite toward the end of 1996 (shortly before I moved to London to direct the London Mennonite Centre).

Another interesting and little-known irony related to Green's claim that I am "forcing Bonhoeffer into a Mennonite framework" is that in 1937, the year *Nachfolge/Discipleship* was published, it was Bonhoeffer who needed to teach twentieth-century Mennonites about discipleship. For according to Mennonite historian Albert Keim, in recent history prior to the 1940s, "'discipleship' was not yet a Mennonite word."[9] As strange as it may seem, it was two German-speaking, non-Mennonite Christians who helped these descendants of sixteenth-century Anabaptists to recapture the New Testament language of discipleship in the twentieth century. To be honest, more influential than Bonhoeffer was the Austrian Jewish-Christian Robert Friedman. Friedman was a scholar of sixteenth-century Anabaptism. In the early 1940s he convinced Harold Bender, an influential Mennonite theologian and church leader, that discipleship was one of the key teachings of sixteenth-century Anabaptists. Friedman was so convincing that by December 28, 1943, when Bender gave his presidential address to the American Society of Church History at Columbia University on "The Anabaptist Vision," discipleship had, by Bender's account, become one of the

---

9. Keim, *Harold S. Bender*, 324. I believe he is speaking only of US Mennonites. I had previously noticed an interesting fact: Bonhoeffer and Bender were in a (large) class together on dogmatics at the University of Tübingen.

key tenets of Anabaptism.[10] Friedman had also convinced Bender that Anabaptists emphasized this teaching simply because they saw it in the Gospels, in the teachings of Jesus. By the school year 1950–1951 Bender had added a new course to the curriculum for Goshen College and its seminary—a course entitled "Christian Discipleship." An assigned text was the recently translated *The Cost of Discipleship*, by Bonhoeffer. Also, by 1950 Bender had finally found the time to revise his 1935 dissertation. It was published as *Conrad Grebel, c. 1498–1526: The Founder of the Swiss Brethren, Sometimes Called Anabaptists*.[11] In a chapter added to the published version, Bender said: "Now holy discipleship is the genuine intent of the New Testament, lying at the very center of the original Christian genius. . . . Through the centuries a divine discontent has stirred in the hearts of many Christians, who, having once experienced Jesus could never again be satisfied with the church as it was nor with the prevailing 'Christian' society. This discontent is again stirring deeply today, in Europe perhaps more than in America."[12] In a footnote placed just before these remarks in the main text he refers to Bonhoeffer's *The Cost of Discipleship* and asserts that "in some respects, though not in all, Bonhoeffer would be a good Anabaptist."[13] Between the presenting of "The Anabaptist Vision" lecture in 1943 and the initial offering of this course in 1950–1951, John Howard Yoder would be a student of Harold Bender at Goshen College (a few years before he studied with Karl Barth at the University of Basel).

The previous paragraph suggests that perhaps rather than my trying to make Bonhoeffer into an Anabaptist, Bonhoeffer, in a manner of speaking, helped twentieth-century Mennonites become "Anabaptists." That is to say, he helped Mennonites to recapture the call to discipleship through his own provocative and challenging book, *Discipleship*. One expression of this is John Howard Yoder's book *The Politics of Jesus*. However, not only did Yoder not draw consciously from Bonhoeffer, he in fact specifically distinguished his own approach from Bonhoeffer's. Michael DeJonge and Michael Mawson have pointed to differences between Yoder and Bonhoeffer, in regards to both *The Politics of Jesus* and an essay by Yoder on Bonhoeffer.[14] However,

---

10. By the following year this lecture became a published essay in *The Mennonite Quarterly Review*, as well as a booklet published by the Mennonite Church, Herald Press. Over the next few decades this essay would be quite influential among Mennonites.

11. Bender, *Conrad Grebel*.

12. Bender, *Conrad Grebel*, 210.

13. Bender, *Conrad Grebel*, 280.

14. DeJonge, *Bonhoeffer's Reception of Luther*, 149–54; and Mawson, "Politics of Jesus." The essay by Yoder to which they refer is "Christological Presuppositions of Discipleship." It would be worthwhile to enter into a critical discussion with them, but

one should not make too much of this. Yoder was brilliant. But his essay on Bonhoeffer was not one of his better efforts. It is unfortunate that the editors who published Yoder's essay for the first time in 2010 did not include a more accurate historical footnote.[15] Originally written in 1970, this essay was to be included in a book of essays on Anabaptism and Bonhoeffer. This was an incredibly busy time in Yoder's life, thus I imagine the essay was written very quickly. Among other things, before his essay was even submitted to the editor (by his assistant at the seminary in Elkhart, Indiana), Yoder left for Argentina to serve there for a year as a visiting lecturer. As it happened, not only was that book never published, but Yoder's essay was lost until 1984. A few years after Yoder rediscovered his essay, a few Bonhoeffer scholars (including Clifford Green) recommended that Yoder present his essay as a lecture at the Bonhoeffer Society meeting in 1988. Before he presented it as a lecture, Yoder slightly reframed the argument, but did not, so far as I know, do any fresh research. He had never recovered the footnotes for the essay; I found seventy-three of the seventy-five (partial) footnotes in the year 2009.

So, the previous paragraph provided a historical note on Yoder's single essay on Bonhoeffer. But it is also to suggest the following. Once I had begun doing my own substantial research on Bonhoeffer, in 1989, I barely referenced Yoder's then unpublished essay. In fact, as much as anything, I find his essay misleading. Perhaps I should add that Hauerwas has done serious research on Bonhoeffer over the years; we have on occasion discussed Bonhoeffer. But we have simply been doing our own independent work, coming to similar but not identical conclusions. By now, it may be the case that Bonhoeffer is the one area of academic theological knowledge where I can claim to know more than Hauerwas. But all of this is to say that neither Yoder nor Hauerwas has especially influenced my interpretation of Bonhoeffer.

However, I have very recently had something clarified through rereading the exchange around Bonhoeffer and pacifism between Clifford Green and Larry Rasmussen, an exchange that was occasioned by the rerelease in 2005 of Rasmussen's 1972 book, *Dietrich Bonhoeffer: Reality and Resistance*.[16] As I recently read this interesting exchange, I remembered that in

---

I will not do so here.

15. I am the one who conveyed the essay to the editors via the Yoder family. I sent along an extended memo on the history of the essay. I don't know whether the editors received it.

16. Green, "Review of *Dietrich Bonhoeffer*" (with a response from Larry Rasmussen). The book was originally published in 1972; it was rereleased in 2005, with no revisions.

my research in 1989 I was significantly influenced by Rasmussen's book, since it was the only book-length treatment of Bonhoeffer's "pacifism" as it related to involvement in the conspiracy. And because of this influence, I believe I did exactly what Green says one should not do, namely started such a study of Bonhoeffer not only with the word "pacifism," but "defining it in a more or less standard way," unfolding everything from there.[17] Again, ironies abound. For, under that influence, I still agreed at that time with Bethge and Green.

But that was 1989. By 2009, as I worked on *Bonhoeffer the Assassin?*, I began to realize the true significance of Green's claim that we distort our understanding of Bonhoeffer if we approach his understanding of peace by beginning with what Green refers to as a standard definition of pacifism, unfolding everything from there. So, I was determined not to do that in *Bonhoeffer the Assassin?* What do I mean by saying this? Green, in his 2015 review of my book, states something that is *importantly* false. He claims: "The heart of the book is about non-killing, i.e. nonviolence, i.e. pacifism as so defined."[18] Well, no, it is not. Green couldn't know this, but I specifically chose two of my former students to write the theological chapters because I knew they would, quite appropriately, make Christ *and not* pacifism central to their chapters. And that is exactly what they did in their four chapters on the Barcelona lecture, *Discipleship*, and *Ethics*. These chapters provide the heavy, weight-bearing theological framework that supports the whole of the book's argument. Green affirmed that these "are the strongest parts of the book."[19] He also affirmed two of my three biographical chapters as providing "a generally reliable overview in concise compass" of Bonhoeffer's life.[20] In retrospect, it could be that I worked too hard in the third of my biographical chapters to distance Bonhoeffer from personal involvement in attempts to kill Hitler. Or maybe I simply did not word certain sentences carefully enough. For what is, once again, ironic is that, though I gave more detail, I was basically claiming something similar to what Green himself claims, namely that "no scholar or careful readers of Bonhoeffer believe that he was an 'assassin,' i.e. personally involved in attempts to kill Hitler."[21] Well, there is one difference. Green is stating this as a factual observation: no "careful reader" of Bonhoeffer *does* believe he was personally involved in attempts to kill Hitler. I would instead say, no careful reader of Bonhoeffer *should*

---

17. Green, "Review of *Dietrich Bonhoeffer*," 159.
18. Green, "Peace Ethic or 'Pacifism,'" 201–8.
19. Green, "Peace Ethic or 'Pacifism,'" 202.
20. Green, "Peace Ethic or 'Pacifism,'" 201.
21. Green, "Peace Ethic or 'Pacifism,'" 202.

believe that he was personally involved. The difference is not trivial. For, I have observed that many serious theological academics, with more than a passing knowledge of Bonhoeffer, believe that *somehow* or *in some way* Bonhoeffer *was* involved personally in attempts to kill Hitler. So, I—unlike Green—have felt compelled to offer details regarding what Bonhoeffer did and did not do in relation to attempts to kill Hitler. Recently, I was surprised (and delighted) that my account of Bonhoeffer's "involvement" in the conspiracy largely agrees with that of Victoria Barnett in a 2019 essay, despite the fact that she too seems to dismiss my writings out of hand.[22]

Despite the fact that Green commended the authors of *Bonhoeffer the Assassin?* for six strong chapters (out of seven), "the book is deeply problematic" for him, I assume, basically because of our claim that Bonhoeffer was a pacifist.[23] Green's writings quite decidedly name Bonhoeffer's "peace ethic," *not* his pacifism. Given that it is problematic for Bonhoeffer to allow any principle to replace Jesus, then there appears to be some logic to the claim that Bonhoeffer could not be a pacifist. That is because by "the standard definition" the word *pacifism* implies a principled approach to ethics— i.e., always in principle being opposed to war (and, typically, violence in general).

In a paragraph in the concluding chapter of *Bonhoeffer the Assassin?* I offered reflections specifically on the word *pacifist* as applied to Bonhoeffer. In a few sentences there I expressed my concern (shared by Green) that Bonhoeffer's approach to ethics should be seen as defined by the centrality of Jesus Christ, not by principles. As I said there: "I've come to believe that Barth and Bonhoeffer both were right to make theological claims— especially regarding the God known in Jesus Christ—central. And then their instinct was right that if we substitute *any* abstraction for this central theological claim—even pacifism, peace, or social justice—we are likely to skew a proper understanding of our faith and call to faithfulness. And, then, in the midst of attending to this theological carefulness, we still must use specific, contextually relevant language to call for faithfulness."[24] In other words, it is vitally important that we ask *why* Bonhoeffer is against employing principles in relation to ethics. What is he against? And what is he for? He is *for* always retaining the centrality of Jesus Christ in our approach to the moral life. In terms of ethical knowledge and obedience, it is about Jesus

---

22. Barnett, "Bonhoeffer and the Conspiracy." And yet she seems to reject my 2013 book out of hand as "wishful thinking, not scholarship" (quoted in Green, "Hauerwas and Nation," 15n58), apparently because I believe that memories of informal conversations might not be accurate memories (especially when convictions differ significantly).

23. Green, "Peace Ethic or 'Pacifism,'" 202.

24. Nation et al., *Bonhoeffer the Assassin?*, 228.

and nothing more! One can easily find passages in *Discipleship* that say precisely this. But then, what is also true is that Bonhoeffer repeatedly names the particular moral entailments of the claim that God reveals himself to us centrally in the person of Jesus—including the call to love enemies and embrace nonviolence. It is this that the 2013 book and the present book attempt to make clear—through both biographical narrative and theological reflections. Bonhoeffer is *against* allowing these moral entailments to become autonomous, freeing them from their dependence on the God revealed through Jesus Christ.

However, it continues to be intriguing to me that in the main I agree with Green. We agree that there is a continuity in Bonhoeffer's approach to ethics, especially regarding peace, from 1931 to the end of his life. We also agree that theology—especially the God known through Jesus Christ—is what is central for Bonhoeffer's approach to ethics. Furthermore, we agree that Bonhoeffer very specifically was opposed to reducing ethics to principles.

So, there is irony again. Back when I agreed with Green (and Bethge) that Bonhoeffer was never a pacifist but rather held to a strong peace ethic, I did what Green said should not be done (taking cues from Larry Rasmussen): I assumed "a standard definition of pacifism" and unfolded everything from there. However, beginning around 2009 I increasingly allowed Bonhoeffer's approach to theology (and thus ethics) to shape my interpretation of him (and what he meant by pacifism). Precisely because I know the writings of John Howard Yoder, I am aware that there are numerous (theo-)logical approaches to pacifism. Not all are rooted in principles. There would be several ways to attempt to name Bonhoeffer's own approach to pacifism. One would be to compare his approach to the type that Yoder names as "The Pacifism of Proclamation," which is represented by the German theologian Hans-Werner Bartsch.[25] However, in revisiting the book *Nevertheless*, I was surprised that of the twenty-nine types of pacifism Yoder describes, it is the brief description of his own version of pacifism—"The Pacifism of the Messianic Community"—which probably comes closest to fitting Bonhoeffer.[26] But perhaps the best characterization of Bonhoeffer's pacifism would be a combination of Yoder's brief self-description and a theologically consistent Barthian approach (with Lutheran accents).[27]

---

25. Yoder, *Nevertheless*, 62–67; also see Bartsch, "Foundation and Meaning."

26. Yoder, *Nevertheless*, 133–38. Also see Davis, "Pacifism as a Vocation," in *Warcraft and Fragility of Virtue*, 27–51.

27. See Yoder, *Karl Barth and Problem of War*.

But help me understand this. Bonhoeffer said in a letter in 1936 to a long-time friend that sometime before 1933 he came to see pacifism as self-evident. In a number of public lectures, beginning in the summer of 1931, Bonhoeffer consistently said it was wrong for Christians to kill in war—suggesting in one lecture that we should not balk at using the word *pacifist* to describe what he is naming. Along with this, he became a regular advocate for conscientious objection to war. He himself went to great lengths to avoid serving as a combatant in the military (and was sentenced to prison on those grounds). He worked to secure an invitation from Gandhi to study nonviolent resistance so that he could "resist Hitler in a Christian manner." In a book on discipleship, he gives a detailed argument for why Christians should love their enemies and embrace nonviolence, even when it costs them their lives, even when it seems an extraordinary thing to do—because their Lord commands it and enables their faithfulness. He echoes these specific teachings in his unfinished manuscript on ethics (and affirms the basic thrust of *Discipleship* from prison in 1944). In every segment of his short life, beginning in 1931, those who knew him and heard him speak publicly—Jean Lasserre, who lectured with Bonhoeffer on peace in Mexico in 1931; Theodore Heckel, a German church authority who heard Bonhoeffer speak on a number of occasions and interacted with him personally during much of the 1930s; Lawrence Whitburn, one of his parishioners who became a friend, in London, 1933–1935; Joachim Kanitz and Wolf-Dieter Zimmermann, both students of Bonhoeffer in Berlin and at Finkenwalde; Herbert Jehle, who was converted to pacifism through Bonhoeffer; Franz Hildebrandt, his "closest and most like-minded friend"; Paul Lehmann in the summer of 1939; and Karl Barth, who met with Bonhoeffer at least six times between 1940 and 1942—all claim that Bonhoeffer was an advocate for pacifism. His personal, bodily "involvement" in the conspiracy against Hitler amounted to putting out "peace feelers" to seek assurances from Allied powers that they would not take advantage of Germany if top officials were removed from power. The only "evidence" that Bonhoeffer affirmed the attempts to kill Hitler are memories (of non-pacifists) of informal conversations. But I'm the one with the biased hermeneutic, because I say he was a pacifist?

Has anyone ever accused Clifford Green (among others) of forcing Bonhoeffer into a non-pacifist, mainstream Protestant framework? Or Geffrey Kelly, Burton Nelson, and Charles Marsh (among others) of attempting to force Bonhoeffer into a Niebuhrian framework?

But, of course, it is not enough to provide an account of my journey as a way of showing that I have written not out of a distorting hermeneutic, but rather have sought to allow Bonhoeffer's life and writings to determine my views. In other words, it is important to show the fruit of my hermeneutic. This book as a whole is my latest attempt to do that very thing.[28]

Irony once again seems like the right word. Why? Because, on many occasions I have pointed to Green's brief summary of Bonhoeffer's "peace ethic" as an almost perfect summary of my views (except with the replacement of the term *peace ethic* with *pacifism*):

> Bonhoeffer's Christian peace ethic is intrinsic to his whole theology. It cannot be separated from his Christology, his understanding of discipleship and the Sermon on the Mount, his way of reading the Bible, and his understanding of the gospel and of the church. It belongs to the heart of his faith. Accordingly, it cannot be reduced to a principle. It is not a discrete option on a menu of ethical "positions." It is not a separate interchangeable part that can be removed from his theology and replaced by something else called, perhaps, "realism," or even "responsibility." His peace ethic is woven throughout his theology and discipleship as a whole. It can't be removed without shredding the whole cloth.[29]

Once I shifted from being captive to Rasmussen's "standard" way of talking about pacifism, I have sought to reflect in my writing on Bonhoeffer exactly what Green suggests in this paragraph.[30] Peace—what Bonhoeffer referred to as pacifism—is fundamentally for Bonhoeffer a theological matter. It truly flows from his commitment to the centrality of Jesus, his understanding of discipleship, the church, and the Scriptures. All of these are, as Green suggests, inseparably woven together. Then, what I finally allowed myself to accept is that the problem was with the hermeneutical stranglehold that Eberhard Bethge had on all of our interpretations of Bonhoeffer. It begins with his denial of Bonhoeffer's straightforward claim that he had come to see pacifism as self-evident. But then it continues with Bethge's seeing major discontinuities in Bonhoeffer's ethical thought—so that by 1940 he has become a (Niebuhrian-type) realist. According to Bethge, Bonhoeffer no longer believes what he said in *Discipleship* three years earlier; the time to discuss violence and nonviolence was over. What this means, then, is that

---

28. I should also mention that Jens Zimmermann's essay "Bonhoeffer and Non-Violence" is a thoughtful engagement with my writings. I believe that with a combination of the book as a whole, including this essay, I have responded to most, if not all, of his questions.

29. Green, "Pacifism and Tyrannicide," 45. I was originally planning to quote this passage in the conclusion of *Bonhoeffer the Assassin?* I should have.

30. Yoder's book *Nevertheless* shows quite clearly that there is no one "standard" way to define pacifism theologically.

some biographers, standing on the shoulders of Bethge, simply straightforwardly say, like Charles Marsh, that he was a Niebuhrian. Or, like the son of a Confessing Church leader Ferdinand Schliengensiepen that Bonhoeffer basically returned to the beliefs he articulated in 1929 in Barcelona: "God will sanctify murder."

I would never claim that Bethge has shredded the whole cloth, but he has certainly done it significant damage. I want to preserve the whole (theological) cloth. We need it!

Appendix 2

"Christianity Stands or Falls with Its Revolutionary Protest against Violence"[1]

How Could Dietrich Bonhoeffer, a Lutheran, Make Such a Claim?[2]

Mark Thiessen Nation
and Stanley Hauerwas

Abstract

Like many theologians, we have been drawn to the life and writings of Dietrich Bonhoeffer for most of our lives. He was not only a fascinating individual from an interesting family, but he also lived his short life in the midst of one of the most destructive regimes in modern history. The richness of his theological writings takes on an even deeper resonance because of the intense challenges he faced in Nazi Germany; and he confronted them with great courage and integrity. Both of us have written previously on Bonhoeffer. Contrary to accusations, especially from Michael DeJonge, neither

---

1. Bonhoeffer, DBWE 13, 402.

2. This essay was originally written as a response to Michael P. DeJonge, "Bonhoeffer's Non-Commitment to Nonviolence." His essay was later expanded as "Anabaptists and Peace," in DeJonge, *Bonhoeffer's Reception of Luther.*

of us has ever imagined that he had the freedom to make Bonhoeffer into an Anabaptist. Rather, both of us have attempted to be fair to the sources. In fact, both of us have had our minds changed regarding Bonhoeffer and peace. Within the last ten years it is precisely a broader and more careful reading of Bonhoeffer's collected writings, combined with a more thorough examination of the resistance movement, that has led to our present conclusions. That is, we have come more fully to accept Bonhoeffer's own assessment in prison that there was considerable continuity in his life and thought, especially after his time in New York City at the beginning of the 1930s. And in addition, we see his statement from prison that he continued to stand by what he had written in *Discipleship* as an implicit reaffirmation that he continued to see the call to nonviolence and love of enemies—what he termed *pacifism*—as self-evident. Coming to these conclusions we fully acknowledge the following. First, for Bonhoeffer, these are centrally theological matters. More specifically, whatever he means by "pacifism" must be understood within the context of his whole theology, which must include an awareness that he was a Lutheran theologian deeply influenced by Karl Barth. Second, however we name his theological identity, his convictions regarding peace set him apart from virtually all of his fellow German theologians and pastors. Thus, we should not imagine we have captured who he was by simply being reminded that he was a Lutheran theologian. In this essay we simply try to name honestly the trajectory of his life and thought related to peace. There is much else yet to be discussed.

A Consistent Trajectory Initiated by a Transformation

This essay will do what authors like Michael DeJonge have not done: show the consistent trajectory in Bonhoeffer's life and thought regarding peace, a trajectory that is basically consistent from 1931 to the end of his life.[3] We will name this trajectory in three ways. We will show, first, that Bonhoeffer's opposition to violence, rooted in his commitment to love enemies and informed by his deep engagement with the Sermon on the Mount, is consistent from 1931 to 1945. Second, this conviction was specifically expressed through his advocacy for and—when it became relevant—embodiment of conscientious objection from 1932 forward. And third, most central—to himself and to us—is the way in which his set of moral commitments was rooted in his understanding of the command and enabling power of God

---

3. Bonhoeffer himself points to the consistency in his life and thought in 1944 (DBWE, 8, 352–53, 358). Though there will be some documentation of the argument offered throughout this essay, for fuller documentation the interested reader should consult Nation et al., *Bonhoeffer the Assassin?*, and the present book.

embodied in the person and work of Jesus Christ and expressed through the visibility of the church. Along the way, we will reflect briefly on the challenges raised about this trajectory. We will end by offering reflections on the claim that we have attempted, anachronistically, to make Bonhoeffer into a Yoderian Anabaptist rather than read him in his own context as a Lutheran, influenced by Barth.

Fortunately for us, Bonhoeffer names the "transformation" that happened in his life that initiated his straight trajectory. In a letter to his friend, Elizabeth Zinn, on January 27, 1936, he speaks of the "great liberation" that happened in his life sometime before 1933. He says that he experienced a new kind of freedom through "the Bible, but especially the Sermon on the Mount." Among other things that changed for him was a deep conviction "that everything depended on the renewal of the church and of the pastoral station." Additionally, he says that "Christian pacifism," which only recently he had argued against with passion, now seemed "utterly self-evident."[4] We acknowledge Bonhoeffer did not often use the word *pacifist*, but we think that if anything that actually strengthens our case.[5] It does so because it makes clear that from the beginning he did not think pacifism was a position one assumed that required further theological justification. Rather, from the time he first became aware that he was a pacifist he discovered he was so because of Jesus Christ; his pacifism and his christological convictions were inseparable.

Theological Groundwork

In fact, once we notice his transformation we can also see how his two graduate theses paved the way for his transformed life and thought. It is as if he was developing the necessary theological groundwork for him to respond faithfully to Nazism and the then almost inevitable war.

We see this already in his doctoral thesis, *Sanctorum Communio*, finished in July 1927. We notice the creative way Bonhoeffer draws from Troeltsch, armed with Barthian sensibilities. Troeltsch's understanding of the relationship between ecclesiology and insights about the "world" helped Bonhoeffer avoid the temptation to abstract an ethic from theology. Rather, in his own way Bonhoeffer reflected Troeltsch's fundamental insight about how the church was situated in the world; this situatedness shaped his convictions in a manner that eventually made his commitment to costly

---

4. Bonhoeffer, DBWE 14, 134.

5. See Nation's reflections on the use of the term *pacifist* in Nation et al., *Bonhoeffer the Assassin?*, 228–30.

discipleship almost inevitable. For already here we see Bonhoeffer saying, "Our present church is 'bourgeois.' The best proof remains ... that the proletariat has turned its back on the church, while the bourgeois (civil servant, skilled worker, merchant) stayed.... Sermons are thus aimed at people who live relatively securely and relatively stable morally."[6] So, even in this early work we see Bonhoeffer trying to imagine a church that will form people's lives in ways that matter decisively for the way they live in the world. Put differently, in *Sanctorum Communio* we observe Bonhoeffer's effort to articulate the social dimensions of the church in a way that has theological integrity—a way that is captive not to normal bourgeois sensibilities but to the word of God that frees the church to be faithful in its life together and in its witness to the larger world.

In retrospect we think it is clear that his thesis paved the way for Bonhoeffer to see the great significance of the church. It should not be surprising that the church he discovered in New York City looked like the church of *Sanctorum Communio*, made up of people who knew they were in tension with the world. His later move to create the sort of "new monastic" community that existed at Finkenwalde also stands in continuity with his early insights.

Bonhoeffer's commitment to nonviolence and his emphasis on the visibility of the church are necessary correlatives. The significance of those connections is manifest in the two sections devoted to the visible church-community in *Discipleship* and are given expression through his taking the time to write *Life Together*, reflecting on what he had learned from his communal experiment at the seminary. In other words, he was envisioning the church as *polis*.[7]

Sanctorum Communio was Bonhoeffer's first effort to reflect his indebtedness to the theology of Karl Barth, which he had initially encountered in 1925. In 1930, when Bonhoeffer wrote his habilitation thesis, *Act and Being*, Barth's theology is again in focus, though once again Bonhoeffer goes beyond Barth. Drawing on an account of being as activity, Bonhoeffer shows how no "ethic" can be separated from theology because the command of God is always to be found in the flesh of this person called Jesus Christ. This way of understanding the Word of God made flesh allowed Bonhoeffer, at the beginning of the 1930s, to embrace Barth's aversion to a principled approach to ethics while beginning to name both a continuity in the revelation of God to us *and* a continuity in the body of Christ (where Christ is truly present). All of this served as preparation for the life-changing experiences

---

6. Bonhoeffer, DBWE 1, 273.
7. Bonhoeffer, DBWE 4, 261–2.

Bonhoeffer would have in America. But this would be given full, clear theological expression only after his year in New York and after several years of living with the Sermon on the Mount.

"We Should Not Balk Here at Using the Word 'Pacifism'"

Since one of the implications of his "transformation" was that pacifism was seen by him as "self-evident" then we are given chronological parameters for knowing when this happened. For as recently as 1929 Bonhoeffer's views on war were similar to those of most Germans of his time. In February of that year, in a lecture on ethics in Barcelona, Spain, Bonhoeffer gave a rationale for killing in war: "I will defend my brother, my mother, my people, and yet I know that I can do so only by spilling blood; but love for my people will sanctify murder, will sanctify war."[8] Eberhard Bethge says Bonhoeffer would never speak in these terms again. In fact, he would speak in quite different terms after his time in New York City, 1930–1931.

At least two factors seem formative for Bonhoeffer's "grand liberation" that began during this time. First, he became friends with the pacifist French Reformed pastor Jean Lasserre, a fellow international student at Union Seminary. Second, he became actively involved in Abyssinian Baptist Church, a dynamic African American congregation. What followed from this? According to Jean Lasserre, Bonhoeffer advocated for pacifism publicly in lectures in Mexico in the summer of 1931.[9] Our first textual record of such advocacy is from 1932.[10] There is, for instance, his lecture at the ecumenical Youth Peace Conference in Czechoslovakia on July 26, 1932, "On the Theological Foundation of the Work of the World Alliance." "The broken character of the order of peace," says Bonhoeffer, "is expressed in the fact that the peace demanded by God has two boundaries: first, the truth; second, justice [*Recht*]. A community of peace can exist only when it does not rest on *a lie* or on *injustice*. Wherever a community of peace endangers or suffocates truth and justice, the community of peace must be broken and the battle must be declared."[11] These statements show that the young Bonhoeffer is not naïvely advocating for peace. Nor is he willing to live comfortably with a false peace that simply serves as a cover for lies protecting

---

8. Bonhoeffer, DBWE 10, 372. Chapter 4 of *Bonhoeffer the Assassin?* is devoted to this lecture. It is discussed briefly within ch. 3 of the present book.

9. Nation et al., *Bonhoeffer the Assassin?*, 22n17. Of course the time in New York City affected Bonhoeffer in various ways. Here, however, we are emphasizing his advocacy for pacifism.

10. The first instances are from Feb. 1932 (Bonhoeffer, DBWE 11, 246–57; 419–33).

11. Bonhoeffer, DBWE 11, 365; emphases his.

injustices. Nevertheless, he also doesn't want to be misunderstood as subtly endorsing violence, when "necessary." Bonhoeffer continues:

> Today, however, there is a widespread and extremely dangerous error that says that in the *justification of struggle* there is already a justification for war, that this contains the *fundamental Yes to war*. The right to wage war can be derived from the right to struggle no more than the right to inflict torture can be derived from the necessity of legal process in human society. . . . Our contemporary war does not fall under the concept of battle because it means certain *self-destruction of both warring sides. For that reason today it is utterly impossible to characterize it* as an order of preservation toward revelation, simply because it is absolutely destructive. . . . Today's war destroys soul and body. Because there is no way for us to understand war as God's order of preservation and therefore as God's commandment, and because war needs to be idealized and idolatrized in order to live, today's war, the next war, must be *condemned* by the church. . . . We must face the next war with all the power of resistance, rejection, condemnation. . . . We should not balk here at using the word 'pacifism.' Just as certainly we submit the ultimate *pacem facere* to God, we too must *pacem facere* to overcome war.[12]

Before the year was out Bonhoeffer would give two similar lectures at other ecumenical conferences. Moreover, he would continue to be a strong advocate for what he—not we—referred to as pacifism over the next several years of his involvement in the ecumenical movement. It is true that some of Bonhoeffer's rhetoric in these lectures is contextual and thus seems context dependent. And yet it also seems to go beyond that—condemning not just today's war, but *the next war* as well.[13] But it is Bonhoeffer's book *Discipleship* that provides the fullest theological framework for understanding his call to love enemies and embrace nonviolence while also challenging any claim that Bonhoeffer consistently contextualized his critique of violence.

It challenges this claim partly because it is an expression of Bonhoeffer's desire to give more permanent form to his convictions expressed through his lectures on discipleship at the Finkenwalde seminary. In August 1937, shortly before the seminary was forcibly closed by the Gestapo, Bonhoeffer submitted the manuscript of these lectures to a book publisher. A book by

---

12. Bonhoeffer, DBWE 11, 366–67; emphases his.

13. Contrary to what DeJonge claims, there are brief comments on the contextual nature of this early lecture by Bonhoeffer in *Bonhoeffer the Assassin?*, 30–33; the subject is treated more fully in chs. 4 and 5 of the book. (Also, now see the relevant sections of ch. 3 of the present book.)

definition is not a merely "contextual" document. Bonhoeffer knew it would speak of the gospel's claim on our lives in various contexts and in ongoing ways. Moreover, there is no evidence he thought you could make conflicting claims at different times and places.

To deal adequately with the argument of *Discipleship* would require more space than we have here. In fact, ironically, it is DeJonge's book, *Bonhoeffer's Theological Formation*, that helped galvanize our argument regarding *Discipleship* in our chapter on it in *Bonhoeffer the Assassin?*.[14] The center of the unleashed power of this sermonic book is the act and being of God becoming one in the Person of Jesus Christ, the Redeemer and Lord who both saves and commands. This Word of God made flesh is the same yesterday, today, and forever. Thus, this Lord both issues commands that seem extraordinary and empowers us to live this extraordinary life. Toward the end of over ten pages of reflections on love of enemies, Bonhoeffer says:

> It is the great mistake of a false Protestant ethic to assume that loving Christ can be the same as loving one's native country, or friendship or profession, that the better righteousness and *justitia civilis* are the same. Jesus does not talk that way. What is Christian depends on the "extraordinary." That is why Christians cannot conform to the world, because their concern is the περισσόν. What does the περισσόν, the extraordinary, consist of? It is the existence of those blessed in the Beatitudes, the life of the disciples. It is the shining light, the city on the hill. It is the way of self-denial, perfect love, perfect purity, perfect truthfulness, perfect nonviolence. Here is undivided love for one's enemies, loving those who love no one and whom no one loves. . . . It is the love of Jesus Christ himself, who goes to the cross in suffering and obedience. It is the cross. What is unique in Christianity is the cross, which allows Christians to step beyond the world in order to receive victory over the world. The *passio* in the love of the crucified one—that is the "extraordinary" mark of Christian existence.[15]

In the spring of 1935, while serving as a pastor in London, Bonhoeffer preached sermons that were moving toward the teaching on discipleship he would do in the Finkenwalde seminary. His sermons on the Sermon on the Mount have been lost. But in other sermons he also addressed violence. For instance, in a sermon on 2 Corinthians he makes the extraordinary claim that, "Christianity stands or falls with its revolutionary protest against

---

14. Nation et al., *Bonhoeffer the Assassin?*, 125–60.
15. Bonhoeffer, DBWE 4, 144–45.

violence."[16] Lawrence B. Whitburn, one of his congregants in London, said that Bonhoeffer's opinion in favor of pacifism "was so marked and clear in his mind" that a discussion of the subject "soon developed into an argument"—though not in such a way that it damaged their friendship.[17] This is consistent with the fact that by the beginning of 1935 there was apparently something about Dietrich's understanding of faith and the Christian community that led his brother, Karl-Friedrich, to perceive him as a fanatic.[18] Dietrich responded to his brother by speaking of how much the Sermon on the Mount had transformed him. One of the inner circle of his first cohort of students at the Finkenwalde seminary, Joachim Kanitz, comments that "it became clear to us on the basis of this Bible study [of the Sermon on the Mount, given by Bonhoeffer] that it is not possible for Christians to justify killing or to justify war."[19]

Some scholars would admit that Bonhoeffer was clear on nonviolence between 1932 and 1938 (especially 1935–1937). For it is during this time that the textual evidence is clearest. In addition to *Discipleship* there is the straightforward claim by Bonhoeffer himself, in January 1936, that he had come to see pacifism as "utterly self-evident." It is intriguing that the most significant "counter-evidence," in terms of texts, comes from this time period. But it also comes in *certain forms*: catechetical instructions and homiletical exercises. So, in a catechetical exercise Bonhoeffer suggests that one might say: "*How are Christians to act in war?* There is *no* revealed commandment of God here. The church can never give its blessing to war and weapons. The Christian can never participate in unjust wars. If the Christian takes up arms, he must daily ask God for forgiveness for this sin and pray for peace."[20] Joachim Kanitz (later a soldier) heard him give this lecture. And yet he still tells us that Bonhoeffer taught them pacifism. It is not hard for many of us pacifists to imagine that Bonhoeffer, here and in relation to Remembrance Day, was giving advice relevant to those who did not embrace his pacifism. What instructions could he give for them, in their future pastorates, when most of them will not have been convinced to be pacifist?[21]

For those who acknowledge that Bonhoeffer seemed to be pacifist through 1938, the claim is often made that he had departed from his earlier

16. Bonhoeffer, DBWE 13, 402.
17. Whitburn, "Bonhoeffer without His Cassock," 80.
18. Bonhoeffer, DBWE 13, 284–85.
19. Nation et al., *Bonhoeffer the Assassin?*, 10.
20. DeJonge, "Bonhoeffer's Non-Commitment to Nonviolence," 381.
21. Now see the more detailed discussion in ch. 3 of the present book.

commitment to nonviolence by 1939 or 1940 (or that he recontextualized his peace ethic). And here there are three types of evidence: texts, memories of things Bonhoeffer said in private conversations, and his "involvements in the conspiracy."

First, we will look briefly at texts. Early in this period, in the winter of 1940, Bonhoeffer seemed delighted to continue to share his book *Discipleship* with others.[22] But the most significant textual evidence comes from the working manuscripts of his book on ethics, written between 1940 and 1943. Without question there are complicated issues involved in these unfinished, unpolished creative efforts to reframe ethics. However, what we continually find remarkable is that, in what are thought to be the first four chapters of this work, one sees substantial echoes of what we have already noted— the centrality of Jesus Christ who, among other things, calls us to love our enemies.[23] The passages on responsibility and guilt in the *Ethics* are often thought to reflect Bonhoeffer's recognition of the necessity of violence, but Bonhoeffer was a person of keen insight who could just as well recognize that a commitment to nonviolence would not free one so committed from responsibilities or guilt.[24]

Bonhoeffer very specifically criticizes any "realistic" approach to matters like force that are not centered in the reality known in Jesus Christ.[25] Here again, as in *Discipleship*, the Sermon on the Mount has a significant role in his argument. For instance, he says, "The Sermon on the Mount is either valid as the word of God's world-reconciling love everywhere and at all times, or it is not really relevant for us at all."[26] Furthermore, he says, "The Sermon on the Mount as the proclamation of the incarnate love of God calls people to love one another, and thus to reject everything that hinders fulfilling this task—in short, it calls them to self-denial. In renouncing one's own happiness, one's own rights, one's own righteousness, one's own dignity, in renouncing violence and success, in renouncing one's own life, a person is prepared to love the neighbor."[27] Thus Bonhoeffer in 1942.

---

22. Bonhoeffer, DBWE 16, 102.

23. For a detailed discussion, see the present book, ch. 5.

24. Again, see ch. 5 of the present book. But also see Nation et al., *Bonhoeffer the Assassin?*, chs. 6 and 7.

25. Nation, "Blanket License," 147–49; also see ch. 5 in the present book.

26. Nation, "Blanket License," 149.

27. Bonhoeffer, DBWE 6, 242. (It is really rather surprising that DeJonge, to counter such claims, would highlight passages from Bonhoeffer's *Ethics* that are from the essay "Natural Life" (DeJonge, "Bonhoeffer's Non-Commitment to Nonviolence," 381–82). Assuming Bonhoeffer is still deeply influenced by Barth, then this essay must be seen in light of the first four chapters, which seem much more Barthian (in Bonhoeffer's own

About two years later, May 1944, in one of his very few somewhat sermonic writings from prison, "Thoughts on the Day of Baptism of Dietrich Wilhelm Rüdiger Bethge," Bonhoeffer offered the following reflections. He mentions that even as his namesake is being baptized,

> We too are being thrown back all the way to the beginnings of our understanding. What reconciliation and redemption mean, rebirth and Holy Spirit, love for one's enemies, cross and resurrection, what it means to live in Christ and follow Christ; all that is so difficult and remote that we hardly dare speak of it anymore. In these words and actions handed down to us, we sense something totally new and revolutionary, but we cannot yet grasp it and express it. This is our own fault. Our church has been fighting during these years only for its self-preservation, as if that were an end in itself. It has become incapable of bringing the word of reconciliation and redemption to humankind and to the world. . . . [The church needs] conversion and purification. It is not for us to predict the day—but the day will come—when people will once more be called to speak the word of God in such a way that the world is changed and renewed. It will be in a new language, perhaps quite nonreligious language, but liberating and redeeming like Jesus' language, so that people will be alarmed and yet overcome by its power—the language of a new righteousness and truth, a language proclaiming that God makes peace with humankind and that God's kingdom is drawing near.[28]

Around the same time, in a letter to Eberhard Bethge in 1944, Bonhoeffer says that he still stood by what he wrote in *Discipleship*.[29]

"For Christians, Any Military Service Is Forbidden"

It will hardly do for DeJonge to dismiss the historical argument presented in *Bonhoeffer the Assassin?* by simply saying, in a footnote, that we are promoting "wishful thinking."[30] The book has clarified some factual matters that *need* clarifying. For instance, regarding Bonhoeffer's promotion of conscientious objection. Bonhoeffer specifically advocated for conscientious objection to war beginning at least as early as December 1932. In a

---

unique way).

28. Bonhoeffer, DBWE 8, 389–90.

29. Bonhoeffer, DBWE 8, 486. If Bonhoeffer had come to see his previous affirmation of pacifism as naïve, he could easily have said so here.

30. DeJonge, "Bonhoeffer's Non-Commitment to Nonviolence," 380.

lecture on "Christ and Peace" to the German Student Christian Movement, Bonhoeffer said that "the command, 'you shall not kill,' the word that says 'Love your enemies,' is given to us simply to be obeyed. For Christians, any military service, except in the ambulance corps, and any preparation for war is forbidden."[31] Over the next five years Bonhoeffer would be actively involved in ecumenical gatherings throughout Europe. He consistently kept the issue of conscientious objection before these gatherings, often being a formal advocate, sometimes simply making sure it was an agenda item that did not get lost. In the spring of 1935, during the time he was starting the seminary in Germany, the military draft was reintroduced. He encouraged his students to seriously consider conscientious objection. In addition to his own encouragement, he brought two other conscientious objectors to speak at Finkenwalde. Eberhard Bethge commented on how unusual this was. It was basically unheard of from a Lutheran theologian![32]

In 1939 when Bonhoeffer knew he would be drafted into the military, after consultation with friends, he decided to return to the US, mostly to avoid conscription. He then returned to Germany after a little less than a month in New York City. After returning he first sought to become a military chaplain. His application was denied. After that happened, it appears that his brother-in-law Hans von Donahnyi told him that if he went to work for the Abwehr, the military intelligence agency, he could receive what was referred to as a *uk* status, which would classify him as ineligible to be drafted for military service because his work with the Abwehr was essential for the welfare of Germany. This way he did not have to swear an oath of allegiance to Hitler or kill on the front lines in the war. Thus, for this reason he went to work for the Abwehr. His status was apparently repeatedly under threat during his time in the agency, from October 1940 to early March 1943; for his bosses submitted repeated requests on his behalf that he continue to receive a *uk* status. Both Eberhard Bethge and Sabine Dramm, in her book *Dietrich Bonhoeffer and the Resistance*, note this. We now know that at both his trial and his brother-in-law's trial, a key issue for the judge was that Bonhoeffer was effectively living as a conscientious objector, which after 1939 was a capital offense. For the judge suspected that his work was not essential to the welfare of Germany and thus his "work" with the Abwehr was a ruse to keep him "entirely, partially, or temporarily from fulfillment of military service, [which] subverts military power."[33]

---

31. Bonhoeffer, DBWE 12, 260.
32. Bethge, "Dietrich Bonhoeffers Weg," 118–20.
33. Bonhoeffer, DBWE 16, 444.

Bonhoeffer "the Assassin"?

Then there is the matter of Bonhoeffer's involvement in the conspiracy. We can't tell you the number of people we have known over the years who believed it was simply a "fact" that Bonhoeffer was arrested on April 5, 1943, *because* he was substantially involved in one of the two efforts to kill Hitler in March of the same year; the proximity suggests the connection. But that is *absolutely* not true. How do we know? Because *no one* was arrested in connection with these attempts; the authorities did not discover them.[34] So, why was he arrested? Because he was involved in an effort to save the lives of fourteen Jews. It is also typically assumed that Bonhoeffer was imprisoned because of "involvement" in efforts to kill Hitler. Again, not true. Now that we have a summary of the court proceedings we can see that what convinced the judge to imprison Bonhoeffer was that he was avoiding military service and helping others to avoid such service. Furthermore, it is assumed that Bonhoeffer's execution confirms that he *must* have been involved in attempts to kill Hitler. Only those ignorant of the Nazi court system would imagine that. Thousands of people were executed after the attempt on Hitler's life in July 1944 (more than a year after Bonhoeffer was arrested). The vast majority were not involved in efforts to kill Hitler. Peter Hoffman, perhaps the foremost expert in the world on the conspiracies against Hitler, has referred to Bonhoeffer's work for the Abwehr, quite appropriately, as putting out peace feelers. "[Bonhoeffer] urged his friends . . . to use their influence to ensure that the Allies would call a halt to military operations during the anticipated coup in Germany."[35] Since 1936—long before anyone imagines that Bonhoeffer was involved in any efforts to kill Hitler—Bonhoeffer had been labeled "a pacifist and enemy of the state."[36] That designation was sufficient, so far as the Nazi justice system was concerned, to execute him.

Finally, there are memories that in informal conversations Bonhoeffer affirmed the killing of Hitler—or even said he was willing to kill Hitler himself. In *Bonhoeffer the Assassin?* Nation claims that we should assign more weight to texts and established facts than to memories derived from informal conversations. In saying this he is taking cues from Eberhard Bethge himself. For Bethge questions the accuracy of Bishop George Bell's memory that Bonhoeffer had referred to Hitler as the antichrist, even though Bell is relying on a diary he kept. Bethge critically reflects on this supposed memory

---

34. It should be added that it's highly unlikely that he had anything to do with either of these two attempts on Hitler's life, period (Nation et al., *Bonhoeffer the Assassin?*, 71–97 and ch. 1 of the present book).

35. Cited in Nation et al., *Bonhoeffer the Assassin?*, 75.

36. Cited in Nation et al., *Bonhoeffer the Assassin?*, 17.

by saying that Bonhoeffer did not believe that Hitler was the antichrist. And he says we can test this claim by examining texts written by Bonhoeffer. However, Bethge does concede, "If that rather crude theological expression could really have encouraged his friends, Bonhoeffer perhaps would have used it verbally."[37] Perhaps Bethge knew what anyone knows who has ever interviewed people about memories of informal conversations. The contexts for conversations, nature of relationship, tones of voice, facial expressions—not to mention the biases of those who are recounting memories—are some components of what are necessary for truly understanding what was originally meant in informal conversations as reported by others. Besides that, most of us are not as careful in informal conversations. Especially if we are among friends, reflecting candidly about quite painful and difficult matters, we might honestly vent emotions, overstate the case, or use terms we would never use in more carefully prepared comments, for various reasons. So, likewise, in informal conversations with friends who were also opposed to the extreme nationalism and abuses of the Hitler regime, Bonhoeffer could easily have said things in support of his friends in ways that were imprecise or simply vented his emotions, which might not be truly expressive of his own settled convictions.[38] He had no idea his words would be quoted or paraphrased many years later.

However, in addition to assigning greater weight to formal writings and established facts, we also have to wrestle with conflicting memories. Paul Lehmann recalls a conversation he had with Bonhoeffer just before he left the US in July of 1939 to return to Germany. They had both recently read a book on the horrendous situation in Germany. Lehmann tells Bonhoeffer that this book had caused him to abandon his pacifism, whereas Bonhoeffer said that it had only confirmed *his* commitment to pacifism.[39] Emmi Bonhoeffer, one of Dietrich's sisters-in-law, recounts a conversation she had with Dietrich sometime after he had returned to Germany in 1939: "How is that with you Christians?" she asks. "You will not kill but that another one does it, you agree and are glad about it. Why is that?" Dietrich responds:

---

37. Bethge, *Dietrich Bonhoeffer*, 723.

38. Mark has taught a course with Carl Stauffer, assistant professor of justice and development studies, a long-time pacifist who lived in Zimbabwe and worked in several African countries in the region. Stauffer says that he can easily imagine having been misunderstood by those who didn't know his own convictions regarding nonviolence because of venting among friends on occasions, e.g., about Robert Mugabe and his horrible acts as president of Zimbabwe. I have in my personal files his own reflections on this, with the title taken from a question posed by one of his friends: "Is it right for me to be praying for the death of my president?"

39. Nation, *Bonhoeffer the Assassin?*, 79.

"One should not be glad. But I understand what you mean."[40] Bonhoeffer met with Karl Barth on at least six occasions between 1940 and 1942. Barth was a trusted theological ally; Bethge says Bonhoeffer told him "the whole truth."[41] A decade later Barth summarized his twin perceptions drawn from their conversations. On the one hand, "the Lutheran theologian Dietrich Bonhoeffer belonged to these circles [of those willing to kill Hitler]." On the other, "he was really a pacifist on the basis of his understanding of the Gospel."[42] Franz Hildebrandt, whom Bethge referred to as Bonhoeffer's "best and most like-minded friend," after he was told in 1945 that Bonhoeffer was involved in efforts to kill Hitler, said that he was sure he was not involved."[43]

Bonhoeffer the Anabaptist?

When Michael DeJonge claims that we are attempting to make Bonhoeffer into a Yoderian pacifist or an Anabaptist we're reminded of the criterion of dissimilarity in the approach to the study of the Gospels. We *know* Jesus said it if a teaching is dissimilar to the Judaism from which he came or the early church which followed him—as if he was not formed by Judaism or did not decisively shape his followers? The reality is that Yoder studied with Barth, and Hauerwas and Nation are deeply influenced by Barth. Though he came to a somewhat different conclusion, Barth saw the same thing in the New Testament that Bonhoeffer did: "According to the sense of the New Testament we cannot be pacifists in principle, only in practice. But we have to consider very closely whether, if we are called to discipleship, we can avoid being practical pacifists, or fail to be so."[44] Of course it is also the case that Yoder and, perhaps even more, Hauerwas and Nation have been significantly influenced by Bonhoeffer.

In an earlier essay in which DeJonge criticized us, he said, "I do not mean to suggest that seeing his peace statements in the Lutheran tradition tells us everything we need to know about Bonhoeffer's thoughts on peace, violence and war."[45] Understatement is the first word that comes to mind after reading this sentence. Or put differently, Karl Barth famously said

---

40. Emmi Bonhoeffer, interview, in Boehlke, *Dietrich Bonhoeffer*, beginning at approximately 1:03:00.
41. Bethge, *Dietrich Bonhoeffer*, 727.
42. Barth, *Doctrine of Creation* (CD III/4), 449.
43. Green, "Pacifism and Tyrannicide," 46.
44. Barth, *Doctrine of Reconciliation* (CD IV/2), 550.
45. DeJonge, "How to Read Bonhoeffer's Peace Statements," 163.

that Bonhoeffer's book *Sanctorum Communio* was "a theological miracle."[46] Perhaps similar words would be appropriate for *Discipleship*. In its time it offered a unique—and it should be said *radical*, almost inexplicable—appropriation of Luther and Barth through offering a fresh reading of Scripture. Barth was willing, later, to give *Discipleship* his wholehearted endorsement by basically paraphrasing it in the fourth volume of his *Church Dogmatics* when he offered his own account of discipleship. Two contemporary Lutherans, Marva Dawn and Bernd Wannenwetsch, along with an assist from Frederick Dale Bruner, have tentatively convinced us that there are radical streams within Luther's own writings that can give rise to a book like *Discipleship*. But it should go without saying that it was anything but common within Nazi Germany! It is also worth noting that Yoder's *The Politics of Jesus* is, so far as we know, more like *Discipleship* than any other book written between 1937 and 1972 (not least because Yoder had a deep appreciation of Bonhoeffer's book).[47] Eberhard Bethge, in 1937, said Franz Hildebrandt, a Jewish-Christian, was Bonhoeffer's "best-informed and most like-minded friend." Was Hildebrandt still Bonhoeffer's most "like-minded" friend when he, in 1984, said that if there was one book every pastor should read it was *The Politics of Jesus*?[48] And was this Methodist confusing himself with an Anabaptist? Or was he simply calling us to the same discipleship found in the New Testament that his friend Dietrich was calling us to?

But let us end our reflections by slightly modifying what Franz Hildebrandt said about pacifism, in his introduction to John Howard Yoder's 1959 essay "Peace without Eschatology":

> What is commonly said [about Bonhoeffer the conspirator] . . . would "be just as possible, if Christ had never become incarnate, died, ascended to heaven, and sent His Spirit." . . . In a theological and ecclesiastical climate . . . where any literal application of the Gospel is suspect of "Schwärmertum" and where only the ex-pacifist is respectable, it will take some time and not a little humility to admit, especially for those trained in the school of the great Reformers, that at this point in question the Mennonite minority has been, and still is right: "not because it

---

46. Godsey, *Theology of Dietrich Bonhoeffer*, 21.

47. Nation: But let me also say very clearly: every time I read *Discipleship* afresh—perhaps especially when I am discussing it with students—I can *feel* (I think that's the right word) the substantial difference between Bonhoeffer's Lutheran take on the New Testament and Yoder's Mennonite take (and in some ways I favor the former).

48. Nation: I heard Hildebrandt make this extemporaneous statement during his lecture at the Fiftieth Anniversary of the Barmen Confession Conference, held in Seattle, WA, in April 1984.

(nonresistance) works, but because it anticipates the triumph of the Lamb that was slain."[49]

---

49. Cited in Nation et al, *Bonhoeffer the Assassin?*, 232. Hildebrandt's original statement referred to "what is commonly said from pulpits about peace."

Appendix 3

Jesus, Bonhoeffer, and Christoform Hermeneutics

Scot McKnight

How you read the Bible will determine your position on just war theory or pacifism just as it will determine where you stand with respect to international terrorism.[1] Maybe "determine" will cause some to resist a bit—nonviolently, of course—so I will say one's hermeneutic for reading the Bible will "at least shape" one's view of how Christians engage in international wars. One can complicate such a Bible reading focus, but only slightly, by approaching it from the angle of the "old" vs. "new" vs. "apocalyptic" Paul perspectives. An "old" or "covenant theology" perspective fits quite comfortably with the Lutheran and Reformed approaches to the Christian and the law, with its discussions about the three uses of the law. A "new" perspective will find a more salvation-historical dynamic, if not also a fair amount of discontinuity, more permissible. The apocalyptic Paul folk often enough see such a disruption in history that salvation-history becomes a worrisome hermeneutic that gives way to an apocalyptic reading. Namely, if all is new in Christ, *even the Old Testament laws about war and capital punishment*, which are species of the same genus, as well as *the narratives about war* are reengaged from the perspective of new creation in the cross and resurrection of Jesus.

---

1. I am grateful for comments on this essay from John Nugent.

I have briefly sketched a specialization of New Testament studies because *how one reads the Bible* will determine if one can even *permissibly* be a pacifist on the basis of the Bible. No Christian arguing for just war escapes a biblical hermeneutic; to avoid thinking about one's hermeneutic is to play a game of pretend. Frankly, the Old Testament evidence, if taken as normative at some level or taken as revelation of how God engages his own being and attributes in this world, makes any kind of pacifism difficult, or to put it less delicately, impossible. That is how I read most old perspective scholars. But the new perspective and the apocalyptic hermeneutics offer a different, and in my mind *far more plausible*, hermeneutic for how to read the Bible. That is, *each offers plenty of opportunity for discontinuity and disruption* because Jesus was the Messiah, Jesus was both crucified and raised, Jesus now rules over all creation, and this King Jesus *rules as the one who embodies and reconstitutes all of reality in what is often called "cruciformity."* On that my argument rests: Jesus's death and resurrection *radically alters morality* for those who are caught up in that cruciform vision. This essentially disruptive, new-creation hermeneutic does not end the discussion, for Romans 13 at least points an accusing finger at simplistic pacifist theories. But this kind of hermeneutic at least calls us to consider the whole while standing on a different platform.

In what follows I will offer, first, a brief case for a specific kind of pacifism using a Christoformity or cruciformity hermeneutic, and then, second, I will present a brief case that Dietrich Bonhoeffer sustained a specific kind of pacifism throughout his life *by anchoring his later statements in a christoform hermeneutic.*

A Case for Christoformic Hermeneutics in Jesus[2]

I have argued that one's hermeneutic determines where one ends up on the pacifism vs. just war theory debate. In the discussion before us, "just" in "just war theories" is not defined by the Torah of Moses or the teachings of Jesus and the apostles but by a tradition that emerged with particular clarity in Augustine and which was then developed in the church traditions of Aquinas, Luther, and Calvin—and beyond—but even more importantly in the international community of those concerned with international war and peace and justice. Just war is very reasonable on paper but never executed

---

2. Of the many expositions of pacifism that could be listed, I offer this selection of influential studies: Trocmé, *Jesus and Nonviolent Revolution*; Sider, *Christ and Violence*; Yoder, *Politics of Jesus*; Yoder, *Nevertheless*; Yoder, *Christian Witness to State*; Yoder, *Original Revolution*; Yoder, *Nonviolence*; Wink, *Naming the Powers*; Wink, *Unmasking the Powers*; Wink, *Engaging the Powers*; and Hauerwas, *Performing the Faith*.

in practice. For the theory on paper, I quote just war defender Nigel Biggar's summary statement, who begins by saying

> let me pause here briefly to set out [just war's] basic criteria. These fall into two classes, one regarding the justice of going to war in the first place (*ius ad bellum*) and the other regarding justice in the course of fighting (*ius in bello*). The six criteria of *ius ad bellum* are: just cause, legitimate authority, right intention, last resort, proportionality, and prospect of success. The criteria of *ius in bello* are proportionality and discrimination.[3]

The criteria here are not established on the basis of the Bible, nor are they established on the basis of the teachings of Jesus or the apostles. Israel's wars against the Philistines, to name but one example, were not drawn up as just war actions, and I don't think anyone argues Jesus taught just war. Augustine at least had his eye on the Old Testament laws about justice (as well as being thoroughly conversant with the Roman system of justice that would be eventually known as the *Digest of Justinian*). At the level of hermeneutics, one must observe, the just war theory goes well beyond the Bible. In fact, it goes *against the Bible*. For sure, some would contend the theory of justice at work in just war theory derives from the Bible's sense of justice. Perhaps so, and perhaps not so much. Once again, there is only one theory of war as practiced by God's people in the Bible, and there is no theory of war for how non-Israelites were to conduct themselves. Whether one calls the wars of God's people in the pages of the Old Testament *crusader theory* or some kind of *divine right Machievellian theory* does not matter, because whatever one calls it, the takeover of the Holy Land was not done on the basis of just war theory. This happened because Israelites believed God had told them the land was theirs. Let us not then pretend that just war theory is biblical, for it so adjusts what is found in the Old Testament, not to ignore Revelation, that it no longer resembles war in the Bible. Just war theory then is hermeneutics. I shall now depart from this discussion, leaving it to others to develop and defend.

There is not space here to develop how Jesus uses the Old Testament, nor even to explore a text like Jesus urging his disciples to show mercy instead of requiring the *lex talionis* as was the case in Deuteronomy 19:21 (cf. Matt 5:38–42). What I want to do instead is focus on the cruciform hermeneutic of Jesus that instructs on how to read the Bible from the Christ event out.[4] That is, a hermeneutic that teaches us that we comprehend the Bible's narrative only once we have comprehended the significance of Jesus's

---

3. Biggar, *In Defence of War*, 3.
4. Yoder, *Politics of Jesus*, 112–33; Camp, *Mere Discipleship*, 81–106.

life, death, burial, resurrection, ascension, and exaltation. The implication of this is that we learn to see the deepest reality of the Bible in the cross and resurrection. At a most crucial turning point in the narrative of Mark, Jesus declares to his disciples that he is the Son of Man, surely an evocation of Daniel 7, and that he will suffer on the cross and be raised. Peter, ever so knowledgeable about the Hebrew Bible, will have none of this and puts Jesus in his place; Jesus returns the favor by putting Peter back in his former place as a student who doesn't know how to read the Bible. Then Jesus makes the astounding hermeneutical move: *as he is the crucified and resurrected one, so the disciples are to live in that crucifixion and resurrection as well.* His words are "whoever wants to be my disciple must deny themselves and take up their cross [Luke adds 'daily'] and follow me" (Mark 8:34). They didn't put this together well, so Jesus rebukes them two chapters later when they clamor and debate about greatness and their desire to rule over others. To which Jesus responds by saying the greatest is the servant, which is the essence of his own life: "For even the Son of Man did not come to be served, but to serve, and to give his life a ransom for many" (10:45).

After his resurrection, on the road to Emmaus, Jesus *hermeneuts* the Bible for the discouraged disciples. I quote from Luke 24:25-27:

> He said to them, "How foolish you are, and how slow to believe all that the prophets have spoken! Did not the Messiah have to suffer these things and then enter his glory?" And beginning with Moses and all the Prophets, he explained to them what was said in all the Scriptures concerning himself.

Jesus here explains the whole Bible as leading to a Messiah of suffering and then glory. To a Messiah who ruled by way of the cross, not by way of the sword. To a Messiah to whom the whole of Scripture points. The narratival thread for Jesus is a cruciform reality that teaches redemptive suffering, not redemptive violence.

This narrative explains why Jesus focuses on love of neighbor, in what I have called the Jesus Creed (Mark 12:28-34), why Jesus teaches his followers that they are to show mercy in justice (Matt 5:38-42), why they are to act in preemptive forgiveness (6:12), and most especially why they are to seek to turn their enemies—those who persecute them—into neighbors (5:43-48). This narrative also shows why Peter taught the slaves to endure suffering on the template of Christ's own suffering (1 Peter 2:18-25) and why Paul urged a baptismal existence of death and resurrection (Col 2:20-3:11). The cross, in other words, became their soteriology and their ethics. They learned to live in cruciformity in following Christ, and this cruciformity became the umpire's rule book in knowing how to live in the earliest churches. They were no longer under Moses or under Caesar; they were under King Jesus.

Dietrich Bonhoeffer put it this way: "Jesus releases his community from the political and legal order, from the national form of the people of Israel, and makes it into what it truly is, namely, the community of the faithful that is not bound by political or national ties."[5] This ethic of cruciformity was not pragmatism or realism propped up with an ideological apparatus; this was kingdom theory. Instead, Jesus believes the central ethic is to love God and to love others, and his cross is the means and method of life, including making enemies into neighbors and showing mercy where others would want revenge. Again, Bonhoeffer: "Evil will become powerless when it finds no opposing object, no resistance, but, instead, is willingly borne and suffered. Evil meets an opponent for which it is not a match."[6]

The hermeneutic of Jesus, to put a very complicated discussion into short propositions, is that all of law has come to its fulfillment in him; the him in whom it is fulfilled is the him who lives the incarnate life for others, who was crucified without resistance, who was raised in vindication, and who is now exalted to rule over all creation. The express words of Jesus were that his followers embrace and live by the cross (Mark 8:34), and thus cruciformity is the door one must enter if one wants to enter into the kingdom ethic of Jesus. In that kingdom Jesus, not Caesar, rules, and that rule is effectively operative in the redeemed people of Jesus, the church, and they are summoned to become Christlike by Christoformity or cruciformity. They are called then to a different order of life by the one who has conquered this world's order of life by a cross, not a sword (Col 2:15). No text reveals the narrative hermeneutic and ethic of Jesus more than Philippians 2:6–11.

Practicalities aside, this is what the hermeneutic of Jesus looks like to me. The church has been seduced at times by Peter's own seduction. On the Mount of Transfiguration, when Moses and Elijah appeared, Peter suggested to Jesus that he might set up three tents—one for Jesus, one for Moses, and one for Elijah. The Lord rebuked Peter, for he thereby made Jesus an equal to what was not equal: to the lawgiver and to the prophet. The Father's voice was "Listen to Jesus. Turn from Moses and Elijah to see their fulfillment in Jesus." That same temptation is offered and accepted by many in the church today who instead of listening to the crucified one listen instead to the *lex talionis* of the lawgiver.

---

5. Bonhoeffer, DBWE 4, 132.
6. Bonhoeffer, DBWE 4, 133.

This cruciform reality of Jesus, which goes to the heart of the Bible's narrative and central message, has led me to these positions:[7]

> I cannot kill a non-Christian, for whom Christ has died and to whom I am called to preach the gospel, for the State; that would be rendering to Caesar what is God's and deconstruct the kingdom mission.
>
> I cannot kill a fellow Christian for the State; that would be rendering to Caesar what is God's. My first allegiance is to the king and to his kingdom people.
>
> I am called to cooperate with the State to the degree it is consistent with the kingdom; I cannot in good conscience cooperate with the State when it is inconsistent with the kingdom; that would be to render to Caesar what is God's.
>
> I cannot ask in the first instance if this is practicable. I am to ask in the first instance what it means to follow Jesus.
>
> The Jesus Creed, which forms the bedrock for Jesus's statement about the *lex talionis*, is radical beyond calculation: it calls us to love the neighbor and the enemy. Love or violence seem to be the two major options.
>
> The cross reveals how God himself deals with injustice and violence; by absorbing and bearing it away, the sin is removed and the mask of injustice stripped away to reveal injustice. It was through the cross that Jesus was vindicated in resurrection and exaltation, and that same promise and christoformity is what Jesus expects of his followers in Mark 8:34–9:1.

What does this look like in everyday reality? In times of terrorism? Even more, what does this look like when the powers of an empire are breathing down your neck and watching your every move and opening your every mail? What does it look like in Dietrich Bonhoeffer?

Bonhoeffer and Christoform Hermeneutics

There is much to be said about Bonhoeffer's life, about his historical context as the son of a well-known psychiatrist in Berlin, about his theological education and major influences—from Harnack, Seeberg, and Barth—about a professional and ecclesial theologian[8] in the swirl of the German Christians and the Confessing Church, about the Bethel and Barmen Declarations as early attempts to block Hitler's power-mongering, about his own work in

---

7. From McKnight, *Sermon on the Mount*, 132.

8. That Bonhoeffer's theology was ecclesial has been emphasized in refreshing ways by Hauerwas, *Performing the Faith*.

the ecumenical movement, about his provocative theory about "religionless Christianity" or the "world come of age," and then about the intricate and at times mysterious involvement of Bonhoeffer with his brother-in-law in the German Abwehr (the Third Reich's military intelligence agency that became safe harbor for those in the resistance movement)[9] and their expectation of what the German churches would do when Hitler was removed[10]—all of this can be found in the standard biographies and studies.[11] I have to lock down in this context on one theme—Bonhoeffer's christological hermeneutic that led to his sort of pacifism[12]—and keep my attention on that theme alone.

We need to be alert to the usual course of action for those who think Bonhoeffer was a pacifist through and through: prove both that Bonhoeffer was a pacifist earlier in his life and public ministry and then also later in his theological writings and letters and all the way through to his hanging at Flossenbürg. To be sure, many today think Bonhoeffer shifted from a pacifist approach to a kind of Niebuhrian realism approach, but I agree that Mark Thiessen Nation has made a case for Bonhoeffer remaining pacifistic.[13] However, I want to ask a slightly different question: we will move from "Was Bonhoeffer a pacifist all the way through his theological career?" to "How did Bonhoeffer's stance toward Hitler and Germany's war with the world *embrace a christoform hermeneutic*?" But I will build on what has been established by Mark Thiessen Nation by exploring the hermeneutic of Bonhoeffer. Furthermore, because the question is not reducible to "Was he or was he not a pacifist?," we will run on parallel lines with Trey Palmisano's

---

9. I don't know that Karl Barth ever did affirm Bonhoeffer's location in the Third Reich's machine. Thus,

> According to a February 1955 communication from Karl Barth and Charlotte von Kirschbaum to Jørgen Glenthøj, during the conversation in September 1941, Karl Barth had directly asked Bonhoeffer, "Dear Bonhoeffer, I wish to ask you openly, 'Why are you actually here in Switzerland?'" In response Bonhoeffer "spoke openly of the plans for Hitler's removal and of the attempts to create a new government and to struggle for a peace plan."

See the letter to Karl Barth, May 17, 1942, in DBWE 16, 277–78, here 278n3.

10. See "Unfinished Draft of a Pulpit Pronouncement following the Coup" and "Draft Proposal for a Reorganization of the Church after the 'End of the Church Struggle,'" in DBWE 16, 572–74, 574–580.

11. Bethge, *Dietrich Bonhoeffer*; Schlingensiepen, *Dietrich Bonhoeffer*; Marsh, *Strange Glory*.

12. Pacifism then is not an abstraction; there are a variety of pacifisms and Bonhoeffer's, I argue, emerges from his theology of *Stellvertretung*. On the varieties of pacifism, see Yoder, *Nevertheless*; Hauerwas, *Performing the Faith*, 169–83.

13. Nation et al., *Bonhoeffer the Assassin?*

proposal that Bonhoeffer's kind of pacifism needs to be examined through his method of doing ethics and more especially through his Christology.[14]

Bonhoeffer was a pacifist earlier in life, at least from 1932 on. First, in 1929, while an assistant pastor in Barcelona to a German-speaking Lutheran church, Bonhoeffer defended military killing in these words in which are some themes he would develop in a christoform hermeneutic in the too few of years of his life that would follow:

> In such cases, I no longer have the choice between good and evil; regardless of which decision I make, that decision will soil me with the world and its laws. I will take up arms with the terrible knowledge of doing something horrible, and yet knowing I can do no other. I will defend my brother, my mother, my people, and yet I know that I can do so only by spilling blood; but love for my people will sanctify murder, will sanctify war. As a Christian, I will suffer from the entire dreadfulness of war. My soul will bear the entire burden of responsibility in its full gravity. I will try to love my enemies against whom I am sworn to the death, as only Christians can love their brothers. And yet I will have to do to those enemies what my love and gratitude toward my own people commands me to do, the people into whom God bore me. And finally I will recognize that Christian decisions are made only within the ongoing relationship with God, within a constantly renewed surrender of oneself to the divine will. I can rest assured that even if the world does violence to my conscience, I can make only one decision, namely, the one to which

---

14. Palmisano, *Peace and Violence*. In particular, Bonhoeffer's ethical method is not by way of deontology—the formulation of timeless and contextless rules or principles—but by way of Christ's own embodiment in the world and our entering into relationship with Christ who utters the command within the confines of that relationship, and in which relationship a person discerns how to act in the moment. (Such an approach is neither Kierkegaardian nor situation ethical, but—as I am arguing—Christoformity.) This is not to say I agree with each point of Palmisano, though his decentering of the questions is important. In fact, his focus on method and Christology almost permits him to reinterpret lines from Bonhoeffer other than how I would read them, not least in his reading of *Discipleship*. Palmisano's radicalization of pacifism at times into "absolute" pacifism, while important, also permits him to minimize some evidence or exaggerate other evidence. Yet, I still contend his focus on method and Christology remains an enduring insight. Bonhoeffer's pacifism must be located outside deontology and in Christology. I shall discuss a conversation below that illustrates Bonhoeffer's method, Christology, pastoral theology, as well as his kind of highly personalized pacifism. It is a pity that Palmisano was not able to enter into dialogue with Nation et al.'s *Bonhoeffer the Assasin?*

God leads me in the sacred hour of encounter between my will and God's will, in the hour in which God conquers my will.[15]

At Union Theological Seminary in New York City in 1930–1931, Bonhoeffer befriended Jean Lasserre, who was himself a convinced and convincing (to Bonhoeffer at least) pacifist, and most would argue that it was this friendship that led to Bonhoeffer's pacifism.[16] It was in his time at Union, then, that Bonhoeffer became convinced that pacifism was how to live in the modern world as a follower of Jesus. The next year in his lectures in ecumenical work, all with the clouds looming of social revolutions and war, Bonhoeffer clearly articulates his pacifistic stance. I give what I think is a forthright statement of his theological conclusions. In December 1932 before the German Student Christian Movement, Bonhoeffer expressed pacifism in classical form:

> The commandment "You shall not kill," the word that says, "Love your enemies," is given to us simply to be obeyed. For Christians, any military service, except in the ambulance corps, and any preparation for war, is forbidden.[17]

In 1936, in a letter dated January 27 to Elizabeth Zinn (future wife of the great New Testament scholar Günther Bornkamm), Bonhoeffer confessed he had only recently been converted through the Bible and especially the Sermon on the Mount, and he called this his "grand liberation." He then said this:

> For me everything now depended on a renewal of the church and of the pastoral station . . . Christian pacifism, which a brief time before—at the disputation where Gerhard [Jacobi, a congregant of Zinn's] was also present!—I had still passionately disputed, suddenly came into focus as something utterly self-evident. And thus it went, step-by-step. I no longer saw or thought about anything else.[18]

Bonhoeffer's pacifism is confirmed by others. Joachim Kanitz, a student of Bonhoeffer at Finkenwalde, said that during one semester at the school

---

15. From a lecture at the church called "Basic Questions of a Christian Ethic," dated Feb. 8, 1929. See Bonhoeffer, DBWE 10, 372.

16. Nelson, "Relationship of Jean Lasserre," 71–84. Bethge does not believe Bonhoeffer ever became a "convinced pacifist"; see Bethge, *Dietrich Bonhoeffer*, 153. Against Bethge, see Marsh, *Strange Glory*, 213–16. The evidence is against Bethge.

17. A lecture called "Christ and Peace" and based on student notes taken at that time. See Bonhoeffer, DBWE 12, 260.

18. Bonhoeffer, DBWE 10, 134.

"we worked on the exegesis of the Sermon on the Mount... [and] it became clear to us on the basis of this Bible study that it is not possible for Christians to justify killing or to justify war." Kanitz also spoke of the "pacifism that Bonhoeffer had taught us."[19] Eberhard Bethge, Bonhoeffer's student, then close friend, and for decades the official biographer of Bonhoeffer, records a story about the unfriendly Bishop Theodor Heckel informing the church leaders that Bonhoeffer could "be accused of being a pacifist and enemy of the state."[20] In his well-known section on God as creator of life and the fundamental demand to protect all life, Karl Barth said of Bonhoeffer both that he was a "pacifist" and one driven by the extreme circumstances to participate in the overthrow of Hitler. He says Bonhoeffer was a pacifist "on the basis of his understanding of the Gospel."[21] What was not up for question in this context in Barth was Bonhoeffer's pacifism but how Bonhoeffer processed his pacifism and his involvement in Germany in a manner that was both against Hitler but for the faithful in the church of Germany.

Bonhoeffer remained pacifistic all the way to his death at Flossenbürg. Having said that, we must observe that some contend that Bonhoeffer through his contacts with Reinhold Niebuhr at Union adapted his theology by adopting some of Niebuhrian realism and in so doing shifted away from his pacifism.[22] That is, he joined the plot to assassinate Hitler. Perhaps the most arresting piece of evidence in the Bonhoeffer works about the assassination occurs in a conversation reported later by Wolf-Dieter

---

19. Quotations of Kanitz taken from Nation et al., *Bonhoeffer the Assassin?*, 10–11.

20. From Bethge, *Dietrich Bonhoeffer*, 512.

21. Barth, *Doctrine of Creation* (*CD* III/4), Study Edition 20, 120. Barth probes the justifiability of tyrannicide, approval of which runs right through Western history from Cicero, who thought a virtuous man should *in extremis* commit the act, onwards.

22. A good example is Marsh, *Strange Glory*. It must be observed that Bethge, too, believes the same: see Bethge, *Dietrich Bonhoeffer*, 677–78. But Bonhoeffer's comments at times veered away from pacifism into a grievous tolerance, as was the case with some of his former students and also with his nephew, Hans-Walter Schleicher, who had recently been inducted into the German military. So in his letter to Schleicher on Oct. 10, 1942: "One should also probably beware of *wanting to have a shared experience* of the war and its horrors; for who, lightheartedly wishing such a thing for himself, really knows how he will respond in the decisive hour? But to be called, to participate in the community, contributing and bearing one's share, whatever that may be—that is, I believe, fairly firm ground on which to stand and to endure even difficult things. And if from time to time one recalls these things and is finally able to live completely from the awareness that this being called is ultimately not accidental, but is God's own way for our lives, then I think one can go very confidently into the unknown. Of course, life in the new community will then also be given very definite and inviolable boundaries, and one's inner reality collapses utterly if one crosses these boundaries out of false solidarity" (Bonhoeffer, DBWE 16, 365).

Zimmermann.[23] As an illegal pastor in Werder on the Havel, Zimmermann reports that in 1942 Bonhoeffer and some friends joined Zimmermann for an evening at his home. A dramatic moment occurs when Werner von Haeften asks a silencing question. As a staff lieutenant in the Third Reich's Army High Command, von Haeften turns to Bonhoeffer and asks:

> Shall I shoot? I can get inside the Führer's headquarters with my revolver. I know where and when the conferences take place. I can get access.

Zimmermann tells us the conversation over that question "lasted for many hours." But Zimmermann also summarized Bonhoeffer's question about assassinating Hitler:

> Bonhoeffer explained that the shooting by itself meant nothing: something had to be gained by it, a change of circumstances, of the government. The liquidation of Hitler would in itself be no use; things might even become worse. That, he said, made the work of the resistance so difficult, that the "thereafter" had to be so carefully prepared.

Zimmermann continues by turning back to von Haeften's measured comments. He was "from an old officers' family, was a gentle type, enthusiastic, idealistic, but also a man of Christian convictions who believed in inherited traditions. He was one of Niemöller's confirmands." Zimmermann reports that at this point von Haeften "suddenly developed enormous energy" and pushed harder, wanting to know what was most right to do. "Bonhoeffer, on the other hand, exhorted him over and over again to be discreet, to plan clearly and then to see all unforeseen complications through. Nothing should be left to chance." One senses the emotional moment when von Haeften again pushes for an answer: "Shall I . . . ? May I . . . ?" At this moment Bonhoeffer's response is both calculated and revealing of both his non-principle approach to pacifism and the very personal nature of discernment for such a moment as his. "Bonhoeffer," Zimmermann concludes, "answered that he could not decide this for him. The risk had to be taken by him, him alone. If he even spoke of guilt in not making use of a chance, there was certainly as much guilt in light-hearted treatment of the situation. No one could ever emerge without guilt from the situation he was in. But then that guilt was always a guilt borne in suffering."

Some infer from this one-of-a-kind exchange that Bonhoeffer could not have been a pacifist because, given the opportunity, he backed off from the opportunity to declare a principled pacifism. I have myself at times

---

23. For what follows, see Zimmermann, *I Knew Dietrich Bonhoeffer*, 190–92.

pondered this very conversation in such a manner, but the rest of the evidence in Bonhoeffer's works leads me to conclude this is not the best read of the von Haeften conversation. Rather than evidence for complicity in the assassination conspiracy or even more of a lack of principled pacifism, I see here Bonhoeffer's reticence to say "Yes, by all means!" as well as his own personal discernment for how he himself was to engage the German situation in the Third Reich. What Bonhoeffer thought right for himself he would not impose on others. So, I'm not convinced the von Haeften conversation reveals either Bonhoeffer's supposed realism nor his shift from pacifism and am convinced, with Mark Thiessen Nation,[24] that he stayed much closer to his christoformic pacifism.

On March 25, 1939, in a letter to Bishop George Bell, Bonhoeffer openly stated he was a conscientious objector:

> I am thinking of leaving Germany sometime. The main reason is the compulsory military service to which the men of my age ([born] 1906) will be called up this year. It seems to me conscientiously impossible to join in a war under the present circumstances.... Perhaps the worst thing of all is the military oath which I should have to swear. So I am rather puzzled in this situation, and perhaps even more, because I feel, it is really only on Christian grounds that I find it difficult to do military service under the present conditions, and yet there are only very few friends who would approve of my attitude.[25]

I have already quoted above twice from *Discipleship*, a book written in 1937 from the Finkenwalde years, indicating that Bonhoeffer was pacifistic at that time in his life. In 1939 Reinhold Niebuhr wrote to Henry Smith Leiper, a leader in the World Council of Churches, and informed him that "Bonhoeffer is due for military service in July and will refuse to serve."[26] Niebuhr was busy at work seeking to get Bonhoeffer out of Germany to the USA to preserve Bonhoeffer's life and gain a formidable intellect for Union seminary; Leiper offered Bonhoeffer a lectureship.

Nor was Bonhoeffer arrested for any involvement in the conspiracy or any assassination attempt.[27] There are a number of elements at work in his arrest: (1) the successful Operation 7 to remove some Jews from Germany

---

24. Nation et al., *Bonhoeffer the Assassin?*

25. Bonhoeffer, DBWE 15, 156–57. His conscientious objection is found in other places, including the "Memorandum to the Ecumenical Youth Commission" on Jan. 29, 1935; see Bonhoeffer, DBWE 13, 289–90.

26. May 1, 1939, in Bonhoeffer, DBWE, 161.

27. On the arrest, see Bethge, *Dietrich Bonhoeffer*, 780–87.

shows some connection to Bonhoeffer; (2) that action was sufficient not only for arrest but could be seen as treason. (3) The Gestapo was in a power struggle seeking to bring down Admiral Canaris and the German Abwehr (military intelligence) and so was doing its own kind of investigations, provoked in part by incriminating interrogations of Consul Schmidhuber and Captain Ickradt and complicated by the Abwehr's demand for its own independence and secrecy. But, (4) that accusation of conspiring to provide safe rescue for some Jews was legally cleared in interrogations through the "explanations" of both von Dohnanyi and Bonhoeffer.[28] In the end, (5) and this can be judged from the indictment against Bonhoeffer, he was arrested and kept in prison for eighteen months because (a) he was accused of deceitfully avoiding military service and (b) he attempted to keep others from military service.[29] In other words, his arrest confirms his pacifism and ought to prevent anyone from thinking he was arrested because of the conspiracy or even his involvement in an assassination attempt.

Yet, there was a notable focusing of his theory of pacifism as his theology began to mature, and it gives me the opportunity to explore his christoform hermeneutics as a way around the debate about how pacifist he was in prison. So, yes, I do think he remained a pacifist, but that is not quite the best way to approach the man; his pacifism was not abstract, not a *Prinzip*,[30] but a Christocentric hermeneutic. Bonhoeffer operated with one of the most radical christoform hermeneutics I have ever seen, and perhaps the most consistently pacifistic christoform hermeneutics in the history of the church. His "pacifism" was rather a christoformic way of life that transcended an ethical posture. I am convinced that Bonhoeffer's Christocentrism lines up with the New Testament's Christocentrism and in particular can be seen as another instance of what the apostle Paul was saying in Colossians 1:24 when he said, "Now I rejoice in what I am suffering for you, and I fill up in my flesh what is still lacking in regard to Christ's afflictions, for the sake of his body, which is the church." In other words, neither of them broaches anything sacrilegious and both are instances of a missional Christoformity.[31]

---

28. Famously, on a note on Canaris's desk was a note explaining the reasons for the failed assassination attempts and stating that Josef Müller would accompany Bonhoeffer to Rome to give such explanations. This implicates Bonhoeffer in knowledge of, but not participation in, the assassination attempts.

29. First in the "Indictment by the Reich War Court" and second in the "Indictment by the Senior Reich Military Prosecutor," in Bonhoeffer, DBWE 16, 435–46.

30. Is Bonhoeffer's aversion to *Prinzip* a derivation from Hegel's distinction between *Moralität* and *Sittlichkeit*, or is it derived from Kierkegaard's more existentialist ethic?

31. I defend this pastoral-missional view in my commentary on Colossians (see

Bonhoeffer's Christology was formed in both his dissertation, *Sanctorum Communio*, and then even more in his conclusions about God's freedom in Christ in his *Habilitationschrift*, *Act and Being*. What one encounters in the Sermon on the Mount, a highlight of Bonhoeffer's *Discipleship*, is a christologically grounded word from God.[32] But in Bonhoeffer's *Ethics* and in *Letters and Papers from Prison* this view comes into fuller maturity.[33] In what follows I want to build a case for Bonhoeffer's kind of pacifism as the inevitable effect of a christoformic hermeneutic. Without his Christology there would not have been his pacifism. To get there we have to pull together some important themes in his most mature theological years.

First, Bonhoeffer was against "principles" or "rules" as they are often presented, so when it came to pacifism he would have been less comfortable saying "I'm a pacifist in every situation" (as an abstraction) and would have said, "In this context my christoform hermeneutic leaves me no other option than to resist and suffer." Discernment rather than law-making or undeviating principle-formation was his method of knowing what to do in a concrete situation.[34] In a lecture on the "Path of the Young Illegal Theologians of the Confessing Church," given on October 26, 1938, Bonhoeffer expressed his mind forcefully on this matter.[35] He opens with "Scripture evidence applies only to the truth of a doctrine, but never to the correctness of a path."[36] The issue in need of discernment was the illegal theologians he was training, but the problem was too many wanted Scripture to be a pathfinder for the future:

> We expect from Scripture such concrete directives that we are released from acting on faith; one wants to see the path before walking on it. One demands the certainty that the path will certainly be pleasing to God before starting the journey. One says: if we could be absolutely certain on the basis of Scripture that the path of the Council of Brethren is pleasing to God, then we would follow it. Demonstrate this from Scripture and we will follow. Thus I want to have the scriptural evidence in my pocket as the guarantee for my path. But the Bible can never fulfill this kind of request either, because it is not intended to be an insurance policy for our paths, which may become dangerous.

McKnight, *Colossians*).

32. Bonhoeffer, DBWE 1; Bonhoeffer, DBWE 2; Bonhoeffer, DBWE 4.
33. Bonhoeffer, DBWE 6; Bonhoeffer, DBWE 8.
34. Perhaps most famous in the Bonhoeffer works is the fragment of an essay called "What Does It Mean to Tell the Truth?," in Bonhoeffer, DBWE 16, 601–8.
35. In Bonhoeffer, DBWE 15, 416–37.
36. Bonhoeffer, DBWE 15, 419.

> The Bible does only one thing: it calls us to faith and obedience in the truth that we know in Jesus Christ. Scripture points not to our paths but to the truth of God. Let no one among you think after this meeting today that he can go home armed with scriptural evidence that justifies his decision for the Council of Brethren; if so, he misunderstands both the Scripture and the essence of faith. The scriptural evidence does not spare us from faith but actually leads us into the venture of faith and obedience to God's word, and it strengthens us in this. According to Scripture we do not first know and comprehend the way and then decide to follow it; it is rather the one who is on the journey who knows that he is on the right way. Knowledge comes only in action and decision. Only he who is in truth will recognize the truth. Jesus says: "Anyone who resolves to do the will of God will know whether the teaching is from God" (John 7:17). For this reason, scriptural evidence can be provided only along the way, that is, for the one who believes.[37]

Hence in his *Ethics*, much of it written in a monastery at Ettal prior to his imprisonment and then some in his parents' home in Berlin, he puts it in his more classical form:

> To begin quite generally, what is at stake are the times and places that concern us, that we experience, that are realities for us. What is at stake are the times and places that pose concrete questions to us, set us tasks, and lay responsibilities on us. . . . Against this, however, is the fact that we are placed objectively by our history into a particular context of experience, responsibility, and decision, from which we cannot withdraw without ending up in abstraction.[38]

Second, Bonhoeffer himself had to discern his way through the complexities of his giftedness as a theologian and the invitation to teach at Union in NYC with the developing and explosive tensions in Germany. Though he had a place at Union, Bonhoeffer's famous month in a room at Union—seemingly spent pacing and smoking and writing and pondering and praying—Bonhoeffer intuited that he had to return to Germany, knowing the ambiguity and suffering the return would entail. He told Henry Smith Leiper upon his offering to Bonhoeffer a lectureship in the USA that the "only thing that makes me hesitate at the present moment of decision

---

37. Bonhoeffer, DBWE 15, 420–21.
38. Bonhoeffer, DBWE 6, 100–101.

is the question of loyalty to my people at home."³⁹ The calmness of this line comes just after his arrival in the USA but does not match the intensity of Bonhoeffer's month in NYC. That very day in his journal he wrote:

> Since yesterday evening my thoughts cannot get away from Germany. I would not have thought it possible that one at my age after so many years abroad can become so agonizingly homesick. . . . I would have liked to take the next ship. . . . The full force of self-reproaches about a wrong decision comes back up and is almost suffocating. I was filled with despair.⁴⁰

Consequently, what he had said would be one year maximum turned into an immediate return. He informed Paul Lehmann on June 30, 1939, the American perhaps most behind his presence in the USA at Union, that return was necessary because "the political situation is dreadful, and I must be with my brothers when things become serious."⁴¹ Similar things were said to Reinhold Niebuhr at about the same time: "I have come to the conclusion that I have made a mistake in coming to America. I must live through this difficult period of our national history with the Christian people of Germany. I will have no right to participate in the reconstruction of Christian life in Germany after the war if I do not share the trials of this time with my people."⁴²

But it was what Bonhoeffer next said to Niebuhr that shapes his christoform hermeneutic: "Christians in Germany will face the terrible alternative of either willing the defeat of their nation in order that Christian civilization may survive, or willing the victory of their nation and thereby destroying our civilization. I know which of these alternatives I must choose; but I cannot make that choice in security."⁴³ This is our *third* observation: Bonhoeffer intentionally reentered the German church struggle and knew it entailed suffering. Just nine months earlier, while in Germany, he had already outlined his theory of suffering:

> Therefore, whoever hates affliction, renunciation, crisis, slander, and imprisonment in his life might otherwise talk about the cross with big words, but nonetheless he hates the cross of Jesus and has no peace with God. But whoever loves the cross of Jesus

---

39. Letter June 15, 1939, in Bonhoeffer, DBWE 15, 183. Also see his journal for June 18, 1939 (DBWE 15, 225).
40. Bonhoeffer, DBWE 15, 222.
41. Bonhoeffer, DBWE 15, 209.
42. Bonhoeffer, "To Reinhold Niebuhr," DBWE 15, 210.
43. Bonhoefer, DBWE 15, 210.

Christ, whoever has found peace in his cross, also begins to love the affliction in his life. And finally he will be able to speak with Scripture: "but we also boast in afflictions."[44]

It was this suffering for the sake of others and his isolation from his fellow suffering brothers that tortured him when he was at Union the following summer (mentioned above). We have now opened the lid to see his christoform hermeneutic: at the heart of God in Christ is the suffering of Christ— Christ has suffered for all, and all suffering has been borne by Christ; thus, to enter into the German struggle and suffer for it is to enter into *a vicarious and representative action on behalf of others*. This is Bonhoeffer's kind of pacifism: the choice in the moment to enter into suffering (rather than violence) for the sake of others in order to bring redemption, the redemption Christ has already established but which needs to be realized in the concrete earthly realities of that moment.

In so entering into the church struggle Bonhoeffer would be stained with *guilt*, but it is a guilt into which Christ has entered, a guilt Christ has borne away, and it is an entrance that requires of the believer the faith that God will bring forgiveness and redemption. In entering into the church struggle he throws himself upon the mercy of God for the guilt he must carry. This guilt of Bonhoeffer was not a shift from pacifism to realism, and neither was it a choice to join in the plot to assassinate Hitler. We don't have that evidence. Instead, it was a choice to enter into the subversion of German nationalism for the sake of the German church, a choice to enter the Abwehr in order to subvert the Wehrmacht, a choice to take upon himself the condition of the German people's sinful violence in order to end that violence through the cross. Hence in his *Ethics* he says, "God wills to be guilty of our guilt; God takes on the punishment and suffering that guilt has brought on us. God takes responsibility for godlessness, love for hate, the holy one for the sinner."[45] This note of responsibility ties us back to his concept of loyalty as well as to the deep wells of his ethical theory about freedom:

> History arises out of accepting this responsibility for other human beings or for entire communities or groups of communities. . . . The moment a person accepts responsibility for other people—and only in so doing does the person live in reality— the genuine ethical situation arises. . . . To act out of concrete responsibility means to act in *freedom*—to decide, to act, and

---

44. From his "Sermon on Romans 5:1–5" at Gross-Schlönwitz on Sept. 3, 1938, in Bonhoeffer, DBWE 15, 473.

45. Bonhoeffer, DBWE 6, 83.

to answer for the consequences of this particular action *myself* without the support of other people or principles.[46]

This act of freedom in faith brings with it the promise of God's grace:

> But civil courage can grow only from the free responsibility of the free man. Only today are Germans beginning to discover what free responsibility means. It is founded in a God who calls for the free venture of faith to responsible action and who promises forgiveness and consolation to the one who on account of such action becomes a sinner.[47]

It is here that we need to name our *fourth* observation, his theory of vicarious representative action [*Stellvertretung*].[48] Dietrich Bonhoeffer interprets his own acts of suffering as *Stellvertretung*, a term known to most theologians through atonement theory. That is, his actions of entering into Germany's condition make him guilty but in a christoformic manner that is simultaneously responsible. This is not imitation of Christ nor is it some kind of moral theory of principles; rather, it is an entering into what Christ already did: "Jesus Christ is the very embodiment of the person who lives responsibly. He is not the individual who seeks to attain his own ethical perfection. Instead, he lives only as the one who in himself has taken on and bears the selves of all human beings. His entire life, action, and suffering is vicarious representative action [*Stellvertretung*]."[49] On the next page he turns the idea over only slightly to clarify when he says, "All human responsibility is rooted in the real vicarious representative action of Jesus Christ on behalf of all human beings."[50] Bonhoeffer's theory of moral *Stellvertretung* then is essentially a christoform hermeneutic that permits discernment of how to live in his German condition.

Already in the summer of 1938, in a Bible study on temptation, Bonhoeffer expressed his theory in these terms, and these terms clarify the kind of pacifism Bonhoeffer upheld:

---

46. Bonhoeffer, DBWE 15, 220–21.
47. From the famous essay "After Ten Years," in Bonhoeffer, DBWE 8, 41.
48. In about April 1941, Bonhoeffer wrote a paper on church and state in which he said government too was a "vicarious representative" of God (Bonhoeffer, DBWE 16, 504). The entire essay deserves extensive discussion, but not in this context. Bonhoeffer thinks government's responsibility is to pave the way for the church to accomplish its mission, but he believes this because of his Christocentrism.
49. Bonhoeffer, DBWE 6, 231.
50. Bonhoeffer, DBWE 6, 232.

> The Christian, however, recognizes in suffering that there is guilt, judgment. What kind of guilt is it that [Christians] recognize in judgment? It is the guilt of all flesh that the Christian bears until the end of life, but beyond this it is at the same time the guilt of the world in Jesus that Christians must bear and endure in suffering. In this way the Christian's suffering of judgment in communion with Jesus Christ becomes a vicarious suffering for the world.[51]

This was not suicide, he would later contend,[52] but the good vicarious action that could lead to the redemption of Germany, an idea he expressed to Niebuhr and which we cited above, but some of it deserves repetition: "Christians in Germany will face the terrible alternative of either willing the defeat of their nation in order that Christian civilization may survive, or willing the victory of their nation and thereby destroying our civilization."[53] That is, his *Stellvertretung theory of pacifism* is redemptive because it enters into Christ's redemptive vicarious representative act on the cross. I begin with *Discipleship*:

> Even though Jesus Christ has already accomplished all the vicarious suffering necessary for our redemption, his sufferings in this world are not finished yet. In his grace, he has left something unfinished . . . in his suffering, which his church-community is to complete in this last period before his second coming. This suffering will benefit the body of Christ, the church. Whether this suffering of Christians also has power to atone for sin (1 Peter 4:1) remains an open question. What is clear, however, is that those suffering in the power of the body of Christ suffer in a vicariously representative [*stellvertretend*] action "for" the church-community, "for" the body of Christ. They are permitted to bear what others are spared.[54]

And then he picks this up again in *Ethics*:

> In this guilty yet sinless Jesus Christ all vicarious responsible action has its origin. . . . Those who act responsibly, seek to avoid

---

51. Bonhoeffer, DBWE 15, 386–415, here 409. Bonhoeffer does not question the uniqueness of Jesus's sufferings; see his circular letter to the Finkenwalde students on Nov. 29, 1942 in Bonhoeffer, DBWE 16, 378.

52. Bonhoeffer, DBWE 6, 197. "Human beings have freedom toward death and the right to death, in the sense of sacrifice, but only when the good sought through sacrifice, and not the destruction of one's own life, is the reason for risking one's life."

53. Bonhoeffer, DBWE 15, 210.

54. Bonhoeffer, DBWE 4, 222.

> becoming guilty, divorce themselves from the ultimate reality of history, that is, from the redeeming mystery of the sinless bearing of guilt by Jesus Christ, and have no part in the divine justification that attends this event. They place their personal innocence [*Unschuld*] above their responsibility for other human beings and are blind to the fact that precisely in so doing they become even more egregiously guilty. They are also blind to the fact that genuine guiltlessness is demonstrated precisely by entering into community with the guilt of other human beings for their sake. Because of Jesus Christ, the essence of responsible action intrinsically involves the sinless becoming guilty.... Only where a person becomes guilty out of love and responsibility does their action have a part in the justification pertaining to Jesus Christ's sinless guilt-bearing.[55]

More than once I have had to put his book down to take in the expansiveness of his pacifistic stance while at the same time knowing he has stretched theological categories to their maximum. He humanizes when he anchors his stance in love:

> Originating from Christ alone, there is now human action that is not crushed by conflicts of principle, but springs instead from the already accomplished reconciliation of the world with God. It is an action that, completely free of tragic or heroic overtones, soberly and simply does what is in accord with reality. It is an action of vicarious representative responsibility, of love for the real human being, of taking on oneself the guilt that burdens the world.[56]

The question he presses upon us even today is not "Should I be a pacifist?," but instead "How can I be Christ in my context?" He puts it this way: "By being responsible for Christ, who is life, before human beings, and only thus, I simultaneously take responsibility for human beings before Christ. I *simultaneously* represent Christ before human beings, and represent human beings before Christ."[57]

One's commitment in love to another person forms a bond with that person, and in that bond becomes manifest a vicarious representative act that connects the situation to the deepest reality in Christ, and in so doing I become a free, responsible human being for another. Bonhoeffer believed that this sort of action would save Germany's church while destroying the

---

55. Bonhoeffer, DBWE 6, 234.
56. Bonhoeffer, DBWE 6, 238.
57. Bonhoeffer, DBWE 6, 256.

Third Reich, but he also glimpsed only in the dark what that church would look like. What it would be, he believed, was solely responsible before the Lord Jesus Christ.[58]

Conclusion

My own commitment to crises like global terrorism is to work from the church out rather than to march onto the lawn in Washington, DC. Nor is my approach to work just war theory over and over until we perfect it for countries who will flout the theory's newest articulations. Just war theory is but a glimpse of what Christoformity can mean in our world. It settles for far too little because it fails to engage the christoform hermeneutic that Christ brings. Our approach to pacifism then is not a philosophical abstraction but instead a corollary to Christology. My approach is to pray, preach, teach, and write in the direction that urges my fellow Christians to walk a path that is rarely walked, the path of a christoform hermeneutic that permits us to discern how best to bring Christ's redemption into our world. A Bonhoeffer kind of Christoformity summons us to subvert the violence of war and the systemic structures that prop it up, not by way of philosophical reason but by way of christological faith, and that kind of life works toward a lasting redemption of our world.

---

58. See both his Finkenwalde circular letters on Nov. 22, 1941 and probably in Apr. 1942 (Bonhoeffer, DBWE 16, 237, 265).

Appendix 4

A Hidden Life
Directed by Terrence Malick
(Fox Searchlight Pictures, 2019)

I have been aware of the story of Franz Jägerstätter since at least the late 1970s. His life was, so far as I know, unique. He was an Austrian Catholic peasant who took a firm stance against becoming a soldier for the Nazis after they took control of his home country in 1938. More specifically, when he faced conscription into the German army he refused not only to kill in the military but also to swear an oath of loyalty to Adolf Hitler, as was required. As is made clear in the 1964 biography by Gordon Zahn, Jägerstätter refused to kill (and swear an oath) precisely because of his strong Catholic faith.[1] In fact, Zahn makes it clear that his convictions about this war were very much expressions of a profound spiritual renewal Jägerstätter underwent beginning around 1934 or 1935. His convictions regarding an unjust war were simply one dimension of his life of devotion to Christ and the church. Zahn quotes liberally from Jägerstätter's writings in his biography; the final chapter is, in fact, comprised of selections from his writings.[2] However, as of 2009 we also have an English translation of all of Jägerstätter's writings, which simply confirm Zahn's portrayal of this Catholic peasant who believed his faith required him to be a conscientious objector to Hitler's war (as well as to express the varied dimensions of his fervent Catholic faith).[3]

---

1. Zahn, *In Solitary Witness*.
2. Zahn, *In Solitary Witness*, 180–216.
3. Jägerstätter, *Letters and Writings from Prison*.

Since this is a fascinating and unique story in the midst of the Nazi era, I was quite excited when I heard, in 2018, that the respected director Terrence Malick was making a movie based on Jägerstätter's life. Released in 2019, it was in early 2020 that it was first screened in Harrisonburg, Virginia. Having now watched the film twice (and the first hour, three times), I offer the following reflections.

I am haunted by this movie. Beauty is the only word sufficient to name the first reason for the haunting I experience. Malick is known for creating beautiful scenes in his films. And he has done it again. I love evocative theme music. And that is the way I would describe the theme music created by James Newton Howard for this film. It creates or captures (which is the right way to put it?) just the right mood in so many scenes throughout this three-hour film. Visually the beauty is conveyed through the interplay of the majestic scenery of the beautiful mountains and streams that surround the rural Austrian village of Radegund, the simple life of these peasant farmers, and the quality of the loving relationships of the Jägerstätter family—Franz, Fani, and their three daughters, along with Fani's sister and Franz's mother, who also live with them.

But a part of what sustains the beauty is the realism of the film. Throughout the film we are brought into the daily, mundane, but meaningful life of this family. We see the joys of the children playing with each other and with both parents. We observe the close, pleasure-filled loving bond of Franz and Fani. But we can also see that everyday life is hard—filled with work that requires continual, strenuous efforts. Their hands work the dirt to plant vegetables and operate the scythes to produce feed for their farm animals. We can see that their simple clothing is practical and often soiled from the daily, insistent work of their small farm. Only on special occasions are clean, bright clothing and celebration present. And we see that hard decisions are indeed tough, causing conflicts and pain within the family. By the time such knowledge is relevant, we *know* that an absent husband and father would make what is already demanding labor almost overwhelmingly burdensome. (One wonders how Fani could possibly have managed the practical tasks during Franz's absence had her sister and mother-in-law not lived with her.)

The beauty of the loving relationship between Franz and Fani is conveyed partly through the letters they exchange while Franz is absent—first in military training in 1940, then in military prison in 1943. Especially during this latter period—which is painful for both Franz and Fani—they both write careful, sensitive, mostly positive letters to be encouraging to each other. And yet the viewer is made aware of the lonely and often brutal existence of Franz in prison, as well as the challenging circumstances Fani faces because of the added work compounded by the stress of knowing the fate her husband awaits (conscientious objection being a capital offense, as both of them well knew).

But now we come to the second reason for the haunting I feel because of this film. *Disappointing* is the word that leaps to mind here. Ironically, my sense of disappointment was deepened precisely because Malick's directing skills are very much on display in this film. He could have made such a wonderful film about this extraordinary—even unique—story. But, alas, he has not truly succeeded in this, I am afraid. That is, he has not honestly portrayed the key elements of the story of Franz Jägerstätter that make it unique and thus very much worth telling. What do I mean?

I kept wanting the film to help the viewer know *why* Jägerstätter was refusing both to be conscripted into the military and give an oath of loyalty to Hitler. For after all, he knowingly goes against the wishes of virtually everyone around him. The (drunken) village mayor tries to shame Franz in front of other villagers, saying that everyone but Franz is going along with the National Socialists. Why is he making it difficult for his family, the village, and the mayor? Franz meets with his local priest and then later the bishop. Both try to convince him that he has a responsibility to the fatherland and to his family. And at least initially his wife also is quite troubled by his decision. So, standing alone, he makes this decision. And he does so—as he well knows—at what is likely to be a tremendous cost both to himself (imprisonment and beheading) *and* his family (the loss of a husband and father, along with the shame his disgraceful death would bring). *Why* is the question that begs to be asked. And the film—if it is to tell the unique story of this conscientious objector—needs to help us answer this question. But it mostly does not.

You see, it is significant that Jägerstätter is not a pacifist. This means that he is not opposed to all war. And certainly, Catholics were not normally given to opposing the swearing of an oath of loyalty to a leader. So, what led this one man to take this inflexible stance, with such great cost to himself and his family that he dearly loved?

Two realities needed to be conveyed by the film. The first would be to give the viewer some sense of the horrors perpetrated by the Nazis, especially the military. But also, to let us know that Franz was aware of such horrors—the excessive violence and gross injustices, obvious violations of righteous and just behaviors that he would resist to the point of being willing to die and leave his family bereft of a father and husband. There are hints of what these might be, but only hints. This cinematic drama opens with a brief clip from film of Hitler being welcomed, probably by Austrians, as he annexed their country. This shows the strong support Hitler received as he "welcomed" his home country to join with Germany. We have to bracket our (post-World War II) knowledge of Hitler in order to remember that to most late-1930s Austrians there is nothing especially nefarious about these scenes. Another film clip regarding the war efforts of Germany are seen by Franz when he is in a military training camp in 1940. Again, we need to remember this is not a pacifist watching this film. With that in mind, again there is nothing objectionable about the footage he is watching. It is a rather standard depiction of war.

There are also very brief words spoken by acquaintances of Franz that suggest questions one might have about the effects of National Socialism on life in Austria and the war being fought. After a man from the village is conscripted, Franz asks him if he believes in what they're fighting for. The man responds by saying "not really." In one of his two or three "speeches" in the village pub, the mayor rants about immigrants ruining the country. So, this is indicative of xenophobia (and perhaps racism or anti-Semitism). But this is a local villager speaking, not National Socialists who have taken over the country. The local mill operator seems quite critical of the Nazis. He on one occasion says: "Don't they know evil when they see it? The mask is off. I fear for my family . . . We're used to it now. Crime. Shame." Local villagers utter "Heil, Hitler" as they greet Franz on the walkway. The blacksmith is once shown speaking to Franz, saying that he has seen terrible things in Vienna: hate, killing of children and the insane. Traki, a local baker, seems to speak in strong, exaggerated terms. On one occasion he says: "The whole world is sinking." "They've asked you to take an oath to the antichrist; I know." "Is this the end of the world? The death of the light?" Also, early in the film, Fani observes planes overhead, but without comment from her. Again, these seem to me to be hints. But enough to clarify why Franz was deeply convinced of the evils of National Socialism? Even when none of the other villagers apparently saw any or all of this as reason to resist National Socialism in the way Franz does?

The other reality that needed to be conveyed by the film was who Franz was in 1939 and beyond. Why did he in particular come to such strong convictions about this that he was willing to lose his own life and cause his family to suffer because of his fatal choice? As portrayed in the film, Franz is a man of few words. The following are more or less the sum total of words Franz uses in the film to provide a rationale for his behaviors. After watching the footage of the war mentioned above, Franz asks: "What's happening to our country?" About twenty-six minutes into the film Franz meets with his local priest. Franz says: "Father, if they call me up, I can't serve. We're killing innocent people. Raiding other countries. Preying on the weak. Now the priests are calling them [the soldiers] heroes, even saints.

The soldiers that do this. It might be that the others are heroes. The ones who defend their homes against the invaders."[4] The priest then seeks to talk him out of his conscientious objection. He asks him if he's considered the consequences for his family. He reminds him that he will almost certainly be executed. And he tells him that his sacrifice will benefit no one. But he will speak to the bishop about his case.

Franz, when asked by villagers, refuses to contribute to the collection to help veterans and their families. He has also apparently refused to accept subsidies offered to families like his by the National Socialists. The mayor chides him for both of these responses.

Franz later meets with the bishop. Franz: "If God has given us free will, are we not responsible for what we do? If our leaders are not good, if they are evil, what do we do? I want to save my life, but not with lies." The bishop then urges him that he has a duty to the fatherland; the church tells him so. Then he paraphrases a portion of Romans 13:1–7. A little later Franz is shown pausing to look thoughtfully at a statue of the crucified Christ along the pathway.

Franz is again shown in the area cathedral, this time with Ohlendorf, a man who is repainting some of the walls. Some of the best theological lines in the film come from this painter, speaking to Franz, who is for some unexplained reason simply watching. As the painter does his work, he speaks to Franz: "What we do, is we just create sympathy. We create . . . we create admirers. We don't create followers. Christ's life is a demand. We don't want to be reminded of it. So, we don't have to see what happens to the truth. A darker time is coming. And men will be more clever. They won't fight the truth; so, just ignore it. I paint their comfortable Christ, with a halo over his head. How can I show what I haven't lived? Someday I might have the courage to venture; not yet. Someday I'll paint the true Christ."

Shortly after Franz has been called up for military duty he reflects on his likely fate: "Does a man have a right to let himself be put to death? For the truth? Could it possibly please God? He wants to have peace. Happiness. Not bring suffering on ourselves."

So, this is as close as the film gets to helping the viewer know "why" this one man resolutely stood totally opposed to the National Socialists: he would not give an oath of loyalty to Hitler nor would he kill in their army. Even presented with the possibility of serving in a nonviolent capacity, such as working in a hospital, he still refused to swear an oath of loyalty (upon penalty of death).

4. This is one of the few instances where the script signals that the writer has read Jägerstätter's writings. For portions of these words are directly taken from Jägerstätter, *Letters and Writings from Prison*, 208.

Having carefully viewed the film a second time, I can see that there are more hints about the why than I noticed in my first viewing in the theater. However, the story as told through the film does not satisfactorily answer the why question. Or, put differently: it is hard to imagine why Jägerstätter was so resolute in his stance, given the tremendous costs. More specifically, the story as told by Malick has mostly muted the deep convictions that made Jägerstätter who he was, especially as they related to his opposition to National Socialism. That is, Malick has mostly left the viewer ignorant of the passionate Catholic convictions of this man. Who would have imagined from the film that Franz had experienced an apparently life-altering religious awakening in late 1934 or early 1935? And according to his biographer, Gordon Zahn, a sociologist and Catholic peace activist, this was crucial to his opposition to National Socialism. From 1935 forward not only was Franz a fervent Catholic, he was also very active in the local parish. In fact, it is quite possible that Franz was deeply influenced by Father Karobath, his priest, to whom he was quite close and who had been exiled from the community in 1940 because of speaking out against the Nazi regime in that year. Franz's faith—a theologically specific Catholic expression of faith—is ever present in his writings. And we now have over one hundred pages of essays on a variety of subjects in English, mostly expressive of his faith. But very little of this is present in the film.

Now don't get me wrong. A truly quality film should not be overly didactic. However, I would argue that Malick managed to give a couple of characters in the film, such as the painter in the cathedral and the mayor, substantial "speeches" that seem to convey more of their character than is true for Jägerstätter. But beyond that, there were many natural opportunities where, without being overly didactic, Franz could have been shown to reveal his deep convictions. His wife wanted desperately to know why he was making this decision that was so costly. He met with both his priest and the bishop. He said some words to them. But given the purpose of the meetings, more words would have been quite appropriate. The painter in the cathedral opened up an avenue of exploration that could have led naturally into Jägerstätter's conveying some of his similar convictions. But nothing; he is silent (which is more often true than not, throughout the film).

Surely, for background, Malick read Zahn's biography. Some film critic indicated that the film is based on the 2009 collection of Jägerstätter's writings. If so, there are many passages to draw from. In some "brief reflection on the current era" Jägerstätter offers the following remarks: "It is of course very sad today that so many people do not recognize, or do not want to recognize, the dangerous situation in which we find ourselves. Many people claim to be blameless. God will eventually judge to what extent they truly are."[5] He goes on to say that those in power who seduce are more blameworthy than the seduced. Later, in 1942, he writes some reflections on whether or not the German war is a typical war or rather a revolution of sorts. He argues it is the latter. "I believe that many people have forgotten what the Holy Father said about National Socialism in his encyclical many years ago, namely, that National Socialism is even more dangerous than Communism. Since Rome has not withdrawn this judgment, I believe that it is not likely a crime or a sin if someone as a Catholic were to refuse the current obligation for military service—even though a person who refuses military service is surely looking at death. Is it not more Christian for someone to give himself as a sacrifice than to have to murder others who possess a right to life on earth and who want to live in order to save their lives for a short while?" "I can never and shall never believe that we Catholics must make ourselves available to do the work of the most evil and dangerous anti-Christian power that has ever existed."[6] "What kind of Catholic would venture to declare that these military campaigns of plundering which Germany has undertaken in many lands and is still leading, constitute a just and holy war?"[7]

And then there are the brief quotes that form a list of over two hundred sayings, compiled by Jägerstätter in 1943, entitled "What Every Christian Should Know."[8] Among them: "Love of enemies is not a weakness of personal character but a heroic power of the soul and the initiation of the divine model. (See Matt. 5:43ff.)" "Those who want to find the right way to eternal well-being should not walk with the majority of people who are usually timid about making sacrifices, and they should not entrust themselves to leaders whose actions differ from their words. (See Matt. 7:15ff.)" "Authentic spirituality comes about not by talking about God, but by living according to God's command. Without this obedience, even wonderful acts mean nothing. (See Matt. 7:21ff.)" "Our bond with God's will must be stronger than our love of our family and relatives. (See Mark 3:31–35.)" "The disciples of Jesus must learn to perceive the suffering of their master as unavoidable and to apprehend the religion of Jesus as the religion of the cross. (See Mark 8:31.) The salvation of the soul takes precedence over everything else." "In Christ's kingdom there are no rigid rights. Rather, self-giving love is the highest authority. In place of self-seeking, Christ upholds selflessness. Christ never spoke well of injustice and acts of violence. A higher readiness

---

5. Jägerstätter, *Letters and Writings from Prison*, 171 (notebooks, 1941–1942).

6. Jägerstätter, *Letters and Writings from Prison*, 189–90.

7. Jägerstätter, *Letters and Writings from Prison*, 207.

8. Jägerstätter, *Letters and Writings from Prison*, 214–33. The quotes in this paragraph come from these pages.

to sacrifice oneself is required of Christians than of nonbelievers. (See Luke 6:27–35.)" "Religious belief is a whole. Someone cannot accept one individual in love but reject another. Belief flows forth not from nationality and race but from a living faith in Christ. . . . (See Eph. 2:11–21.)" "The watchword of Christians amid conflict is not 'Resist power with power,' but 'Resist power with patience and perseverance in faith.' (See the Letter of Jude, verse 20.)"

Once again, I don't believe the film should have been overly didactic. But the rich set of writings we have by this modestly educated Catholic peasant help answer the *why* question. They provide a rationale for why this man was willing to sacrifice his life and place hardships on the family he loved. And their articulation might well have made sense in this rural, Austrian, Catholic community—at least to serious Catholics. Without such a rationale the film is seriously deficient. The well-written script as it exists could have, within its three hours, artfully woven selections from these writings into dialogues that would have made a good film a truly great film—about a unique and extraordinary human being, whose reasons for living, and in this case resisting, were rooted in deeply held Catholic convictions that collided with the Nazi ideology that had taken over his country and seduced his own village.

Bibliography

Ahlers, Rolf. *The Barmen Theological Declaration of 1934: The Archeology of a Confessional Text*. Lewiston, NY: Edwin Mellen, 1986.

Balfour, Michael, and Julian Frisby. *Helmuth von Moltke: A Leader Against Hitler*. London: Macmillan, 1972.

Barkai, Avraham. *From Boycott to Annihilation: The Economic Struggle of German Jews 1933–1943*. Translated by William Templer. Hanover, NH: University Press of New England, 1989.

Barnes, Kenneth C. "Dietrich Bonhoeffer and Hitler's Persecution of the Jews." In *Betrayal: German Churches and the Holocaust*, edited by Robert P. Ericksen and Susannah Heschel, 110–28. Minneapolis: Fortress, 1999.

———. *Nazism, Liberalism, and Christianity: Protestant Social Thought in Germany and Great Britain 1925–1937*. Lexington, KY: University Press of Kentucky, 1991.

Barnett, Victoria J. "Bonhoeffer and the Conspiracy." In *The Oxford Handbook of Dietrich Bonhoeffer*, edited by Philip G. Ziegler and Michael Mawson, 65–75. Oxford, UK: Oxford University Press, 2019.

———. *For the Soul of the People: Protestant Protest Against Hitler*. Oxford, UK: Oxford University Press, 1992.

Barth, Karl. *The Doctrine of Creation Part 4*. Edited by G. W. Bromiley and T. F. Torrance. Translated by A. T. Mackay et al. Vol. 3 of *Church Dogmatics*. Edinburgh: T & T Clark, 1961.

———. *The Doctrine of Creation Part 4, Sections 55–56*. Edited by G. W. Bromiley and T. F. Torrance. Translated by A. T. Mackay et al. Vol. 3 of *Church Dogmatics*. Study Edition 20. London: T & T Clark, 2010.

———. *The Doctrine of Reconciliation Part 2*. Edited by G. W. Bromiley and T. F. Torrance. Translated by G. W. Bromiley. Vol. 4 of *Church Dogmatics*. Edinburgh: T & T Clark, 1958.

———. *Fragments Grave and Gay*. Edited by Martin Rumscheidt. Translated by Erich Mosbacher. London: Fountain, 1971.

———. "The New World in the Bible." In *The Word of God and Theology*, edited and translated by Amy Marga, 15–29. London: T & T Clark, 2011.

———. *On Religion: The Revelation of God as the Sublimation of Religion*. Translated and introduced by Garrett Green. London: T & T Clark, 2006.

———. *A Unique Time of God: Karl Barth's WWI Sermons*. Edited and translated by William Klempa. Louisville: Westminster John Knox, 2016.

Bartov, Omer. *Hitler's Army: Soldiers, Nazis, and War in the Third Reich*. Oxford, UK: Oxford University Press, 1991.

Bartsch, Hans-Werner. "The Foundation and Meaning of Christian Pacifism." In *New Theology No. 6: On Revolution and Non-Revolution, Violence and Non-Violence, Peace and Power*, edited by Martin E. Marty and Dean G. Peerman, 185–98. London: Macmillan, 1969.

Bender, Harold S. *Conrad Grebel, c. 1498–1526: The Founder of the Swiss Brethren, Sometimes Called Anabaptists*. Scottdale, PA: Herald, 1950.

Berenbaum, Michael, ed. *Witness to the Holocaust: An Illustrated Documentary History of the Holocaust in the Words of Its Victims, Perpetrators and Bystanders*. New York: HarperCollins, 1997.

Bergen, Doris L. *Twisted Cross: The German Christian Movement in the Third Reich*. Chapel Hill, NC: University of North Carolina Press, 1996.

Bethge, Eberhard. "Bonhoeffer's Pacifism: Some Comments by Eberhard Bethge." *International Bonhoeffer Society Newsletter, English Language Section* (Apr. 1978) 6–7.

———. "Christian Political Involvement." In *Bonhoeffer: Exile and Martyr*, 117–36. New York: Seabury, 1975.

———. *Dietrich Bonhoeffer: A Biography*. Rev. ed. Edited by Victoria J. Barnett. Minneapolis: Fortress, 2000.

———. "Dietrich Bonhoeffer and the Jews." In *Ethical Responsibility: Bonhoeffer's Legacy to the Churches*, edited by John D. Godsey and Geffrey B. Kelly, 43–102. New York: Edwin Mellen, 1981.

———. "Dietrich Bonhoeffers Weg vom 'Pazifismus' zur Verschwörung." In *Frieden: Das unumgängliche Wagnis*, edited by Hans Pfeifer, 118–36. Munich: Chr. Kaiser, 1982.

———. *Friendship and Resistance: Essays on Dietrich Bonhoeffer*. Grand Rapids: Eerdmans, 1995.

———. "Resistance and Terrorism: Dietrich Bonhoeffer's Move into the Field of Violence." Unpublished lecture, presented at Bonhoeffer session, American Academy of Religion, Nov. 1978, 22 pp., in John Howard Yoder papers, Archives of the Mennonite Church, Goshen, IN, Box 184.

———. "Turning Points in Bonhoeffer's Life and Thought." *Union Seminary Quarterly Review* 23, no. 1 (Fall 1967) 3–21.

———, and Renate Bethge, eds. *Last Letters of Resistance: Farewells from the Bonhoeffer Family*. Translated by Dennis Slabaugh. Philadelphia: Fortress, 1986.

Biggar, Nigel. *In Defence of War: Christian Realism and Just Force*. Oxford, UK: Oxford University Press, 2013.

Bleuel, Hans Peter. *Sex and Society in Nazi Germany*. Translated by J. Maxwell Brownjohn. Reprint, New York: Dorset, 1996.

Boehlke, Bain, dir. *Dietrich Bonhoeffer: Memories and Perspectives*. Lansdale, PA: Vision Video, 1982. DVD.

Bonhoeffer, Dietrich. *Act and Being: Transcendental Philosophy and Ontology in Systematic Theology*. Edited by Wayne Whitson Floyd and Hans-Richard Reuter. Translated by Martin Rumscheidt. Vol. 2 of *Dietrich Bonhoeffer Works*. Minneapolis: Fortress, 1996.

———. *Barcelona, Berlin, New York: 1928–1931*. Edited by Clifford Green. Translated by Douglas W. Stott. Vol. 10 of *Dietrich Bonhoeffer Works*. Minneapolis: Fortress, 2008.

———. *Berlin: 1932–1933*. Edited by Larry L. Rasmussen. Translated by Douglas W. Stott et al. Vol. 12 of *Dietrich Bonhoeffer Works*. Minneapolis: Fortress, 2009.

———. *Conspiracy and Imprisonment: 1940–1945*. Edited by Mark Brocker. Translated by Lisa E. Dahill and Douglas W. Stott. Vol. 16 of *Dietrich Bonhoeffer Works*. Minneapolis: Fortress, 2006.

———. *Creation and Fall: A Theological Exposition of Genesis 1–3*. Edited by John W. DeGruchy. Translated by Douglas Stephen Bax. Vol. 3 of *Dietrich Bonhoeffer Works*. Minneapolis: Fortress, 1997.

———. *Discipleship*. Edited by Geffrey B. Kelly and John D. Godsey. Translated by Barbara Green and Reinhard Krauss. Vol. 4 of *Dietrich Bonhoeffer Works*. Minneapolis: Fortress, 2000.

———. *Ecumenical, Academic, and Pastoral Work: 1931–1932*. Edited by Victoria J. Barnett et al. Translated by Isabel Best et al. Vol. 11 of *Dietrich Bonhoeffer Works*. Minneapolis: Fortress, 2012.

———. *Ethics*. Edited by Clifford J. Green. Translated by Reinhard Krauss et al. Vol. 6 of *Dietrich Bonhoeffer Works*. Minneapolis: Fortress, 2005.

———. *Fiction from Tegel Prison*. Edited by Clifford J. Green. Translated by Nancy Lukens. Vol. 7 of *Dietrich Bonhoeffer Works*. Minneapolis: Fortress, 2000.

———. *Letters and Papers from Prison*. Edited by John W. DeGruchy. Translated by Isabel Best et al. Vol. 8 of *Dietrich Bonhoeffer Works*. Minneapolis: Fortress, 2009.

———. *Life Together* and *Prayerbook of the Bible: An Introduction to the Psalms*. Edited by Geffrey B. Kelly. Translated by Daniel W. Bloesch and James H. Burtness. Vol. 5 of *Dietrich Bonhoeffer Works*. Minneapolis: Fortress, 1996.

———. *London: 1933–1935*. Edited by Keith W. Clements. Translated by Isabel Best. Vol. 13 of *Dietrich Bonhoeffer Works*. Minneapolis: Fortress, 2007.

———. *Sanctorum Communio: A Theological Study of the Sociology of the Church*. Edited by Clifford J. Green. Translated by Reinhard Krauss and Nancy Lukens. Vol. 1 of *Dietrich Bonhoeffer Works*. Minneapolis: Fortress, 1998.

———. *Theological Education at Finkenwalde: 1935–1937*. Edited by H. Gaylon Barker and Mark S. Brocker. Translated by Douglas W. Stott. Vol. 14 of *Dietrich Bonhoeffer Works*. Minneapolis: Fortress, 2013.

———. *Theological Education Underground: 1937–1940*. Edited by Victoria J. Barnett. Translated by Claudia D. Bergmann et al. Vol. 15 of *Dietrich Bonhoeffer Works*. Minneapolis: Fortress, 2011.

———. *The Young Bonhoeffer: 1918–1927*. Edited by Paul D. Matheny et al. Translated by Mary Nebelsick and Douglas W. Stott. Vol. 9 of *Dietrich Bonhoeffer Works*. Minneapolis: Fortress, 2003.

———, and Maria von Wedemeyer. *Love Letters from Cell 92*, edited by Ruth-Alice von Bismarck and Ulrich Kavitz. Translated by John Brownjohn. Nashville: Abingdon, 1995.

Borg, Daniel R. *The Old-Prussian Church and the Weimar Republic: A Study in Political Adjustment, 1917–1927*. Hanover, NH: University Press of New England, 1984.

Bosanquet, Mary. *The Life and Death of Dietrich Bonhoeffer*. New York: Harper & Row, 1968.

Brimlow, Robert W. *What about Hitler?* Grand Rapids: Brazos, 2006.

Brock, Brian. *Singing the Ethos of God: On the Place of Christian Ethics in Scripture*. Grand Rapids: Eerdmans, 2007.

———. "'Success and Failure': Public Disasters, Works of Love, and the Inwardness of Faithfulness." In *Who Am I?: Bonhoeffer's Theology through His Poetry*, edited by Bernd Wannenwetsch, 47–69. London: T & T Clark, 2009.

Browning, Christopher. *The Origins of the Final Solution*. New York: Bison, 2007.

Bruner, Frederick Dale. *Matthew: A Commentary*. 2 vols. Rev. ed. Grand Rapids: Eerdmans, 2004.

Brunner, Emil. *The Divine Imperative*. Translated by Olive Wyon. Philadelphia: Westminster, 1947.

Bucher, Rainer. *Hitler's Theology: A Study in Political Religion*. Translated by Rebecca Pohl. London: Continuum, 2011.

Bucholtz, Erika, et al., eds. *"Luther's Words Are Everywhere . . .": Martin Luther in Nazi Germany*. Berlin: Topography of Terror Foundation, 2017.

Burleigh, Michael. *Moral Combat: Good and Evil in World War II*. New York: Harper, 2011.

———. *The Third Reich: A New History*. NY: Hill & Wang, 2000.

———, and Wolfgang Wippermann. *The Racial State: Germany 1933–1945*. Cambridge, UK: Cambridge University Press, 1991.

Busch, Eberhard. *Karl Barth: His Life from Letters and Autobiographical Texts*. Translated by John Bowden. Philadelphia: Fortress, 1975.

Camp, Lee C. *Mere Discipleship: Radical Christianity in a Rebellious World*. 2nd ed. Grand Rapids: Brazos, 2008.

Carter, Guy Christopher. "Confession at Bethel, August 1933—Enduring Witness: The Formation, Revision and Significance of the First Full Theological Confession of the Evangelical Church Struggle in Nazi Germany." PhD diss., Marquette University, 1987.

Chalamet, Christophe. *Revivalism and Social Christianity: The Prophetic Faith of Henri Nick and André Trocmé*. Eugene, OR: Pickwick, 2013.

Chickering, Roger. *Imperial Germany and a World Without War: The Peace Movement and German Society 1892–1914*. Princeton, NJ: Princeton University Press, 1975.

Clingan, Ralph Garlin. *Against Cheap Grace in a World Come of Age: An Intellectual Biography of Clayton Powell, 1865–1953*. New York: Peter Lang, 2002.

Cochrane, Arthur C. *The Church's Confession under Hitler*. 2nd ed. Pittsburgh: Pickwick, 1976.

Collins Winn, Christian T. *"Jesus Is Victor!": The Significance of the Blumhardts for the Theology of Karl Barth*. Eugene, OR: Pickwick, 2009.

Conway, John S. "Between Pacifism and Patriotism—A Protestant Dilemma: The Case of Friedrich Siegmund-Schultze." In *Germans Against Nazism: Nonconformity, Opposition and Resistance in the Third Reich: Essays in Honour of Peter Hoffmann*, edited by Francis R. Nicosia and Lawrence D. Stokes, 87–113. New York: Berg, 1990.

———. *The Nazi Persecution of the Churches 1933–1945*. New York: Basic Books, 1968.

Correll, Mark R. *Shepherds of the Empire: Germany's Conservative Protestant Leadership 1888–1919*. Minneapolis: Fortress, 2014.

Cresswell, Amos, and Max Tow. *Dr. Franz Hildebrandt: Mr. Valiant-for-Truth*. Leominster, UK: Gracewing, 2000.

Davis, Grady Scott. *Warcraft and the Fragility of Virtue*. Moscow, ID: University of Idaho Press, 1992.

DeGruchy, John W. *Daring, Trusting Spirit: Bonhoeffer's Friend Eberhard Bethge*. Minneapolis: Fortress, 2005.

———, ed. *The Cambridge Companion to Dietrich Bonhoeffer*. Cambridge, UK: Cambridge University Press, 1999.

DeJonge, Michael P. *Bonhoeffer on Resistance: The Word against the Wheel*. Oxford, UK: Oxford University Press, 2018.

———. "Bonhoeffer's Non-Commitment to Nonviolence: A Response to Stanley Hauerwas." *Journal of Religious Ethics* 44, no. 4 (2016) 378–94.

———. *Bonhoeffer's Reception of Luther*. Oxford, UK: Oxford University Press, 2017.

———. *Bonhoeffer's Theological Formation: Berlin, Barth, and Protestant Theology*. Oxford, UK: Oxford University Press, 2012.

———. "Bonhoeffer's Two-Kingdoms Thinking in "The Church and the Jewish Question." In *Christ, Church and World: New Studies in Bonhoeffer's Theology and Ethics*, edited by Michael Mawson and Philip G. Ziegler, 141–60. London: T & T Clark, 2016.

———. "How to Read Bonhoeffer's Peace Statements: Or, Bonhoeffer Was a Lutheran and Not an Anabaptist." *Theology* 118, no. 3 (2015) 162–71.

———. "Review of *Bonhoeffer the Assassin?*" *Christian Century* (Oct. 30, 2013) 37–39.

Dorrien, Gary. *The Barthian Revolt in Modern Theology: Theology without Weapons*. Louisville: Westminster John Knox, 2000.

———. *The New Abolition: W. E. B. DuBois and the Black Social Gospel*. New Haven, CT: Yale University Press, 2015.

———. *Social Democracy in the Making: Political and Religious Roots of European Socialism*. New Haven, CT: Yale University Press, 2019.

Dramm, Sabine. *Dietrich Bonhoeffer and the Resistance*. Translated by Margaret Kohl. Minneapolis: Fortress, 2009.

Elshtain, Jean Bethke. *Just War against Terror: The Burden of American Power in a Violent World*. New York: Basic Books, 2004.

Ericksen, Robert P. *Theologians under Hitler*. New Haven, CT: Yale University Press, 1985.

Feil, Ernst. *The Theology of Dietrich Bonhoeffer*. Translated by Martin Rumscheidt. Philadelphia: Fortress, 1985.

Fest, Joachim. *Plotting Hitler's Death: The Story of the German Resistance*. Translated by Bruce Little. New York: Metropolitan, 1996.

Frick, Peter, ed. *Bonhoeffer's Intellectual Formation: Theology and Philosophy in His Thought*. Eugene, OR: Wipf & Stock, 2008.

Fritzsche, Peter. *Germans into Nazis*. Cambridge, MA: Harvard University Press, 1998.

Gellately, Robert. *Backing Hitler: Consent and Coercion in Nazi Germany*. Oxford, UK: Oxford University Press, 2001.

Gerlach, Wolfgang. *And the Witnesses Were Silent: The Confessing Church and the Persecution of the Jews*. Translated and edited by Victoria J. Barnett. Lincoln, NE: University of Nebraska Press, 2000.

Gides, David M. *Pacifism, Just War, and Tyrannicide: Bonhoeffer's Church-World Theology and His Changing Forms of Political Thinking and Involvement*. Eugene, OR: Pickwick, 2011.

Gilbert, Martin. *The Holocaust*. New York: Henry Holt, 1985.

Gill, Anton. *An Honorable Defeat: A History of German Resistance to Hitler, 1933–1945*. New York: Henry Holt, 1994.

Gisevius, Hans Bernd. *To the Bitter End: An Insider's Account of the Plot to Kill Hitler 1933–1944*. Translated by Richard and Clara Winston. New York: DaCapo, 1998.

Godsey, John D. *The Theology of Dietrich Bonhoeffer*. London: SCM, 1960.

Gordon, Sarah. *Hitler, Germans, and the "Jewish Question."* Princeton, NJ: Princeton University Press, 1984.

Gracie, David McI. "Our Need for God's Word." In *Meditating on the Word*, by Dietrich Bonhoeffer, translated by David McI. Gracie, 1–23. Cambridge, MA: Cowley, 1986.

Grayling, A. C. *Among the Dead: The History and Moral Legacy of the WW II Bombing of Civilians in Germany and Japan*. New York: Walker, 2006.

Green, Clifford J. *Bonhoeffer: A Theology of Sociality*. Rev. ed. Grand Rapids: Eerdmans, 1999.

———. "Bonhoeffer at Union. Critical Turning Points: 1931 and 1939." *Union Seminary Quarterly Review* 62 (2010) 1–16.

———. "Bonhoeffer's Christian Peace Ethic, Conditional Pacifism, and Resistance." In *The Oxford Handbook of Dietrich Bonhoeffer*, edited by Philip G. Ziegler and Michael Mawson, 344–62. Oxford, UK: Oxford University Press, 2019.

———. "Editor's Introduction to the English Edition." In *Ethics*, by Dietrich Bonhoeffer, edited by Clifford J. Green, translated by Reinhard Krauss et al., 1–44. Vol. 6 of *Dietrich Bonhoeffer Works*. Minneapolis: Fortress, 2005.

———. "Hauerwas and Nation on Bonhoeffer's 'Pacifism': A Literature Overview." *The Bonhoeffer Legacy: Australasian Journal of Bonhoeffer Studies* 3, no. 2 (2015) 1–15.

———. "Pacifism and Tyrannicide: Bonhoeffer's Christian Peace Ethic." *Studies in Christian Ethics* 18, no. 3 (2005) 31–47.

———. "Peace Ethic or 'Pacifism'?: An Assessment of *Bonhoeffer the Assassin?*" *Modern Theology* 31, no. 1 (Jan. 2015) 201–8.

———. "Review of *Dietrich Bonhoeffer: Reality and Resistance* by Larry Rasmussen." *Conversations in Religion and Theology* 6 (2008) 155–65.

———. "Review of *Performing the Faith: Bonhoeffer and the Practice of Nonviolence* by Stanley Hauerwas." *Modern Theology* 21, no. 4 (Oct. 2005) 674–77.

———. "The Text of Bonhoeffer's Ethics." In *New Studies in Bonhoeffer's Ethics*, edited by William J. Peck, 3–66. Lewiston, NY: Edwin Mellen, 1987.

———, et al. "Editors' Afterword to the German Edition." In *Ethics*, by Dietrich Bonhoeffer, edited by Clifford J. Green, translated by Reinhard Krauss et al., 409–49. Vol. 6 of *Dietrich Bonhoeffer Works*. Minneapolis: Fortress, 2005.

Greene-McCreight, Kathryn. *Darkness Is My Only Companion*. Grand Rapids: Brazos, 2005.

Grose, Peter. *A Good Place to Hide: How One French Community Saved Thousands of Lives during World War II*. New York: Pegasus, 2015.

Gutiérrez, Gustavo. *The Power of the Poor in History*. Translated by Robert R. Barr. Eugene, OR: Wipf & Stock, 2004.

Gutteridge, Richard. *Open Thy Mouth for the Dumb: The German Evangelical Church and the Jews 1879–1950*. Oxford, UK: Basil Blackwell, 1976.

Hallie, Philip. *In the Eye of the Hurricane: Tales of Good and Evil, Help and Harm*. Middletown, CT: Wesleyan University Press, 1997.

———. *Lest Innocent Blood Be Shed*. New York: HarperPerennial, 1994.

Harvey, Barry. *Taking Hold of the Real: Dietrich Bonhoeffer and the Profound Worldliness of Christianity*. Eugene, OR: Cascade, 2015.
Hauerwas, Stanley. *Performing the Faith: Bonhoeffer and the Practice of Non-Violence*. Grand Rapids: Brazos, 2004.
Haynes, Stephen R. *The Battle for Bonhoeffer: Debating Discipleship in the Age of Trump*. Grand Rapids: Eerdmans, 2018.
———. *The Bonhoeffer Legacy: Post-Holocaust Perspectives*. Minneapolis: Fortress, 2006.
———. *The Bonhoeffer Phenomenon: Portraits of a Protestant Saint*. Minneapolis: Fortress, 2004.
Helmreich, Ernest Christian. *The German Churches under Hitler: Background, Struggle, and Epilogue*. Detroit: Wayne State University Press, 1979.
Hildebrandt, Franz. "Barmen: What to Learn and What Not to Learn." In *The Barmen Confession: Papers from the Seattle Assembly*, edited by Hubert G. Locke, 285–302. Lewiston, NY: Edwin Mellen, 1986.
———. "Foreword." In *Peace without Eschatology?*, by John H. Yoder, 3–4. Scottdale, PA: A Concern Reprint, 1959.
———. "An Oasis of Freedom." In *I Knew Dietrich Bonhoeffer*, edited by Wolf-Dieter Zimmermann and Ronald Gregor Smith, 38–40. Reprint, London: Fontana, 1973.
Hinlicky, Paul R. *Before Auschwitz: What Christian Theology Must Learn from the Rise of Nazism*. Eugene, OR: Cascade, 2013.
Hockenos, Matthew D. *Then They Came for Me: Martin Niemöller, the Pastor Who Defied the Nazis*. New York: Basic Books, 2018.
Hoffman, Peter. *The History of the German Resistance 1933–1945*. 3rd ed. Montreal: McGill-Queen's University Press, 1996.
Holland, Scott. "First We Take Manhattan, Then We Take Berlin: Bonhoeffer's New York." *Cross Currents* (Fall 2000) 369–82.
Holmes, Christopher. "'The Indivisible Whole of God's Reality': On the Agency of Jesus in Bonhoeffer's *Ethics*." *International Journal of Systematic Theology* 12 (2010) 283–301.
Hook, Brian S., and R. R. Reno. *Heroism and the Christian Life: Reclaiming Excellence*. Louisville: Westminster John Knox, 2000.
House, Paul R. *Bonhoeffer's Seminary Vision: A Case for Costly Discipleship and Life Together*. Wheaton, IL: Crossway, 2015.
Huber, Ryan. *Dietrich Bonhoeffer's Ethics of Formation*. Lanham, MD: Lexington, 2020.
Jägerstätter, Franz. *Letters and Writings from Prison*. Edited by Erna Putz. Translated by Robert A. Krieg. Maryknoll, NY: Orbis, 2009.
Jantzen, Kyle. *Faith and Fatherland: Parish Politics in Hitler's Germany*. Minneapolis: Fortress, 2008.
Jehle, Frank. *Ever against the Stream: The Politics of Karl Barth, 1906–1968*. Translated by Richard and Martha Burnett. Grand Rapids: Eerdmans, 2002.
Jenkins, Julian. *Christian Pacifism Confronts German Nationalism: The Ecumenical Movement and the Cause of Peace in Germany, 1914–1933*. Lewiston, NY: Edwin Mellen, 2002.
Jenkins, Philip. *The Great and Holy War: How World War I Became a Religious Crusade*. New York: HarperOne, 2014.
Johnson, Eric A. *Nazi Terror: The Gestapo, Jews, and Ordinary Germans*. New York: Basic Books, 1999.

———, and Karl-Heinz Reuband. *What We Knew: Terror, Mass Murder, and Everyday Life in Nazi Germany*. London: John Murray, 2005.

Jones, Nigel. *Countdown to Valkyrie: The July Plot to Assassinate Hitler*. London: Frontline, 2008.

Kaiser, Joshua A. *Becoming Simple and Wise: Moral Discernment in Dietrich Bonhoeffer's Vision of Christian Ethics*. Eugene, OR: Pickwick, 2015.

Keim, Albert N. *Harold S. Bender, 1897–1962*. Scottdale, PA: Herald, 1998.

Kelly, Geffrey B. "An Interview with Jean Lasserre." *Union Seminary Quarterly Review* 27, no. 3 (Spring 1972) 149–60.

———, and F. Burton Nelson. *The Cost of Moral Leadership: The Spirituality of Dietrich Bonhoeffer*. Grand Rapids: Eerdmans, 2003.

Kierkegaard, Søren. *The Journals of Kierkegaard*. Edited and translated by Alexander Dru. New York: Harper & Row, 1959.

Kirkpatrick, Matthew D. *Attacks on Christendom in a World Come of Age: Kierkegaard, Bonhoeffer, and the Question of "Religionless Christianity."* Princeton Theological Monograph Series. Eugene, OR: Pickwick, 2011.

Koontz, Claudia. *The Nazi Conscience*. Cambridge, MA: Belknap Press of Harvard University Press, 2003.

Kühne, Thomas. *Belonging and Genocide: Hitler's Community, 1918–1945*. New Haven CT: Yale University Press, 2010.

Lasserre, Jean. *War and the Gospel*. Translated by Oliver Coburn. Scottdale, PA: Herald, 1974.

Leuner, H. D. *When Compassion Was a Crime: Germany's Silent Heroes 1933–1945*. London: Oswald Wolff, 1966.

Liebholz-Bonhoeffer, Sabine. *The Bonhoeffers: Portrait of a Family*. New York: St. Martin's, 1971.

Luckner, Gertrude. "Untitled Remarks." In booklet from International Theological Symposium on the Holocaust (Oct. 15–17, 1978) 8–10. Philadelphia: National Institute of the Holocaust, 1979.

Ludwig, Hartmut. *Suddenly Jews: The Story of Christians Whom the Nazi Racial Laws Classified as Jews, and of the Good Samaritans Who Came to Their Aid (the Bureau Gruber)*. Translated and edited by Martin Nicholaus. Berkeley, CA: Duplex, 2015.

Luther, Martin. "On Secular Authority: To What Extent It Should Be Obeyed." In *Christian Life in the World*, edited by Hans J. Hillerbrand, 79–129. Vol. 5 of The Annotated Luther. Minneapolis: Fortress, 2017.

Malick, Terrence, dir. *A Hidden Life*. Century City, CA: Fox Searchlight, 2019.

Marsh, Charles. "Bonhoeffer on the Road to King: 'Turning from the Phraseological to the Real.'" In *Bonhoeffer and King: Their Legacies and Import for Christian Social Thought*, edited by Willis Jenkins and Jennifer M. McBride, 123–38. Minneapolis: Fortress, 2010.

———. *Reclaiming Dietrich Bonhoeffer: The Promise of His Theology*. Oxford, UK: Oxford University Press, 1996.

———. *Strange Glory: A Life of Dietrich Bonhoeffer*. New York: Albert A. Knopf, 2014.

Matheson, Peter, ed. *The Third Reich and the Christian Churches: A Documentary Account of Christian Resistance and Complicity during the Nazi Era*. Grand Rapids: Eerdmans, 1981.

Matthews, John W. *Anxious Souls Will Ask . . .: The Christ-Centered Spirituality of Dietrich Bonhoeffer*. Grand Rapids: Eerdmans, 2005.

Mawson, Michael. *Christ Existing as Community: Bonhoeffer's Ecclesiology*. Oxford, UK: Oxford University Press, 2018.

———. "The Politics of Jesus and the Ethics of Christ: Why the Differences Between Yoder and Bonhoeffer Matter." In *The Freedom of a Christian Ethicist: The Future of a Reformation Legacy*, edited by Brian Brock and Michael Mawson, 127–43. London: T & T Clark, 2016.

McGarry, Joseph M. *Christ among a Band of People: Dietrich Bonhoeffer and Formation in Christ*. PhD diss., University of Aberdeen, 2013.

McKnight, Scot. *Colossians*. New International Commentary on the New Testament. Grand Rapids: Eerdmans, 2018.

———. *The Sermon on the Mount*. Story of God Bible Commentary. Grand Rapids: Zondervan, 2013.

McNeill, Genna Rae, et al. *Witness: Two Hundred Years of African-American Faith and Practice at the Abyssinian Baptist Church of Harlem, New York*. Grand Rapids: Eerdmans, 2014.

Metaxas, Eric. *Bonhoeffer: Pastor, Martyr, Prophet, Spy*. Nashville: Thomas Nelson, 2010.

Moberly, Jennifer. "'Felicity to the Original Text'?: The Translation of Bonhoeffer's *Ethics*." *Studies in Christian Ethics* 22, no. 3 (2009) 336–56.

———. *The Virtue of Bonhoeffer's Ethics: A Study of Dietrich Bonhoeffer's Ethics in Relation to Virtue Ethics*. Eugene, OR: Pickwick, 2013.

Mogensen, Jørgen L. F. "Ein Zeuge aus dem KZ-Flossenbürg." In *Dietrich Bonhoeffer Aktuell: Biographie—Theologie—Spiritualität*, edited by Rainer Mayer and Peter Zimmerling, 92–93. Basel: Brunnen, 2001.

Moltke, Freya von. *Memories of Kreisau and the German Resistance*. Translated by Julie M. Winter. Lincoln, NE: University of Nebraska Press, 2003.

Moltke, Helmuth James von. *Letters to Freya, 1939–1945*. Edited and translated by Beate Ruhm von Oppen. New York: Alfred A. Knopf, 1990.

Mommsen, Hans. *Alternatives to Hitler: German Resistance under the Third Reich*. London: I. B. Tauris, 2003.

Moorhouse, Roger. *Killing Hitler: The Plots, the Assassins, and the Dictator Who Cheated Death*. New York: Bantam, 2006.

Morris, Kenneth E. "Bonhoeffer's Critique of Totalitarianism." *Journal of Church and State* 26 (1984) 255–72.

Moses, John A. "Dietrich Bonhoeffer's Repudiation of Protestant German War Theology." *Journal of Religious History* 30 (2006) 354–70.

———. *The Reluctant Revolutionary: Dietrich Bonhoeffer's Collision with Prusso-German History*. New York: Berghahn, 2009.

Mueller, Michael. *Nazi Spymaster: The Life and Death of Admiral Wilhelm Canaris*. New York: Skyhorse, 2017.

Nation, Mark Thiessen. "'A Blanket License to Commit Evil Acts'?: A Fresh Examination of Bonhoeffer's Christological Framing in Ethics." *Perspectives in Religious Studies* 40 (2013) 143–53.

———. "Discipleship in a World Full of Nazis: Dietrich Bonhoeffer's Polyphonic Pacifism as Social Ethics." In *The Wisdom of the Cross: Essays in Honor of John Howard Yoder*, edited by Stanley Hauerwas et al., 249–77. Reprint, Eugene, OR: Wipf & Stock, 2005.

———. "'Pacifist and Enemy of the State': Bonhoeffer's 'Straight and Unbroken Course' from Costly Discipleship to Conspiracy." *Journal of Theology for Southern Africa* 77 (Dec. 1991) 61–77.

———. "The Politics of Compassion: A Study of Christian Nonviolent Resistance in the Third Reich." MA diss., Associated Mennonite Biblical Seminaries, 1981.

———, and Stanley Hauerwas. "'A Pacifist and Enemy of the State': Dietrich Bonhoeffer's Journey to Nonviolence." *ABC Religion and Ethics* (Apr. 19, 2018). https://www.abc.net.au/religion/a-pacifist-and-enemy-of-the-state-bonhoeffers-journey-to-nonviol/10094798. (Revised, retitled, and included as an appendix in this book.)

———, et al. *Bonhoeffer the Assassin?: Challenging the Myth, Recovering His Call to Peacemaking*. Grand Rapids: Baker Academic, 2013.

Neder, Adam. *Participation in Christ: An Entry into Karl Barth's Church Dogmatics*. Louisville: Westminster John Knox, 2009.

Neitzel, Sönke, and Harald Welzer. *Soldaten: On Fighting, Killing, and Dying; The Secret WWII Transcripts of German POWS*. Translated by Jefferson Chase. New York: Alfred A. Knopf, 2012.

Nelson, F. Burton. "The Relationship of Jean Lasserre to Dietrich Bonhoeffer's Peace Concerns in the Struggle of Church and Culture." *Union Seminary Quarterly Review* 40 (1985) 71–84.

Niebuhr, Reinhold. *An Interpretation of Christian Ethics*. New York: Harper and Brothers, 1935.

———. *Moral Man and Immoral Society: A Study in Ethics and Politics*. Reprint, Louisville: Westminster John Knox, 2001.

Niemöller, Martin. "Bringing the Beatitudes Down to Earth." *Sojourners* (Aug. 1981) 15–16.

———. "'What Would Jesus Say?': An Interview with Martin Niemöller." *Sojourners* (Aug. 1981) 12–14.

Northcott, Michael. "'Who Am I?': Human Identity and the Spiritual Disciplines in the Witness of Dietrich Bonhoeffer." In *Who Am I?: Bonhoeffer's Theology through His Poetry*, edited by Bernd Wannenwetsch, 11–29. London: T & T Clark, 2009.

Orbach, Danny. *The Plots against Hitler*. Boston: Mariner, 2016.

Palmisano, Trey. *Peace and Violence in the Ethics of Dietrich Bonhoeffer: An Analysis of Method*. Eugene, OR: Wipf & Stock, 2016.

Pangritz, Andreas. "Dietrich Bonhoeffer and the Jews in Context." In *Christ, Church, and World: New Studies in Bonhoeffer's Theology and Ethics*, edited by Michael Mawson and Philip G. Ziegler, 161–87. London: Bloomsbury T & T Clark, 2016.

———. *Karl Barth in the Theology of Dietrich Bonhoeffer*. Translated by Barbara and Martin Rumsheidt. Grand Rapids: Eerdmans, 2000.

———. *The Polyphony of Life: Bonhoeffer's Theology of Music*. Edited by John W. DeGruchy and John Morris. Translated by Robert Steiner. Eugene, OR: Cascade, 2019.

———. "To Fall within the Spokes of the Wheel." In *Dem Rad in die Speichen Fallen*, edited by Kirsten Busch Nielsen et al., 94–108. Gütersloher, Germ.: Gütersloh, 2014.

Parssinen, Terry. *The Oster Conspiracy of 1938*. New York: HarperCollins, 2003.

Pelikan, Jaroslav. *The Vindication of Tradition*. New Haven, CT: Yale University Press, 1984.

Peterson, Eugene. *Answering God: The Psalms as Tools for Prayer.* New York: Harper & Row, 1989.

Pfeifer, Hans. "Learning Faith and Ethical Commitment in the Context of Spiritual Training Groups: Consequences of Dietrich Bonhoeffer's Post Doctoral Year in New York City 1930/31." *Beiträge zur Dietrich Bonhoeffer-Forschung* 3 (2008) 251–79.

Phillips, Jacob. *Human Subjectivity 'in Christ' in Dietrich Bonhoeffer's Theology: Integrating Simplicity and Wisdom.* London: T & T Clark, 2020.

Probst, Christopher J. *Demonizing the Jews: Luther and the Protestant Church in Nazi Germany.* Bloomington, IN: Indiana University Press, 2012.

Rasmussen, Larry. *Dietrich Bonhoeffer: Reality and Resistance.* Reprint, Louisville: Westminster John Knox, 2005.

———. "The Ethics of Responsible Action." In *The Cambridge Companion to Dietrich Bonhoeffer*, edited by John W. DeGruchy, 206–25. Cambridge, UK: Cambridge University Press, 1999.

———. "Response to Clifford Green." *Conversations in Religion and Theology* 6 (2008) 165–73.

Rasmusson, Arne. "Church and Nation-State: Karl Barth and German Public Theology in Early 20th Century." *Ned Geref Teologiese Tydskrif* 46 (2005) 511–24.

———. "Church and War in the Theology of Karl Barth." In *Living Theology*, edited by Len Hansen et al., 386–98. Wellington, S. Afr.: Bible Media, 2011.

Rees, Laurence. *The Holocaust: A New History.* New York: Public Affairs, 2017.

Reynolds, Diane. *The Doubled Life of Dietrich Bonhoeffer: Women, Sexuality, and Nazi Germany.* Cambridge, UK: James Clarke, 2016.

Roberts, Andrew. *The Storm of War: A New History of the Second World War.* New York: Harper, 2011.

Roon, Ger van. *German Resistance to Hitler: Count von Moltke and the Kreisau Circle.* Translated by Peter Ludlow. London: Van Nostrand Reinhold, 1971.

Root, Andrew. *Bonhoeffer as Youth Worker: A Theological Vision for Discipleship and Life Together.* Grand Rapids: Baker Academic, 2014.

Rowe, C. Kavin. *World Upside Down: Reading Acts in the Graeco-Roman Age.* Oxford, UK: Oxford University Press, 2009.

Ruhm von Oppen, Beate. *Religion and Resistance to Nazism.* Research Monograph 35. Princeton, NJ: Center of International Studies, 1971.

Sauvage, Pierre, dir. *Weapons of the Spirit.* Los Angeles: Chambon Foundation, 1989. DVD.

Sax, Benjamin, and Dieter Kuntz, eds. *Inside Hitler's Germany: A Documentary History of Life in the Third Reich.* Lexington, MA: D. C. Heath, 1992.

Schleunes, Karl A. *The Twisted Road to Auschwitz: Nazi Policy toward German Jews 1933–1939.* Urbana, IL: University of Illinois Press, 1990.

Schliesser, Christine. *Everyone Who Acts Responsibly Becomes Guilty: Bonhoeffer's Concept of Accepting Guilt.* Louisville: Westminster John Knox, 2008.

Schlingensiepen, Ferdinand. *Dietrich Bonhoeffer 1906–1945: Martyr, Thinker, Man of Resistance.* Translated by Isabel Best. London: T&T Clark, 2010.

Schmitz, Florian. "Reading *Discipleship* and *Ethics* Together: Implications for Ethics and Public Life." In *Interpreting Bonhoeffer: Historical Perspectives, Emerging Issues*, edited by Clifford J. Green and Guy C. Carter, 147–53. Minneapolis: Fortress, 2013.

Scholder, Klaus. *The Churches and the Third Reich, Volume One: 1918-1934*. Translated by John Bowden. Philadelphia: Fortress, 1988.

———. *The Churches and the Third Reich, Volume Two: The Year of Disillusionment 1934: Barmen and Rome*. Translated by John Bowden. Philadelphia: Fortress, 1988.

Semelin, Jacques. *Unarmed against Hitler: Civilian Resistance in Europe, 1939-1943*. Westport, CT: Praeger, 1993.

Sider, Ronald J. *Christ and Violence*. Scottdale, PA: Herald, 1979.

Sifton, Elisabeth, and Fritz Stern. *No Ordinary Men: Dietrich Bonhoeffer and Hans von Dohnanyi, Resisters against Hitler in Church and State*. New York: New York Review, 2013.

Singer, Bryan, dir. *Valkyrie*. Beverly Hills, CA: MGM, 2008. DVD.

Snyder, Louis L. *Encyclopedia of the Third Reich*. New York: McGraw-Hill, 1976.

Solberg, Mary M., ed. and trans. *A Church Undone: Documents from the German Christian Faith Movement*. Minneapolis: Fortress, 2015.

Sorum, Jonathan D. "Cheap Grace, Costly Grace, and Just Plain Grace: Bonhoeffer's Defense of Justification by Grace Alone." *Lutheran Forum* 27, no. 3 (Aug. 1993) 20–23.

———. *Following Jesus: Dietrich Bonhoeffer's Recovery of the Gospel of Discipleship*. ThD diss., Luther Seminary, 1994.

Stargardt, Nicholas. *The German War: A Nation under Arms, 1939-1945*. New York: Basic Books, 2015.

Stayer, James M. *Martin Luther, German Saviour: German Evangelical Theological Factions and the Interpretation of Luther 1917-1933*. Montreal: McGill-Queen's University Press, 2000.

Steigmann-Gall, Richard. *The Holy Reich: Nazi Conceptions of Christianity, 1919-1945*. Cambridge, UK: Cambridge University Press, 2003.

Taylor, Derek W. *Reading Scripture as the Church: Dietrich Bonhoeffer's Hermeneutic of Discipleship*. Downers Grove, IL: IVP Academic, 2020.

Thomas, Gordon, and Greg Lewis. *Defying Hitler: The Germans Who Resisted Nazi Rule*. New York: Caliber, 2019.

Tödt, Heinz Eduard. "The Bonhoeffer-Dohnanyi circle in Opposition and Resistance to Hitler's Regime of Violence: Interim Report on a Research Project." In *Authentic Faith: Bonhoeffer's Theological Ethics in Context*, edited by Ernst-Albert Scharffenorth and Glen Harold Stassen, translated by David Stassen and Ilse Tödt, 179–231. Grand Rapids: Eerdmans, 2007.

———. "Dietrich Bonhoeffer's Decisions in the Crisis Years 1929-33." *Studies in Christian Ethics* 18, no. 3 (2005) 107–23.

Trocmé, André. *Jesus and the Nonviolent Revolution*. Rev. ed. Translated by Michael H. Shank et al. Walden, NY: Plough, 2014.

Villiger, Marc, dir. *Heroes: Saving Jewish Lives from the Nazis*. Worcester, PA: Vision Video, 2016.

Voegelin, Eric. *Hitler and the Germans*. Edited and translated by Detlev Clemens and Brendan Purcell. Columbia, MO: University of Missouri Press, 1999.

von Kellenbach, Katharina. *The Mark of Cain: Guilt and Denial in the Post-War Lives of Nazi Perpetrators*. Oxford, UK: Oxford University Press, 2013.

Wallace, Mark I. *The Second Naiveté: Barth, Ricoeur, and the New Yale Theology*. Studies in American Biblical Hermeneutics 6. Macon, GA: Mercer University Press, 1996.

Wannenwetsch, Bernd. *Political Worship: Ethics for Christian Citizens*. Translated by Margaret Kohl. Oxford, UK: Oxford University Press, 2004.

———. "'Responsible Living' or 'Responsible Self'?: Bonhoefferian Reflections on a Vexed Moral Notion." *Studies in Christian Ethics* 18, no. 3 (2005) 125–40.

———, ed. *Who Am I?: Bonhoeffer's Theology through His Poetry*. London: T & T Clark, 2009.

Ward, W. R. *Theology, Sociology and Politics: The German Protestant Social Conscience 1890-1933*. Bern: Peter Lang, 1979.

Wartenburg, Marion Yorck von. *The Power of Solitude: My Life in the German Resistance*. Lincoln, NE: University of Nebraska Press, 2000.

Weber, Max. *Politics as a Vocation*. Translated by H. H. Gerth and C. Wright Mills. Philadelphia: Fortress, 1965.

Webster, John. "The Church as Witnessing Community." *Scottish Bulletin of Evangelical Theology* 21, no. 1 (2003) 21–33.

———. *The Culture of Theology*. Edited by Ivor J. Davidson and Alden C. McCray. Grand Rapids: Baker Academic, 2019.

———. "Discipleship and Calling." *Scottish Bulletin of Evangelical Theology* 23, no. 2 (2005) 133–47.

———. "Discipleship and Obedience." *Scottish Bulletin of Evangelical Theology* 24, no. 1 (2006) 4–18.

———. "The Imitation of Christ." *Tyndale Bulletin* 37 (1986) 95–120.

———. "The Visible Attests the Invisible." In *The Community of the Word*, edited by Mark Husbands and Daniel J. Treier, 96–113. Downers Grove, IL: InterVarsity, 2005.

———. "'Where Christ Is': Christology and Ethics." In *Christology and Ethics*, edited by F. LeRon Shults and Brent Waters, 32–55. Grand Rapids: Eerdmans, 2010.

———. *Word and Church: Essays in Christian Dogmatics*. Edinburgh: T & T Clark, 2001.

Weikart, Richard. *Hitler's Religion*. Washington, DC: Regnery History, 2014.

Westphal, Merold. *Kierkegaard's Concept of Faith*. Grand Rapids: Eerdmans, 2014.

Whitburn, Lawrence B. "Bonhoeffer without His Cassock." In *I Knew Dietrich Bonhoeffer*, edited by Wolf-Dieter Zimmermann and Ronald Gregor Smith, 79–81. London: Fontana, 1973.

Williams, Reggie. *Bonhoeffer's Black Jesus: Harlem Renaissance Theology and an Ethic of Resistance*. Waco, TX: Baylor University Press, 2014.

Wind, Renate. *A Spoke in the Wheel*. Translated by John Bowden. Grand Rapids: Eerdmans, 1991.

Wink, Walter. *Engaging the Powers: Discernment and Resistance in a World of Domination*. Minneapolis: Fortress, 1992.

———. *Naming the Powers: The Language of Power in the New Testament*. Minneapolis: Fortress, 1984.

———. *Unmasking the Powers: The Invisible Powers That Determine Human Existence*. Minneapolis: Fortress, 1986.

Wright, J. R. C. *'Above Parties': The Political Attitudes of the German Protestant Church Leadership 1918-1933*. Oxford, UK: Oxford University Press, 1974.

Wright, N. T. *Jesus and the Victory of God*. Minneapolis: Fortress, 1996.

Wüstenberg, Ralf K. "Religionless Christianity: Dietrich Bonhoeffer's Tegel Theology." In *Bonhoeffer for a New Day*, edited by John W. DeGruchy, 57–71. Grand Rapids: Eerdmans, 1997.

———. *A Theology of Life: Dietrich Bonhoeffer's Religionless Christianity*. Grand Rapids: Eerdmans, 1998.

Yoder, John Howard. *The Christian Witness to the State*. Scottdale, PA: Herald, 2002.

———. "The Christological Presuppositions of Discipleship." In *Being Human, Becoming Human: Dietrich Bonhoeffer and Social Thought*, edited by Jens Zimmermann and Brian Gregor, 127–51. Eugene, OR: Pickwick, 2010.

———. *Karl Barth and the Problem of War and Other Essays on Barth*. Edited by Mark Thiessen Nation. Eugene, OR: Cascade, 2003.

———. *Nevertheless: Varieties of Religious Pacifism*. Rev. ed. Scottdale, PA: Herald, 1992.

———. *Nonviolence: A Brief History*. The Warsaw Lectures. Edited by Paul Martens et al. Waco, TX: Baylor University Press.

———. *The Original Revolution: Essays on Christian Pacifism*. Scottdale, PA: Herald, 2003.

———. *The Politics of Jesus*. Rev. ed. Grand Rapids: Eerdmans, 1994.

Zabel, James A. *Nazism and the Pastors: A Study of the Ideas of Three Deutsche Christian Groups*. Missoula, MT: Scholars, 1976.

Zahn, Gordon. *In Solitary Witness: The Life and Death of Franz Jägerstätter*. Boston: Beacon, 1964.

Zerner, Ruth. "Dietrich Bonhoeffer's American Experiences: People, Letters, and Papers from Union Seminary." *Union Seminary Quarterly Review* 31 (1976) 261–82.

Ziegler, Philip G. "Christ for Us Today: Promeity in the Christologies of Bonhoeffer and Kierkegaard." *International Journal of Systematic Theology* 15, no. 1 (Jan. 2013) 25–41.

———. "'Completely within God's Doing': Soteriology as Meta-Ethics in the Theology of Dietrich Bonhoeffer." In *Christ, Church and World: New Studies in Bonhoeffer's Theology and Ethics*, edited by Michael Mawson and Philip Ziegler, 101–17. London: T & T Clark, 2016.

———. "Dietrich Bonhoeffer: A Theologian of the Word of God." In *Bonhoeffer, Christ and Culture*, edited by Keith L. Johnson and Timothy Larsen, 17–37. Downers Grove, IL: IVP Academic, 2013.

———. *Militant Grace: The Apocalyptic Turn and the Future of Christian Theology*. Grand Rapids: Baker Academic, 2018.

———, and Michael Mawson, eds. *The Oxford Handbook of Dietrich Bonhoeffer*. Oxford, UK: Oxford University Press, 2019.

Zimmermann, Jens. "Bonhoeffer and Non-Violence." *Theologica Wratislaviensia* 11 (2016) 197–211.

———. *Dietrich Bonhoeffer's Christian Humanism*. Oxford, UK: Oxford University Press, 2019.

Zimmermann, Wolf-Dieter, and Ronald Gregor Smith, eds. *I Knew Dietrich Bonhoeffer*. Translated by Käthe Gregor Smith. Reprint, London: Fontana, 1973.

www.ingramcontent.com/pod-product-compliance
Lightning Source LLC
Chambersburg PA
CBHW032109220426
43664CB00008B/1185